JOURNEY'S REWARD

*Renaissance Man Robert Runyon,
Pioneer Aviator P. A. Newman, and
Entrepreneurship in the Borderlands*

Doug Perkins

La Rama Press
Austin, Texas

© 2019 Doug Perkins

All rights reserved. No part of this book may be reproduced or transmitted in any form or by any means electronic or mechanical, including photocopying, recording or by any information storage and retrieval system, without written permission from the author, except for the inclusion of brief quotations in a review.

Please send questions to the author at
La Rama Press, PO Box 203272, Austin, Texas 78720-3272
a division of TriTech Ventures LLC

Library of Congress Control Number: 2019908845

Edition ISBNs:
Hardcover   978-1-7339801-0-4
Softcover   978-1-7339801-1-1
E-book   978-1-7339801-2-8

Editor: David Aretha of Yellow Bird Editors
Book Design: Park Place Enterprises, Inc., Fort Worth, Texas
Map Illustrator: Crabtree Design, Red Oak, Texas
Cover Design: Karen Sheets de Gracia

Front cover credits:
- Top: Hedgehog cactus *(Echinocactus setispinus)*, circa 1928. Photographer: Robert Runyon. From author's files.
- Center: Photo of P.A. Newman, two Carrancistas and Cole "30" touring car in southern Tamaulipas, November 1913. Photographer: Robert Runyon. RUN00062, Robert Runyon Collection, Dolph Briscoe Center for American History, The University of Texas at Austin.

    Runyon slogan from author's files.
- Bottom: Pitaya *(Echinocereus enneacanthus)*, circa 1928. Photographer: Robert Runyon. From author's files.

Back cover credits:
- Robert Runyon, 1909, Brownsville. Photographer: Charles Gilhousen. Runyon Family Papers, Dolph Briscoe Center for American History, The University of Texas at Austin.
- Researchers at Rabb Sabal Palm Grove, circa 1925. Photographer: Robert Runyon. From author's files.
- Prentice A. Newman, circa 1900, Runge. Lorraine Owens Family Papers.
- Newman aeroplane in flight, Brownsville, June 3, 1909. Photographer: Charles Gilhousen. Lorraine Owens Family Papers.

La Rama Press
PO Box 203272
Austin, TX 78720-3272

Contents

   Prologue   1
1 Genius and Genes   9
2 The Nurse and The Birth   20
3 Sudden Tragic Losses   26
4 Death Comes on the Night Train   33
5 The Unwritten Law   37
6 Conquest of the Upper Regions   43
7 An Aeroplane of Practical Value   51
8 An Honest, Moral Man   58
9 Mr. P. A. Newman, Texas   67
10 Home of a Successful Aeroplane   73
11 Success, Innovation and Freedom   77
12 Brownsville Boom Timber   85
13 Será Bien Recibido   93
14 Mortal Duel, Bloody Battle   102
15 Los Compañeros de Viaje   112
16 The Revolution in Monterrey   125
17 Photos of Dead Bandits   131
18 Tenemos Perder Para Ganar   139
19 The Entrepreneur with a Scientist's Mind   148
20 The Lower Rio Grande Valley Flora Authority   153
21 Runyon's Huaco, Topsy-Turvy, and Esenbeckia   159
22 The Misty Figure   167
23 Texas Cacti and the Palm Grove   171
24 Brownsville's Stormy Petrel   180
25 Given the Chance to Serve   187
26 The Entrepreneurs' Twilight Years   193
   Epilogue   200
   Acknowledgments   204
   Endnotes   207
   Bibliography   224
   Index   228

Illustrations

*Indicates Robert Runyon photograph

Prentice Alexander Newman   2
Robert Runyon   3
Texas map   8
Hutokah Caylor Newman and children   12
Robert Runyon as boy   18
Newman aeroplane, Fort Sam Houston   48
Arthur and Prentice Newman in 1909   54
Rio Grande Machine Shop*   56
Brownsville rice mill*   56
Charles Gilhousen photos of Newman flight   76
Texas Longhorn steer postcard*   88
Custom postcard folders   90
Cockpit, Matamoros*   90
Casa Mata, Matamoros*   90
Rio Grande ferry skiff*   94
Plaza Hidalgo, Matamoros*   97
Mule-drawn car, Matamoros*   97
Bullfight, Matamoros*   97
Tamaulipas map   101
Federal cannon, Matamoros*   110
Pyre of dead Federals, Matamoros*   111
Echazaretta execution, Matamoros*   111
Amelia Medrano Longoria and Robert Runyon*   113
Amelia Medrano Longoria de Runyon*   113
General Lucio Blanco, Los Borregos*   114
Military convoy to Ciudad Victoria*   118
Constitutionalist officers at jacal*   118
Auto fording Tamaulipas river*   118
Newman and two Carrancistas*   121
Hacienda Las Virgenes*   123
Ciudad Victoria panteón*   123
Ciudad Victoria prisoners*   123
Palacio de Obispado, Monterrey*   127
Spent Federal artillery shells*   127
Dead bandits at Las Norias*   135
Chapa and Buenrostro*   137
Train derailing at Olmito*   137
Carranza at Brownsville bridge*   140
812 E. St. Charles St.*   142
Runyon daughters*   143
Wine glass by Helen Kleberg   146
Robert Runyon   155
Coryphantha runyonii*   160
P. A. Newman   169
Runyon plant chart   179
Robert Runyon   195
Newman and two Carrancistas*   201

Glossary

a la parilla: on the grill
aguacate: avocado
arroz mexicana: Mexican rice
ayuntamiento: the ruling body of a town and surrounding villages
bailes: dances
buen negocia: good business
canasta: basket
capitalista: capitalist, but also a derogatory term used by the Constitutionalist Army
carnes asada y guisada: grilled and stewed meats
Carrancistas: followers of First Chief Venustiano Carranza
chiles rellenos: stuffed chiles
Ciudadano: Title for a citizen
comal: flat pan for heating tortillas
compañeros de viaje: travel companions
corrida de toros: bullfight
Defensa Social: armed volunteer citizens loyal to the Federal cause
Ejército Constitucionalista: Constitutionalist Army
ejidos: land held in common
El Libro de Cocina: The Cuisine Book
el otro lado: the other side of the Rio Grande
Felicistas: supporters of Félix Díaz
frijoles: pinto beans
frontera: the border
galletas: cookies
huaco: vernacular name for *Manfreda* species; also used as remedy for snake bites
huaraches: leather sandals
jacal: a hut made of native materials including *Sabal texana* leaves for the roof
jardín: garden
jopoy: vernacular name used for Berlandier's Esenbeckia
limoncillo: vernacular name in Tamaulipas for Runyon's Esenbeckia
Loma Alta: a small hill in Cameron County's coastal plains known as Jackass Prairie
loma: rising ground, a slope, a small hill
matamorenses: natives of Matamoros, Tamaulipas, Mexico
mezquital: a mesquite forest
monte: brush country; Runyon described it as "forest, uncleared land"
naranjillo: vernacular name in Nuevo León for Runyon's Esenbeckia
Nuevo Santander: name given to northeast Mexico and part of South Texas after its settlement by José de Escandón in the 1740s
paisano: fellow countryman
palma de micharos: vernacular name preferred by Robert Runyon for *Sabal texana*
pantéon: cemetery
paseo: promenade in the plaza where women strolled one direction and men in the other
pawa: regional name, probably Mayan, for a robust variety of borderlands avocado
pipero: a borderlands entrepreneur who used a mule to pull water barrels to customers
plaza: city square
por la carreta: by wagon
porción: an allotment of land
primer jefe: first chief, the title given to Venustiano Carranza
resaca: borderlands term to designate abandoned water courses or river beds, which are sometimes dry; Runyon said its literal definition was ravine
rosbif: roast beef
Rurales: a rural law enforcement body
Santa Cruz: literally, Holy Cross; also terminal point in Matamoros for Rio Grande ferry boats
santo y seña: military password
sendero: dirt path or trail
Será Bien Recibido: "You will be well received"
síndico procurador: a city attorney in colonial Mexico
sopa de fideo: dish of vermicelli, stewed tomatoes and spices
tamales: meat mixture wrapped in corn masa, then covered by a dried corn husk
tardeadas: afternoon parties
Tenemos perder para ganar: literally, "We must lose in order to gain"
tortillas de maíz: corn tortillas
tumbas: tombs
Villistas: followers of Pancho Villa
yerbería: vendor of dried herbs and other beneficial plants

Abbreviations Used in Cutlines
(see page 207 for guide to Endnotes Abbreviations)
RFP, DBCAH: Runyon Family Papers, Dolph Briscoe Center for American History, The University of Texas at Austin
RUNXXXXX, RRC, DBCAH: Photograph file number, Robert Runyon Collection, Dolph Briscoe Center for American History, The University of Texas at Austin

Prologue

Prentice Alexander Newman, a native Texan with ancestral ties that antedated the Republic, and Robert Runyon, a steadfast son of the commonwealth of Kentucky, each stepped onto the train platform at Brownsville, Texas, three weeks apart in winter 1909.

Both men were self-taught American entrepreneurs whose creativity over the next decade would help define the lower Rio Grande Valley as a dynamic region. Each man also possessed a unique, individual style—Newman, thirty-eight, was an engineering specialist, and Runyon, twenty-seven, was a polymath. Nothing illustrated these individuals' respective intellectual expertise more keenly than each man's actions immediately upon reaching this southernmost point on the St. Louis, Brownsville and Mexico (SLB&M) Railway.

Newman detrained at the Brownsville depot, just a few hundred yards from the Rio Grande, on January 14 to meet a pool of potential investors. So, upon arrival, Newman went right from the depot to prepare a pitch he hoped would encourage investors to fund construction of the first viable aeroplane anywhere south of Kitty Hawk, North Carolina.

Newman had credentials. Beginning December 30, 1908, on the Fort Sam Houston parade grounds in San Antonio, Newman held onlookers spellbound through New Year's Day. The attraction was something never before seen in the southwestern United States—a two hundred-pound, twenty-five-foot long, ten-foot high, unpowered biplane with a thirty-five-foot wingspread.

Newman had designed the machine based on research into the Wright brothers' aeroplanes, Flyer, Flyer II and Flyer III. With a colleague's help, Newman built his aeroplane's components in a downtown San Antonio basement over several months before assembling them into an airship at Fort

Prentice Alexander Newman at about 29 years old in 1900 while living in Runge, Texas. Lorraine Owens Family Papers.

Sam Houston. After waiting for favorable weather, on January 2, 1909, Newman piloted his aeroplane through the San Antonio skies and treated two hundred spectators to the stuff of dreams. That accomplishment made Newman the first person to achieve a heavier-than-air flight anywhere south of a line from Kitty Hawk to the Pacific in the post-Wright brothers' era.[1]

At the time, Newman was awaiting trial for murder before the Lavaca County District Court in Hallettsville, Texas. Yet anxiety over a possible sentence of death by hanging could not sidetrack Newman's brilliant engineering mind. During the next twelve months in Brownsville, the specialist conceived and prototyped unique ideas to pace a dynamic year of flight experimentation. Those innovations fleetingly moved Newman to a public relations apex approaching the Wright brothers in 1909's global race to make human flight possible.[2] Even though Newman lost that position just as rapidly, he left a legacy of engineering innovations designed to take piloting out of the realm of technicians and daredevils and within reach of the average human.

Robert Runyon in a 1909 portrait taken by photographer Charles Gilhousen in Brownsville, Texas. RFP, DBCAH, The University of Texas at Austin.

Runyon arrived in Brownsville with a less solid plan. He had traveled by rail from eastern Kentucky to Houston to seek work in late January 1909. On February 9, he started an entry-level job for a railroad service provider under contract to SLB&M's recently launched night train from Houston to the border. Runyon worked onboard through the night hours and saw Brownsville for the first time around 11:15 a.m. the next morning.[3] Upon detraining at the Brownsville depot, he walked through its adjacent large park. His eyes immediately took in the native Texas palms and other exotic plants that thrived in the subtropical climate even in dead of winter. Runyon noted that each species was so drastically different from all plant life he had known in Appalachia. It would take almost a decade before he could fully explore the region's unique flora, but that initial pass through the depot park never left his mind.

In environment, customs, cuisine, and language, the Kentucky native rapidly perceived he had entered a vigorous new and strange world. As a first-time visitor, Runyon did what any Brownsville newcomer might do in those years—he strolled to the boardwalk that led him to the ferry, which transported him across the Rio Grande to Matamoros, Tamaulipas, Mexico. Within two hours of his first arrival in Brownsville, Runyon was in a foreign country, photographing scenes on his vest-sized Kodak. His exposure record for that day registered his wonder at the borderlands' unique turn-of-the-century sights—the narrow gauge rail cars that transported passengers from Matamoros' Santa Cruz ferry terminal to Plaza Hidalgo, the water-delivery entrepreneurs called *piperos*, and the above-ground *tumbas* at the city *panteón antiguo*.[4]

Although Runyon had no defined business or personal strategy on this first trip, he was certain of one short-term goal: he needed this low-level railroad job. Runyon's wife had died suddenly just two months before. Soon after her funeral, he uncharacteristically acted on impulse. He left his young son, William, with his Kentucky in-laws and went searching for a new life in what he called the "Southwest." He would later discover that what he was seeking embraced him at his first step onto the platform at the SLB&M depot.

The vitality of the lower Rio Grande Valley and northeastern Mexico sparked an amazingly long burst of creativity inside this prototypical entrepreneur. Runyon soon would establish himself in Brownsville as a pioneer photojournalist during the Mexican Revolution and the Texas bandit wars. He then became a creative master who used his camera to chronicle everyday life in the lower Valley and northeastern Mexico from 1912 to 1928.

Yet his true innovative legacy did not start until about 1918, the year he began to study and observe native plants in the lower Valley and northeastern Mexico. His rapid grasp of complex botanical science earned him recognition as champion of the region's diverse, unique, and endangered flora. As an entrepreneur with an analytical mind, Runyon advocated over decades for propagating these native plants in public and private landscapes to make the lower Rio Grande Valley more beautiful through its own assets.

In life, Newman and Runyon had little in common. These men were never more than casual acquaintances. Each man pursued unrelated entrepreneurial dreams.

Yet, as contemporaries, Newman and Runyon possessed notable commonalities that entice a weaving together of their stories of innovation and research in science and technology. Each man came to Brownsville after burying a loved young woman following an unexpected death. For decades, both men lived on the same St. Charles Street in Brownsville, and for many years each man innovated within 150 yards of the other. Both men admired and worked closely with the people of Mexico throughout their lives, making long-lasting commercial and personal friendships across the border.

Yet the most telling shared attribute is that each man realized that the Rio Grande delta is fertile for reasons other than its alluvial clay's richness. Valuable resources of sea, river, land, people, and culture combine to make the lower Rio Grande Valley unique. It supports classical entrepreneurs who start a small business to earn a profit in cities, towns, and villages separated only by a river's flow. It celebrates multinational cultures and architecture, a multitude of languages, and constantly emerging and evolving venture opportunities. And, as Newman and Runyon each came to understand, men and women of enterprise could innovate in the borderlands to make society efficient and stronger.

At times, for personal economic reasons, Newman and Runyon fell into a classical entrepreneur category to service the needs of local clienteles.[5] At these junctures, each man operated traditional businesses to accept profit and manage risk. Yet it was a unique brand of entrepreneur—the kind who innovated in technology and science—that united Newman's and Runyon's lives. From 1909 until the late 1960s, one of these men recurrently introduced revolutionary and economically sound ideas founded in technology and science to a wider population. Their milestones are notable and lasting: Newman introduced the monoplane to American aviation that had been focused on airships with two parallel wings on each side; Runyon protected and championed a vast number of endangered plant species, including *Esenbeckia runyonii*, Texas' rarest tree, and *Sabal texana*, Texas' only native palm.

Then, in November 1913, during the height of bloodshed caused by the Mexican Revolution's sweep into northeastern Mexico, the two men's careers linked together as participants in a six-automobile military convoy. The experience became a tense, weeklong journey over *senderos*, since no roads existed anywhere in northeastern Mexico in that era. The round trip, which encompassed more than four hundred miles, sent Newman and Runyon deep into the battle theater of Tamaulipas before they headed back to Brownsville. Newman and Runyon crossed wide and deep rivers in early automobiles, and they passed through war-torn countryside and villages, many of which had been occupied in recent weeks by Federals, then by opposing Constitutionalist revolutionaries. It was a week of challenges for all members of the convoy—including chaos and confusion following the accidental killing of its commanding officer by his own general's sentries.

Runyon, by that time an experienced photojournalist, took several photographs during that trip for newspapers, news syndicates, and his own line of postcards. But the photograph he took of Newman and two *Carrancistas*, all three subjects armed with Winchesters or Mausers and standing next to a requisitioned Cole "30" Touring Car, best symbolizes the entrepreneurial spirit shared by the two Americans. What that image validates is that when everyone else had abandoned the mission after the commanding officer's untimely death, only Newman and Runyon carried on. They called upon entrepreneurial skills of risk management, team building, leadership, opportunism, focus, and determination to finish their assignments before they returned to Brownsville.

Unrealized by Newman and Runyon at that moment is that the photograph also marked a transition in each man's entrepreneurial career. Newman's long, remarkably vibrant burst of innovation had slowed; conversely, Runyon's era of innovation that would drive him the rest of his life had started to emerge.

The following chapters portray Newman's and Runyon's struggles, inspirations, aspirations, and achievements for what each man was—an imperfect yet important American entrepreneur of the last century. Imperfect because neither man enjoyed overwhelming success or recognition in his life; important because both men generated significant innovations that impact daily life in the region even today. In this narrative, entrepreneurs of modern disruptive digital technology enterprises will find parallels in challenges and barriers these two men confronted long before the computer age. Significantly, they'll see that Newman's and Runyon's stories are universal tales of entrepreneurship principles personified.

Readers will understand how and why these men shared and transferred knowledge. Newman offered his technology openly, while Runyon fiercely protected intellectual property from which a single entity—a newspaper or a cabal of elite businessmen—would profit. Yet Runyon also eagerly and willingly shared and transferred, at his own expense, all knowledge that would benefit society at large through his work in botany, conservation and genealogy.

And, finally, readers will understand how these far-sighted innovators uniquely managed and coped with twists of fate that arise in every entrepreneur's everyday life, all the while refusing to allow adversity, rejection, conflict, or failure end their dreams before they themselves were ready to terminate them.

Because Newman was a specialist, his story takes place serially, flowing in chronological order. As a polymath, Runyon's story is more difficult to detail in time sequence. Runyon's chapters occasionally overlap in chronology to examine as much relevant detail as possible about his multiple discrete interests.

Their combined story is one of innovation, yet it is not one of mind-boggling success or quick wealth creation. Rather, it presents the entrepreneur's more common experiences of frugalness, struggle, disappointment, failure, and frustration. It is not a story of war, although battles—military, political, and personal—are integral elements of these men's lives. It is not a story just of photography, aviation, or botany, although these pursuits make up most of the two men's experiences.

What the story does tell is how two different minds study problems and develop solutions. It tells of knowledge creation and its important offspring, knowledge sharing. It is a story of true entrepreneurship and all inherent challenges involved with commercializing human creativity, not the least of which is the entrepreneur's skillfulness in managing risk effectively during times of personal turmoil.

Chapter 1
Genius and Genes

Prentice Alexander Newman arrived in Brownsville in January 1909 with his eyes on the heavens and a dogged resolve to build a heavier-than-air machine that flew under its own power. At the time, the gray-eyed, five-foot-nine, 160-pound Texan had a recent successful aviation test behind him.[6] He flew briefly in San Antonio at an altitude of seventy feet in a glider of his design and construction. That accomplishment brought him to Brownsville as the Southwest's first mover in the race to build a motorized aeroplane.

Newman's goal, though, was not just to fly; the Wright brothers had already achieved that many times over. Rather, his goal was to develop an airship that was as easy to pilot as an automobile was to drive by early 1900s automotive standards.[7]

Newman also arrived in Brownsville with a pledge to stand trial for murder when summoned by the Lavaca County District Court. He had borne the burden of a possible conviction since May 16, 1905, when he and his younger brother, Malcom Arthur Newman, surrendered to Lavaca County law officials immediately after rifling down their late sister's lover.[8]

Yet the brothers spent few hours behind bars for the man's death because they were Newmans, a surname deeply respected in a significantly large portion of south central Texas.

The Newmans' birthright to this privilege began a century before in Illinois territory, where William and Mary Smalley Rabb raised four sons and one daughter. Rabb was a gristmill operator, county judge, and sometime Illinois legislator. On June 12, 1806, the Rabbs' daughter, Rachel, married Joseph Newman in Warren County, Ohio. The couple made their home near the Rabbs, even during Joseph's military service in the War of 1812 and a few Indian conflicts. In Illinois, Rachel and Joseph had their first five children.

By 1818, the Rabb and Newman families migrated to today's eastern Oklahoma. In 1820, Rabb moved again to Jonesborough in Red River County, Texas. While looking for farmland to the south in 1823, Rabb liked what he saw in Spanish territory just east of the Colorado River in today's Fayette County. After Spanish authorities granted Rabb's request, made through empresario Stephen F. Austin, to settle on that site, Rabb and Newman moved their families to the new land. With that relocation, the Rabb and Newman names became enshrined as members of Austin's Old Three Hundred settlers. And, in Texas, the Newmans had five more children.

Rabb and Newman both died in 1831, but by then the two men had created a foundation for the large number of Newman descendants in early Texas.[9]

One of them, William, the oldest son of Joseph and Rachel, was born in Illinois territory in 1810. In 1833, William Newman married Margaret Nelson, and they had two sons who died young. Newman fought for Texas independence in 1836 and received slight wounds at San Jacinto.[10]

Newman's wife died in 1838, and in 1840 he married Martha Ann Shedricks. In 1841, at their home at Egypt in Wharton County, he and his new wife had their first of seven children, Joseph Austin Newman. William and Martha Ann later purchased land in Karnes County and relocated their family near Yorktown on March 28, 1860.[11]

Joseph volunteered for Confederate service in the Texas Cavalry's Thirty-Fifth Regiment, Company D, during the Civil War with brother Ali, but they saw no action. The brothers received discharges in 1865 at Columbus, Texas. In 1870, in Smith County, Texas, Joseph married Hutokah Dodson Caylor, daughter of Michael G. Caylor, a native of Virginia, who served as Smith County's postmaster. The couple first lived in Caylor's home while Joseph performed day labor in northeast Texas and Hutokah kept house. Before the year was out, though, the couple moved to a small Karnes County community originally called Riedelville, a name that later was corrupted to Riddleville. After the turn of the century, it was called Gillett.[12]

Joseph and Hutokah Newman had three children in this community: Prentice Alexander Newman, born January 1, 1871; Lillian May (Lily) Newman, born February 22, 1873; and Malcolm Arthur Newman, who went by his middle name, born December 7, 1877.[13]

In about 1880, family members believe that Joseph moved his family into Mexico, where he gained a job building the Mexican National Railway. By 1881, the International-Great Northern (I&GN) Railroad had terminated its line at Laredo on the border. Joseph gained employment as master of the I&GN roundhouse that same year.[14]

It was in Laredo, where Prentice, Lily and Arthur all attended public schools, that their creative talents impressed the community. Circa 1888, Lily won an essay contest with her impressions of the school's field day tour of the newspaper's printing press.[15] About the same time, young Prentice's experiments in generating motion through steam earned him a reputation as a "mechanical genius." He built a miniature steam engine using a pocketknife and awl as tools on commonplace parts: a copper cartridge casing for the steam cylinder, empty oyster cans for boilers, and copper wire for connecting rods and crank pins. In a mold, Prentice cast sand and lead together to create the flywheel needed to steady the motion of the working parts.

"The engine runs with a noise and snorting almost perfect," wrote an admiring reporter from Galveston who viewed Prentice's innovation in action.

Laredo city officials appreciated Prentice's creation too. They featured his small-scale steam engine in Webb County's pavilion at Fort Worth's Texas Spring Palace in late May 1889. The event, a precursor to the State Fair of Texas, invited each Texas county to set up an exhibit to promote its interests. [16]

Prentice and Arthur took advantage of their father's roundhouse position by studying the railroad's infrastructure. What knowledge the brothers absorbed inspired them to collaborate on building their own small-scaled rail system. Prentice and Arthur incorporated a wood-burning miniature steam engine in a small homemade locomotive that pulled train cars over wire rails. The ingenuity that went into making the thirty-inch train amazed everyone who watched it run in the yard of the Newmans' Laredo home. Arthur's granddaughter, Lorraine Owens, said the train sometimes carried chicks from the family's coop as unwilling passengers.[17]

The Newman brothers' technical creativity was long remembered by Laredo's residents. In 1915, Prentice returned to Laredo after driving through Tamaulipas and Nuevo León, Mexico. Before Newman could depart for his home in Brownsville, a journalist caught up with him. In the next day's story, the reporter described Prentice as "an old time Laredo boy...who attended the public schools of Laredo twenty-five years ago.... Mr. Newman will be well remembered by old timers of Laredo."[18]

Life on the border sent Prentice down two paths that would define his adult years. He and Arthur both became fluent Spanish speakers and both gained a strong appreciation for the Mexican culture. Those qualities played key roles in tying Prentice and Arthur to the borderlands throughout their adult lives.

The second path began as Prentice started reading about the pioneering aviation feats of Samuel Pierpont Langley and Sir Hiram Maxim. He avidly kept up with the two pioneers' aeronautic trials.[19] At the time, based on Prentice's appreciation for steam engines, he likely agreed with Langley's primitive theory that steam was essential to an engine-powered aeroplane.[20]

Hutokah Caylor Newman, far right, had this portrait with her children taken about 1887 when they lived in Laredo, Texas. The Newman children and approximate ages are, from left, Lily, 14, Arthur, 10, and Prentice, 16. George Banker Owens Collection (MGC 1167-GBOC), Midwest Genealogy Center, Mid-Continent Public Library, Independence, Missouri.

By 1892, the Newman family returned to Karnes County and took up residence in Runge, about seventy miles southeast of San Antonio. In the yard of the Newmans' home, a two-story green house at the edge of town, Prentice and Arthur again set up their small-scale steam-engine train.[21] The sight delighted Runge's residents, yet the Newman brothers had more innovations in store for their neighbors.

In Runge, Prentice incorporated all his tacit and explicit knowledge of steam engines in an innovation. In November 1892, the U.S. Patent Office agreed that Prentice's improved automatic control for a steam boiler's feed-pump mechanism was new and useful. Newman, then just twenty-one, received Patent No. 485,976 for his concept that included a whistle to indicate when a faulty pump needed repair.[22]

Prentice also launched his first technology business in 1892. Family accounts say he moved the miniature train to the store to draw traffic to his specialty watch repair business. Yet, because of Prentice's mechanical competency, the business became more of an all-around fix-it shop. With part-time help from Arthur, who attended Runge High School, the brothers built and repaired bicycles, sewing machines, and farm machinery, once even repairing a cotton gin.[23]

The Newman brothers' association with bicycles paralleled the intellectual path of two other brothers named Wilbur and Orville Wright, who opened their bicycle shop in Dayton, Ohio, in 1893, a year after the Newmans. Bicycle manufacturers, including the Newman and Wright brothers, were responding to customers' demands for lighter, more balanced bicycles than previous iterations. Demand grew as manufacturer improvements encouraged high percentages of America's workers to turn to a "wheel," in the parlance of the day, for everyday commutes.

The Wrights advertised with confidence "that no wheel on the market will run easier or wear longer" than their bicycles.[24] Newman had the same idea, but his engineering mind turned to showing customers rather than telling them through advertising. To illustrate the performance of a Newman bicycle, Prentice rode "on his wheel" from Runge to Georgetown and back, a distance of better than 250 miles, in the furnace of an 1898 Texas July.[25] Arthur performed a similar feat on a Newman bicycle, riding round trip from Runge to San Antonio, a distance of 140 miles.[26]

In this era before improved roads, Central Texas' terrain, excessive temperatures, and high humidity made bicycle riding a tough transportation choice for anything but short hops. Yet the bicycle experience later was as valuable to Prentice as it was essential to the Wright brothers in theories of flight.

Prentice was not the only Newman family member for whom life was in flux as the next century drew closer. Before 1895, Lily moved to Cuero to begin nursing school. In 1895, Arthur graduated in Runge's first senior class. And that same year, Joseph and Hutokah Newman, both long past middle age, brought in a baby girl, Daisy Ethelyne, and raised her as their own. Then on October 9, 1901, their family expanded again when Prentice married Pearl P. Williams, daughter of T. S. Williams, a rancher at Cuero in neighboring DeWitt County.[27]

At the time, Prentice considered his main occupation as "General Repairer (watches &c)."[28] But in 1902, he watched growing fascination for the automobile enrapture his fellow Texans. Unlike Wilbur Wright, who believed the automobile had no future because it was noisy and constantly needed repairing, the Newman brothers embraced this transportation technology and quickly found their niche in repairs.[29]

Third-party repairs were vital because early automobile makers failed to integrate into parts manufacturing to fix their vehicles' frequent breakdowns. The burdensome repair role initially fell to the automobile owner who, in turn, put pressure on the automobile dealer to provide reliable service. With no parts manufacturer available, many leading dealers employed a machinist to make and install defective or broken parts. The Newman brothers, born with mechanical talents, quickly became qualified machinists. From 1902 to 1909, that talent provided Prentice, particularly, with employment in several of Texas' major population centers.[30]

His first stop in 1902 was automobile repair school in Dallas, where he and Pearl lived at 586 Elm Street.[31] Before the birth of their first child, a son they named Prentice Alexander Newman Jr., on March 27, 1904,[32] they moved to Fort Worth, where Prentice became machinist at Fort Worth Auto and Livery Stable.[33] The Newmans lived in a rented home at 307 E. Fifth Street near downtown Fort Worth, but soon moved to a boardinghouse at 914 W. Thirteenth Street, a short walk to his Houston street workplace.[34]

Fate might have kept Newman in the automotive field for his entire career except for two events that shook his professional and personal life. The repercussions of the first event were not immediately clear to him. It occurred on December 17, 1903, at Kitty Hawk, North Carolina, when the Wright brothers piloted the first powered flight of a heavier-than-air machine. The second event, much more personal and one that changed his life, occurred on April 27, 1905, back in Runge.

In contrast to Newman, Robert Runyon was far less spontaneous. He rarely made hasty decisions. He analyzed all possible outcomes of any entrepreneurial action he took in life. Yet he also was a true adventurer, attacking challenges eagerly when he had a plan to mitigate risk. On each of his many ventures, Runyon did his homework and knew exactly where to go, who to trust, what to do, and how to leave and return safely. That's not to say he always calculated correctly, but he never suffered a major setback.

Take his move to Texas. The decision was well planned even though it appeared a hasty and illogical path for the twenty-seven-year-old, five-foot-six, 140-pound, blue-eyed Kentucky native.[35]

Runyon's ties to the commonwealths of Kentucky and Virginia, especially the part of the latter that became the state of West Virginia in 1861, extended back to the late eighteenth century. Counting his direct family, his cousins, and in-laws, his personal network in the Appalachian region was legion. Early on, wherever he traveled, he maximized his capacity to build on key lessons and attitudes that he learned from his forebears. Yet, by adulthood, Runyon had not acquired or inherited land or businesses that would convince him to stay in his home area.

Runyon's genealogical research showed that his Runyon ancestors, Huguenot immigrants from France, came to America by way of the Channel Islands before 1668 and settled in New Jersey. Runyon's fourth great-grandfather, Isaac Runyon, and Isaac's wife, Geertje (Charity) Hagerman or Hegeman, moved from New Jersey to Maryland and then to Virginia. During the Revolution, Isaac and his son, John, Runyon's third-great-grandfather, served together in the Virginia militia. Isaac's pension application to the Virginia General Assembly states that he fought at or near the critical March 1781 military engagement with the British at Guilford County Court House in North Carolina.[36] After independence, Isaac and family moved to Tazewell County, Virginia, probably where Isaac died, a pensioner, after 1821.

Runyon once described that era as a time of "universal desire" to explore new lands to the west as earlier tales of the promise of unsettled frontier, related by famous explorers like Daniel Boone, Christopher Gist, James Harrod, and brothers James, George, and Robert McAfee, continued to resound with families in Virginia and the Carolinas. By 1824, John, and several other Runyons, established multiple family lines in Pike County, Kentucky. Runyon's research concluded that each new arrival established roots in much the same pattern: the patriarch chose his tract and used the available poplar trees to build a log house with a "rough stone chimney." A large wood-burning fireplace inside helped families make it through cold winters.

> "The roof usually was made of clapboards riven from Oak trees, sawed into convenient lengths and fastened with iron nails, called 'cut' nails. The house, being built, the settler began the process of clearing some choice bits of land for the raising of crops, chief among which was Indian corn."[37]

In Kentucky, the Runyon family expanded rapidly. John and his wife, the former Betsy Raemer (or Runner), raised six children. One of his sons, Adron, born in 1801, had fourteen children with his wife, the former Jennie Maynard, as well as some illegitimate children with other women.[38] One of Adron's legitimate sons, Mitchell, born in 1830, moved to Catlettsburg, Boyd County, Kentucky, in the winter of 1877 and purchased a small farm. His wife, the former Margaret (Peggy) Taylor, and nine children followed in the spring of 1877. They moved their essential possessions, including a bear trap that went back generations, by barge up the Tug Fork of the Big Sandy River. That relocation entrenched this branch of the Runyon family in the northeast corner of Kentucky. Mitchell's son, Floyd, then had six children with his first wife, the former Elizabeth Lawson, all near Catlettsburg. The eldest son was Robert Runyon, born July 28, 1881.[39]

Family stories about Mitchell left a giant influence on his grandson's life. One of Runyon's earliest memories was seeing an uncle arrive unexpectedly at his home on a "very cold" morning, January 24, 1886. Before the day ended, Runyon learned the content of the message that his uncle had whispered in his mother's ear: Grandfather Mitchell, who had spent the previous day hunting, died during the night.

Mitchell's memorial took place later that year when better weather allowed relatives to travel from his birthplace at Pond Creek in Pike County. The large numbers of family and friends who converged on Catlettsburg to remember Mitchell months after his death impressed Runyon.[40]

During the preaching, he learned his grandfather moved to Boyd County, with its proximity to both West Virginia and Ohio, to give his eight children a better education than they could receive in Pike County. Runyon turned to travel to gain knowledge the rest of his life.

On Runyon's maternal Lawson side, the lines were equally prolific.

The first Lawson immigrants were Anthony and Ann Bilton Lawson of Stanton, Northumberland, England, tenant farmers and both descendants of long lines of the same. In 1817, Anthony and Ann packed up their four sons, three trunks, two chests, one barrel of wearing apparel, beds and bedding, and one hamper of crockery ware and left Newcastle-upon-Tyne on the *Brig Active* for Philadelphia.[41] The family lived initially in Alexandria, Virginia, where Anthony's younger brother, John, had done well as a tavern owner and grocer after emigrating from Northumberland a year earlier.

To support his family in Alexandria, Anthony sold imported and locally grown seeds—for both forage and crops—through general stores in Alexandria and Washington, D.C. By 1820, though, Anthony moved his family deep into the wilds of Virginia and helped settle what today is Logan County, West Virginia. Anthony prospered by buying beaver fur, cattle hides, and wild ginseng from local farmers and hunters, transporting the commodities by flatboats up the Guyandotte River, then connecting to the Ohio River, to access commercial buyers in Pittsburgh. From proceeds, he bought merchandise that he resold at cost-plus to local landowners through his Logan County general store. The business model was common for the times, but Anthony made it profitable by selecting a remote location where he had little competition for buying from, or supplying to, local residents.[42]

Over time, the Lawson family members, all of whom were born in mean English tenant farmer residences, became community leaders, accumulated wealth, and acquired significant land holdings. Anthony and Ann and some of their sons also owned slaves.

The Lawson family, which had a good run of success for several decades after leaving England, eventually ran into a spate of bad fortune prior to the Civil War.

On May 20, 1847, Anthony died of cholera during a return business trip from Pittsburgh to Logan. His sons buried him where he died at Guyandotte, today a neighborhood of Huntington, West Virginia.

In the same year, on December 27, one of Anthony's two slaves beat Anthony's widow to death with fire tongs. Family legend says Ann Lawson was mending the slave's shirt at the time. Authorities never learned the motive of the murder, although the family suspected it was because Anthony had promised freedom to his slaves after both he and his wife were dead. Ann was buried on a hilltop cemetery in Logan. Her murderer was hanged in Logan County's first public execution, and his accomplice was sent out of the United States.[43]

Even before their deaths, Anthony and Ann's oldest son and Runyon's great-grandfather, John Lawson, had moved his family to today's Mingo County, West Virginia. There, he operated both a general store and a logging operation. In 1844, John was killed by a tree that he was felling.

John's oldest son and Runyon's grandfather, George Washington Lawson, became another principal influence on Runyon's life. After their father's death, George W. and his brothers were raised by their mother, Emily, and her second husband, George Smith. Two of his brothers fought for the Confederacy during the Civil War, both of them as officers. Some Civil War historians also place George W. in a single raid, under the command of his younger brother, Melvin, in October 1864 at Peach Orchard in Lawrence County, Kentucky.[44]

Other evidence, however, indicates that George W. focused on more humanitarian pursuits. At the Civil War's onset, Lawson was a miller in Pike County, Kentucky. Yet before war's end, and for decades after, Logan County citizens knew George W. Lawson as a self-educated physician who practiced in rural parts of West Virginia for poor and affluent residents alike. One story says that during the early morning hours of Christmas 1879, Dr. Lawson provided emergency aid to Devil Anse Hatfield's son, Cap, who had been gut-shot at a Christmas Eve party. Cap survived and continued with his father as principal actors in the Hatfield-McCoy feud. Yet another family story also says that Lawson rode through Union lines during the War to deliver a baby.[45]

In 1945, Runyon wrote of his grandfather:

"Dr. George W. Lawson was an outstanding physician of much fame and practiced medicine in Logan County for many years.... He took great pride in the medical profession and was known as one of the most outstanding physicians of his time. He suffered many hardships during the cold and stormy weather to render services to the sick and suffering people living in the mountains of Logan County."[46]

Robert Runyon, the future accomplished professional photographer, gets perhaps his first look inside a formal studio when he stood for this portrait circa 1893 at about 12 years old in Catlettsburg, Kentucky. RFP, DBCAH, The University of Texas at Austin.

Lawson taught his grandson through example how dedication to the study of science allowed a person to contribute to the academic community without an advanced education. Indeed, even though Lawson had no formal training, *The American Medical Directory of 1908* identifies Dr. Lawson as a licensed medical doctor "based on years of practice." The *Directory of Deceased American Physicians, 1804-1929* lists Lawson of West Virginia as an allopath.[47]

Dr. Lawson's daughter, Elizabeth, married Floyd Runyon in Logan County on December 13, 1874. The couple moved first to Pike County, Kentucky, and then returned to Runyon land near Hampton City on the outskirts of Catlettsburg where Robert Runyon was born and grew up. It is unclear how far in school he went. Runyon's political resume from the 1940s states that he received some high school education, and the 1940 census also records him with nine years of schooling.[48]

His career options in northeastern Kentucky after leaving school were scant but well defined. He could farm, log, mine, or work the railroad. Runyon, in fact, would give farming and railroads a try. Yet his interests and passions lay far beyond those choices. He had an internal thirst that compelled him to pursue knowledge and education in multiple avenues.

In his young adult years, politics earned perhaps his most ardent interest as shown by the numbers of local and national election reports he clipped and kept. Before he was old enough to vote, Runyon avidly followed Grover Cleveland's campaign in his 1894 election to the presidency.[49] As a result of that early association, Runyon tied his lifetime's allegiance to the Democratic Party.

Botany, among all natural sciences, also interested him intensely. Any type of plant, beneficial or not, cultivated or wild, garden variety or weed, fascinated him. As a polymath, he would add other pursuits over the decades to come.

Similar to the choice Newman confronted before he moved to Dallas to work on automobiles, Runyon could have stayed home in Kentucky or West Virginia. Yet, also like Newman, an event out of Runyon's control sent his life reeling. His response was to study the situation, get advice, and then make radical and quick change.

Chapter 2
The Nurse and The Birth

A yellow fever panic in the last half of 1903 seized the population of southern Texas. Yellow fever or yellow jack, named for the color of the skin of the affected person, had plagued Texas and Mexico many times in the past, but this event was unique. It was the first major outbreak to threaten northeastern Mexico and southern Texas since medical journals published new theories about the tropical disease's transmission. The newest research pointed to a particular species of mosquito, *Stegomyia fasciata* (today classified as *Aedes aegypti*), as the disease vector. Based on data, officials theorized that the virulent disease spread from Tampico in early May through infected mosquitoes hitching a ride north in a boxcar as well as from infected persons who also traveled by train.

Texas health officials feared a rapid spread when yellow fever hit Laredo hard in September. State and federal authorities acted quickly to limit the disease's reach beyond that old Texas city.[50]

Then something alarming happened: The disease popped up far from the border between San Antonio and Houston at the Bennet Ranch in DeWitt County. Cuero, the county seat, was just ten miles from the ranch. Even more worrisome, Cuero was a four-hour daily train trip from San Antonio and six hours from Houston, the state's two largest cities at the turn of the century.[51]

How yellow fever reached that rural area perplexed local physicians and state-federal health officials. The ranch occupied the west bank of the Guadalupe River. The ranch headquarters, the site of the outbreak, was at the Bennet family compound at Valentinook, the headright of the family's Spanish land grant in the DeWitt Colony.

The official report of Dr. J. M. Reuss of Cuero, attending physician at Bennet Ranch during the outbreak, offered the most plausible account of how yellow fever arrived.

Reuss, seventy-nine, well understood yellow fever's epidemiology based on then-available knowledge. Reuss had been on the front line of the yellow fever epidemic of 1867 that swept through the Gulf Coast at Indianola, where he personally treated almost half of the six hundred citizens eventually infected during the outbreak. Eighty-five Indianola residents died of the disease. Not yet understanding it traveled via the mosquito, Reuss watched yellow fever then invade Galveston, where it killed 725 persons.[52]

Reuss left Indianola between two devastating hurricanes in 1875 and 1886 that ultimately ended the community's existence. He moved his family seventy-five miles inland to Cuero.[53] By 1888, he had established both a medical practice and a community drugstore.[54]

When sickness hit DeWitt County in 1903, Reuss' recent knowledge of mosquito vector research combined with his previous experience proved immeasurable benefits to the area's health.

Reuss' professional account showed that Anne Bennet, the older sister of ranch manager Robert Bennet, invited a friend from Laredo to visit the ranch. A few days later, the lady's young son traveled from Laredo to join her. Both mother and son fell ill, but their attending physician misdiagnosed their conditions as dengue fever. The two visitors fought through their illnesses, recovered, and departed.

Right away, a husband and wife who worked on the ranch both fell ill. Only then did word spread that the visitors had come from Laredo.

Anne Bennet succumbed next. Robert Bennet too came down with fever. He had suffered health problems for several years due to severe attacks of an unidentified illness, so his body had little defense against the infection.[55]

That was when Reuss took charge. He brought Minnie Toerck, a trained nurse from the Salome Hospital, a clinic that Reuss' son, Dr. J. H. Reuss, had established in the mid-1890s in Cuero after graduation from the College of Physicians and Surgeons in New York.[56]

Salome was the first organized hospital in that sector of rural Texas. The region's residents highly regarded Salome because the widely respected Doctors Reuss headed its medical staff. Residents also appreciated that the hospital certificated its nurses following a medical training course. Training protocols were rare in rural Texas health care, but well appreciated for producing qualified health professionals by citizens of DeWitt and surrounding counties.

On day seven of the ranch outbreak, Reuss reported Robert Bennet's death after seeing telltale black vomit—the black hemorrhagic bile that a fevered patient expelled from the stomach at late disease stages. State and federal health officers traveled immediately to the ranch to observe Reuss' autopsy. The findings confirmed yellow fever.[57]

Five days later, a "healthy and robust" young woman living on the ranch took ill. She died six days later. Reuss' autopsy again confirmed yellow fever.

State officials believed the Bennet Ranch's isolated location negated a need for a county-wide quarantine despite the deaths. Instead, the state locked down the ranch so ill persons could not travel and spread infection.

To manage the threat, Reuss fumigated the ranch houses with sulfur powder to control adult mosquitoes and moved ranch owners, ranch hands, their families, and the Salome nurse to a temporary camp on higher ground two miles from Valentinook. The location put needed distance between the Bennet Ranch personnel, the Guadalupe River, and any adjacent mosquito-breeding pools of water.

After confirmation of the cause of deaths, Nurse Toerck immediately covered her arms, face, and neck to protect her skin from mosquitoes as she went about her duties. It was too late. Ten days after arrival, Toerck showed symptoms. Reuss confined her to a separate tent away from the temporary camp.[58]

Reuss then requested that Salome send a volunteer to continue the health care at the ranch. He was gratified to see Lily Newman step forward immediately.[59]

The older Reuss was well aware of Lily's reputation as a nurse who cared deeply for her patients' welfare. Lily had received her nursing certificate from Salome Hospital on April 15, 1903.[60] Even before that, she had been part of a medical team organized by Reuss on May 18, 1902, to bring aid to Goliad in the wake of the deadliest tornado recorded up to that year in Texas history.[61] Lily's brother, Prentice, and his wife, Pearl, also had volunteered.[62]

At the Bennet Ranch, Lily's responsibilities included nursing the infected ranch group as well as Nurse Toerck.[63] Lily took preventive measures upon arrival, donning netting around her face and neck and wearing long leather gloves. Her apparel left no skin exposed to mosquitoes.

The days were long because of Lily's regular meticulous patient treatments under Reuss' medical protocol. Lily bathed the patients' feet in mustard baths and applied mustard plasters to backs and chests. She prepared and dispensed oral doses of calomel and castor oil with diuretic herbal teas brewed from sage and orange leaves. She rubbed patients' bodies with cut lemon to stimulate their skin. When required, she also had to inject some patients with morphine to calm restlessness and administer aconite, an anti-fever herb that Reuss preferred over quinine.

Five days after Lily's arrival, all patients' fevers dissipated. Lily's focus then turned to the nutritional regimen so each patient could move on from a liquid diet. Thirteen days after infection, Lily telephoned the Yoakum newspaper from the ranch with news that Nurse Toerck had recovered.[64] Forty-eight hours after that call, Reuss lifted the ranch restrictions.[65]

At the final assessment, two persons—Bennet and the unnamed young woman—died of yellow fever on the ranch. More than six persons infected by the virus had survived, largely due to Lily's care under Reuss' protocol. By year's end, yellow fever moved out of Texas altogether. It was the last significant outbreak of this disease in the state's history,[66] thanks in part to medical teams like Reuss and Lily who used the new knowledge that identified mosquitoes as carriers.

A few months after the crisis, a group of DeWitt County leaders asked all residents to honor Lily's selflessness. The campaign had a simple rule: No one could contribute more than twenty-five cents so that everyone could afford to participate and, by inference, everyone needed to participate. Before the year ended, the campaign purchased Lily a "costly" gold watch.[67] The inscription read:

"Presented to Miss Lillian Newman by her friends and citizens of Cuero as a recognition of her loyalty to her calling. Nov. 1903."[68]

About the time Texas started battling yellow fever, another young woman far to the north celebrated a milestone that would soon be followed by another. In September 1902, Nora Runyon reached the second anniversary of her marriage to Robert Runyon. And by December she became pregnant with their first child.

The child represented the fourth generation of her family in eastern Kentucky. The former Nora Young's maternal grandfather, John Diuguid Mims, had helped settle northeast Kentucky when it was still a frontier. By 1830, Mims became wealthy within this pristine area.

In those years, the mountains of eastern Kentucky supported abundant wildlife—bear, deer, raccoon, wild turkey, wild pigeon, and pheasants—while its pure streams of water teemed with fish. Settlers supplemented the wild fare by raising cattle, sheep, and hogs for food. The sheep provided wool for weaving cloth, and cattle hides provided leather for shoes. Most settlers also had a horse or two. "Since there were no roads at first, excepting the trails which the men cut among the trees, the only method of travel was on foot or on horseback," Runyon said.

In winter months, settlers utilized a second income stream the land offered them. After crop harvests, they turned their energy toward cutting the fine timber that surrounded their properties. As a boy in the mid-1880s, Runyon remembered seeing "long teams of oxen…haul the logs from the big Yellow Poplar trees to splash dams which had been built across the streams for the purpose of catching heads of water to splash out the logs to the river. They were rafted together in convenience rafts and floated down the river to market at Catlettsburg, Ironton, and other river towns." He said this industry lasted until the forests became depleted in the early twentieth century.

Mims was not interested in farming, logging, or hunting himself, though. He followed the same business model that Anthony Lawson, Runyon's second-great-grandfather, conducted on the Guyandotte River in Logan County, ninety miles to the southeast. Mims bought crop harvests, wool, hides, and wild ginseng gathered by the settlers and transported these commodities up the Ohio River for sale in Pittsburgh. From the profit, he purchased goods to stock his own general store in Pike County from which he serviced settlers and their families. This circular supply chain provided Big Sandy Valley residents with an ever-growing variety of necessities including sugar, salt, coffee, and clothing.

Around 1854, Mims saw potential a little further north in the town of Catlettsburg in Boyd County. After relocating, Mims integrated into the hide tanning process. By adding an extra processing step, Mims captured higher profit from his buyers for each raw hide that he purchased from local farmers. His model soon generated a measure of wealth for the growing Mims family. He already had two children by his first wife, who had died before his move to Boyd County. His second wife had given birth to two sons and one daughter, Nora's mother, Mary Louise.[69]

In 1879, when the Mims family was among the wealthiest occupants in the region, Mary Louise met thirty-three-year-old William Thornton Young of Ohio, a divorced man living in Pikeville. Like Mary Louise, Young came from a retail background although one much less ambitious than the Mims model. Young's father was a dry goods merchant in Adams County, Ohio; Young was a salesman for Singer Sewing Machines.[70]

From the beginning, the Mims family had a low opinion of the salesman as a potential son-in-law, causing Young and Mary Louise to elope.[71] After the wedding, the couple moved to Prestonsburg in Pike County, where Young continued representing Singer products. Despite the Mims family's objections, though, his occupation proved a fit for both husband and wife as they began to raise a family. In 1880, Nora came into their lives, followed in 1883 by a son, Edgar, and in 1887 by a daughter, Ella, after the Young family relocated to Hampton City in Boyd County, the small community located just south of Catlettsburg where the Big Sandy joins the Ohio River.[72] In the new location, Young gained employment as a hardware store clerk.[73] The family's neighbors were Floyd and Elizabeth Lawson Runyon and their children—three boys and two girls by 1897.[74]

Runyon, born half a year after Nora, likely worked and lived apart from his family shortly after quitting school in the ninth grade, sometime after 1895.

Runyon certainly was living on his own near Catlettsburg by 1900. Nora stayed in school until she was nineteen.

By the turn of the century, an attraction grew between Runyon and Nora.[75] On September 16, 1901, the couple slipped across the Big Sandy, probably by steamboat ferry, and traveled to Ironton, Lawrence County, Ohio.[76] Although each was twenty years of age, they attested before the probate judge issuing their wedding license that day to be a year older.[77] Then at 3 p.m. at the Palace Hotel, Justice of the Peace William D. Henry joined them in marriage.[78]

The event sparked Runyon's entrepreneurial drive for the rest of his life. Marriage fueled his polymathy as he began pursuing myriad interests, some for revenue and others to satisfy a thirst for knowledge. After marriage, Runyon also started documenting his life, his interests, and his activities through diaries, journals, and files, archiving even mundane correspondence and business receipts.

Runyon's entrepreneurial impetus may have been preparation for when he and Nora would have children. And farming, coal mining, or logging did not fit his ambition after marriage any better than they had before he met Nora.

With Nora, he had an ally. Her grandfather's model had served her family well for decades. Her father also had worked outside northeastern Kentucky's common careers. As a result, Nora was more liberally minded in allowing Runyon to follow non-traditional job paths than would another Kentucky wife.

At the time, Runyon showed no political aspirations, instead observing how the Democratic Party functioned, election protocol, and how party affiliation put a person in position to run for office. Runyon registered his first vote in the 1902 midterm election in Kentucky and his first vote for president for William Jennings Bryan in the 1904 election. In 1906 and 1908, at his own expense, he observed how politicians hit the stump by driving a candidate to campaign events in a buggy.[79] Yet his political focus was sporadic, for as educational as his early election activities might have been, they cost Runyon money when he needed to grow income.

He began to cure that deficiency by selling insurance. By 1903 Runyon was a representative of the Prudential Insurance Co. of America and a bill collector for the International Law & Collection Company of Dayton, Ohio. He and Nora may have moved briefly to Ironton so that he could better service customers in both Ohio and West Virginia, but, if so, they soon moved back to Kentucky to prepare for their first child.[80]

At 6 a.m. on August 6, 1904, just a few weeks before Runyon and Nora's third anniversary, Dr. L. T. Hood delivered a boy at the Runyon home at 607 E. Carter St. in Ashland. They named the son William Thornton Runyon after Nora's father.[81]

Chapter 3
Sudden Tragic Losses

The Mason brothers, natives of Missouri, fell into the outsider category in the late 1890s when they took up residence in Yoakum in Lavaca County, Texas. The Masons, Frederick and Elmer, who went by Shell, initially had come to south central Texas to investigate various business opportunities.[82]

Yoakum seemed a good location. Since the 1860s, the town's site had been a traditional gathering spot for South Texas herds headed to market up the Chisholm Trail. When the San Antonio and Aransas Pass (SAAP) Railway built tracks through the location in 1887, a town named for SAAP executive Benjamin F. Yoakum blossomed around the old cattle pens.[83] Despite the railroad's importance, though, cotton and livestock paid bills for folks in the country. And to raise fiber and protein, the landowners needed farm and ranch supplies. By 1898, Frederick and Shell had identified that need and built a livery stable and store in Yoakum as "the place to get feed of all kinds."[84]

A fire in January 1905 destroyed the Mason brothers' first concern, but they rebuilt rapidly on Yoakum's best commercial lot. When completed, the feed store expanded to two separate buildings, including a structure entirely made of sheet metal.[85]

Knowing they were outsiders, the Masons worked hard to fit into the community. After Fred married, he and his wife, Margaret, bought a house in town that was cater-corner to the Lane Hotel, billed as "the only first class hotel in Yoakum."[86] Since the house was just a short walk from the feed store, Shell, a bachelor, took a room with his brother and sister-in-law.[87]

Each day, the Masons' servant fixed Shell an early breakfast so he could leave just as the town woke up. A gate, located outside a long gallery that connected the house's kitchen to its pantry, provided access to Lott Street. As he exited the gate, if he glanced toward the Lane Hotel on the opposite corner, he might sometimes see lights in Room No. 2 as an early-rising salesman readied for a morning appointment. From Lott Street, it took a few minutes' walk south to reach the Mason Brothers' feed store on May Street.[88]

Most neighbors considered Shell likable. His customers considered him "a good businessman" with a "jovial disposition." In his personal life, Mason "enjoyed the acquaintance and friendship of a large number of people."[89] Yet in Lavaca County, where many families inherited ranchland from ancestors who came with Austin or Green DeWitt or who fought in the Texas Revolution, the Masons from Missouri always were outsiders.

Nonetheless, some Yoakum residents enjoyed salacious gossip surrounding Shell's private affairs. As a bachelor, Shell had earned a reputation as "somewhat of a 'Don Juan.'"[90] So imaginations and rumors ran wild when Lily Newman started seeing the thirty-one-year-old Mason about 1904, after she had moved to Yoakum to continue her nursing career. At the time, Lily was the last of Joseph and Hutokah Newman's children still living in the area. Prentice was repairing automobiles in North Texas. Arthur had moved to Alice, Texas, where he ran a jewelry business that repaired railroad watches and firearms for a clientele that included Texas Rangers.[91]

Mason and Lily could not keep their relationship secret in DeWitt, Lavaca, or Karnes counties. Even if Lily were not a prestigious trained nurse and a heroine for stemming the spread of yellow fever, her surname alone brought notice.[92] Neighbors found curious the attraction of a reputable young lady to a man they considered a libertine. Before long, whether Lily and Mason wanted it known or not, everyone considered them "sweethearts."[93] As it turned out, they were.

By early 1905, Lily learned she was pregnant. In her mind, that revelation could only lead to a single course of action. When Lily informed Shell of the pregnancy, she asked him to marry her.[94]

Mason agreed. Although Lily's father was alive, Mason chose to gain consent first from Lily's mother. Mrs. Newman gave her permission and immediately began to make Lily's wedding dress. By the haste, it is possible Lily also told her about the pregnancy.

Almost immediately, though, Mason wavered from his pledge and decided to pursue a radically different course. Mason persuaded Lily to meet with Dr. John Boyd, a Yoakum physician, to end the pregnancy. Boyd recommended measures that Lily followed toward the last week of April. That method failed and Lily's health declined rapidly. Any remedy for the botched attempt was beyond Boyd's abilities, so Lily and Mason rushed by train to Houston to seek medical assistance.

They found no relief in Houston, and Lily's already dreadful physical suffering grew worse. Rather than stay the night, the couple returned to Yoakum by night train. Mason hoped that the 10:15 p.m. departure from Houston's Grand Central Depot, with arrival at the Yoakum depot at 3:15 a.m., would lessen chances acquaintances would see him with Lily. His bad luck was to run into W. C. Thrift, a former dry goods merchant in Yoakum, who had moved to Houston a year earlier to start a sale barn. When Thrift hailed the couple on the southbound train, their response took him aback.

Mason did not reply. He drew his hat over his face, feigning sleep, to avoid eye contact. Thrift remembered too Lily's pale complexion and her apparent bodily pain that rendered her physically and mentally unable to acknowledge him.

When the train pulled into the Yoakum depot five hours later, Lily was in grave condition. Mason could have carried Lily to his brother's home or he could have delivered her to her own residence in Yoakum. At either location she could have received needed medical care. Yet, faced with starkly different options, Mason chose a craven course. He lodged Lily "in a house of questionable reputation" to keep anyone from recognizing her.[95] A brothel, though, proved a poor hiding place. Persons did see Lily there, and they described her condition as "sick and helpless."

Shell persuaded Boyd to check on Lily, but the doctor could not ease her suffering. By the next day, Lily ordered Mason to take her to her mother in Runge.

There, Lily's strength dissipated rapidly even after Mrs. Newman brought in two Karnes County physicians, Doctors Joseph Lackey and S. S. Robinson, to attend. If Lily had any good memories of her close relationship with Mason, she forgot them that day. Lily confided to her mother that Mason had treated her "like a dog." Lily said if her mother knew the misery that Mason had caused her life, her mother "would feel like killing him."

On April 27, Lily asked her mother to summon Mason. He made the fifty-mile trip and Mrs. Newman witnessed her daughter beg him to marry her. Mason agreed again, but said he first had to leave for a while. Those were the last words exchanged between the two wretched lovers.

At 9 p.m. that night, Lily died at the age of thirty-two. Mrs. Newman, herself just fifty-five years of age, immediately contacted Prentice in Fort Worth and Arthur in Alice to give them the sad news of their sister's tragic, untimely death.

The news also reached Mason, still in Runge. He returned to the room where Lily's body lay. By then, Lackey and Robinson had brought in a colleague, Dr. John Burns, to conduct an autopsy.

Burns' presence shook Mason. Witnesses described him as visibly nervous. Robinson pulled Mason aside to quell his anxiety, and Mason used the private conversation to protest the autopsy. He told Robinson that when the post-mortem findings became public "hell would be to pay with him." Mason said he needed time to make plans to leave the country altogether and he "entreated and begged" Robinson to postpone the procedure until Mason at least could depart Runge.

When his pleas could not change the doctors' decision, Mason left for Yoakum.[96]

After William was born, Runyon moved his family to Williamson, West Virginia, a new town on the Tug River, a tributary of the Big Sandy. Williamson had several Runyon relatives among its population, among them Runyon's grandfather, Dr. George W. Lawson.[97]

Runyon secured a clerk's position with the Norfolk & Western Railway Company, which had terminated its Pocahontas and Scioda divisions at Williamson just a few years before. Runyon soon moved up to assistant general yardmaster with management duties. His responsibilities included overseeing the efficient switching of rail cars.[98]

During this time, Runyon also enlisted in the West Virginia National Guard for three years. He mustered into service on July 24, 1905, at Parkersburg as a private in Company E, Second Infantry Regiment.[99] That commitment indicated that Runyon expected to stay in West Virginia with his wife and son for several years.

Perhaps it was Nora who yearned to return to her family in Boyd County. Whatever the reason, evidence shows that while Runyon worked in 1906 and 1907 for N&W Railway, he maintained a residence in Boyd County, Kentucky, where he registered to vote. Julia C. Ford, a close cousin, said that when Runyon was in Williamson he lived with his grandfather until Lawson's death on August 1, 1906. His N&W position may have been as needed, allowing him to rotate travel to Williamson for a week and remain home in Boyd County the next week.[100]

Runyon definitely had returned to Kentucky full-time by April 1907 when the West Virginia National Guard dropped him for living "out of bounds" from West Virginia. Although he could not receive a full and honorable discharge because he did not fulfill the full enlistment term, his commanding officer praised him. He wrote on Runyon's discharge papers: "Service Honest & faithful, Character Excellent. Ability above the average."[101]

During these years, Runyon supplemented what he earned from railroad work and his ongoing insurance commissions with a sales representative position with Graham Nursery Company in Rochester, New York. His position promised a thirty percent commission for plants that he sold to a sales area of Kentucky, West Virginia, and Ohio. A year later, he became authorized agent for another Rochester nursery, James B. Nellis & Company. Even later he added Kalamazoo Nursery Company of Michigan to his sales efforts. This latter grower introduced Runyon to the power of promotion by supplying him with abundant printed materials to promote sales.[102]

Runyon's several diverse jobs provided the income stream that he sought. His 1906 record indicates a number of investments he made for his family's future. In July, he bought accident insurance for himself and $100 life insurance policies in his, his wife's, and his son's names. In October, he went to a Catlettsburg jeweler and purchased two fifteen-jewel watches (his a used Elgin and a new Waltham for Nora).[103]

Even so, Runyon constantly sought new revenue ideas. He had become interested in the chemistry of mirroring by studying methods of craftsmen like K. W. MacMasters of Peru, Indiana. In time, Runyon developed a silvering system that he believed could benefit a wider public. He wrote and published *The Mirror Plater's Guide*, an instructional pamphlet he sold for $1 postpaid with customer support for ten cents per inquiry. The guide provided formulas and instructions on how to silver mirrors and chip, etch, foil, and emboss glass.

No copies of this pamphlet exist other than the one in Runyon's files indicating a limited press run. Its acceptance probably was slight as well since Runyon acknowledged his process was difficult to master. "The student should not expect to make first-class mirrors on the first trial and must work it on a small scale till he gets some experience," Runyon wrote. "Silvering mirrors is not a matter of formula, however good, but a trade to itself."[104]

Understanding the technology behind a properly silvered mirror seems to have led Runyon to study a mirror's function in the emerging technology of cameras. In turn, that inspired him to investigate how to create postcards, known as "postals" in the jargon of the day. Kodak had introduced postcard-sized photographic paper in 1902, and by the time Runyon began making postcards four years later, the product had revolutionized personal communication. While some companies mass-produced postcards for the commercial marketplace, Kodak's technology allowed individuals to create their own for personal messages. Runyon quickly absorbed the power of postcards in both applications.

Runyon saved most postals he received from friends, family, and customers. He observed that the postcards carried everyday images—people, buildings, town squares, landscapes, and bridges—from places both familiar and foreign. His analysis also showed he could create his own postcard line as another revenue source. Yet he had to master photography first.

Runyon began producing postcards with photographs he took of friends as early as summer 1906, but his first recorded purchase of a camera came eighteen months later. Runyon's $20 purchase made on December 2, 1907, during a trip to Cincinnati, Ohio, provided him with an Eastman Kodak No. 3-A folding pocket camera that made 3¼ x 5½ inch photographs—ideal for postcard-size images.[105]

Runyon put the camera to work immediately to accelerate his learning curve. Good exposures required handling a multitude of light conditions, so he committed to study and trial-and-error practice to reach competency.

On December 12, he traveled across the Ohio River to take West Virginia landscape scenes including the Chesapeake & Ohio Railway Bridge and the powerhouse. Three days after Christmas he went with friends and his young son up the Cannonsburg Pike. He took scenic views by experimenting with filters and tried his luck with a difficult sunset exposure. On the third day of 1908, he ventured out in frigid temperatures to take action shots of ice skaters at Clyffeside Park in Ashland. On the last day of January, he experimented with photos taken with the subdued light of a winter's day at Ashland's Central Park.

Rupert McClung, a Catlettsburg photographer, developed Runyon's film. After each roll, Runyon critically appraised his progress. Remarkably, the action images taken at Clyffeside Park were the only uniformly well-exposed attempts. The failures mostly were exposure related, but he also blamed old film.

In March, Runyon practiced on models, choosing Nora and her friend, Viola Scott. He chided himself that two photos of Viola didn't come out because of "failure to roll up film." The balance of the photos, though, he rated "all good."[106] During that spring, Runyon also adopted a more professional business approach. In April he returned to Cincinnati and purchased a Remington #6 typewriter to send typewritten correspondence.[107]

Life for the Runyon family pointed toward ever better promise in Kentucky. Runyon committed to his state by volunteering on July 3, 1908, for a three-year term as private in the Kentucky State Guard, Company K, Second Regiment of Infantry.[108] At the same time, he invested renewed vigor in his sales channels. On July 10, 1908, he was elected secretary of the Boyd County Farmers Club to expand his network for plant and seed sales. In autumn 1908, Runyon signed an agent contract with Southern Fire Insurance Company Inc. of Lynchburg, Virginia. In addition, he immersed himself for the first time in public service by winning a race to fill a two-year term as trustee of the sub-district, educational division No. 1, for Boyd County. He also became secretary of the Boyd County Democratic Party executive committee.[109]

Then came the cold winter months of 1908. On December 2, Nora was throwing feed to chickens at their home in Ashland when she noticed she was bleeding.[110] That evening, Runyon took her and William to her parents' home closer to Catlettsburg so Nora could receive care. Overnight, her condition worsened.

At 9:30 a.m. on December 3, Nora's death came without warning; its suddenness stunned Runyon and her family. Nora's obituary stated bluntly that she "dropped dead at the home of her father."[111] In his diary notes for that day, Runyon wrote uterine hemorrhaging as cause of death.[112]

For a man whose planning made life orderly, Runyon suddenly found himself doing just the opposite. He was handling funeral arrangements and contemplating a new future for him and his young son. And he had to do something out of character—he had to act quickly.

Chapter 4
Death Comes on the Night Train

rentice left Fort Worth as soon as news of Lily's death reached him. He traveled to Runge to mourn his sister as well as seek answers about her unexpected death.

Far to the south, Arthur also departed for Runge from his residence in Alice.

After the brothers arrived, Burns released his autopsy findings. His examination showed that Lily had died of blood poisoning caused by an attempt to force premature birth of a child. Prentice asked Lackey to clarify the statement and was told that Lily "actually died from the effects of the attempted abortion." The doctors identified Mason as "father of said unborn child."[113] The report stunned the family, none of whom knew Mason.

On April 29, the day after the autopsy, the Newman family buried Lily at Runge City Cemetery. Every business shuttered its doors during the funeral and public schools dismissed students for the day. Each mourner remembered Lily's devoted attention to her neighbors' care during the region's yellow fever scare two years prior. In her obituary, the town's editor wrote: "Seldom has a death occurred that has brought forth such universal sorrow."[114]

Over the next days, Prentice and Arthur sequestered themselves at their parents' home. Before her last hours, Lily had never hinted to any family member that Mason had treated her badly. Yet when their mother related Lily's deathbed tales of mental abuse, the words fueled anger in the two brothers.

At times, they questioned Lily's friends, and those inquiries led some persons to conjecture that the brothers intended to harm Mason and the doctor who facilitated the abortion attempt. The law authorities in fact did advise Mason and Dr. Boyd of the rumors, although they did not confront the Newmans.[115]

One man privy to all was the Newmans' uncle, W. H. Leckie, a native of Illinois who had moved to Texas after the Civil War and married Martha Newman, sister of Joseph Austin Newman. The Newman children were close to their uncle and aunt. Martha had witnessed Prentice's birth in Gillett thirty-four years earlier. Growing up, the Newman children often spent Sunday afternoons with the Leckies, enjoying ice cream and cookies and participating in song fests. Leckie had watched his nephews and niece turn into adults after they returned to Karnes County from Laredo in the late 1890s.[116] And when the nephews needed him most, Leckie became their confidant.

Despite the dark discussions, Arthur seized the opportunity of being home to marry Lucy Lawson, the daughter of Thomas Jefferson and Lucille G. Lawson, on May 6 in Karnes County.[117] Yet any celebration lasted briefly as Prentice and Arthur soon moved their plan forward.

The first action sent Prentice and Arthur to Yoakum for at least one and perhaps two days. The brothers did not confront Mason on this trip. They later maintained they had not even seen him. It appears this trip's purpose solely was to identify a location, establish the timing, and confirm a method of revenge.[118]

On their return to Runge, they finalized their plan. Prentice, always self-assured, but also quiet and introspective, had undergone a chilling transformation in manner and appearance that concerned family members. He refused to eat or sleep during those woeful days. When he conversed, his topic turned to death. Observers noted he was jumpy, even around close family members, as if he shouldered a heavy burden he would not share.[119] Either during or right after this period, Newman claimed he no longer believed in God.[120]

Acquaintances saw a change in Mason's personality as well. He had adopted a façade of boldness that disguised his mounting stress. When law officials advised Mason of a possible threat from the Newman brothers, "he averred 'that he was from Missouri, and had to be shown.'"[121] To advisers who urged a low profile, Mason stated that he had done nothing wrong. He no longer talked about fleeing the country as he had intimated to Lily's physicians following her death.[122] Mason's plan now seemed to hope time would soften hard resentment of him by the hundreds of neighbors who had loved Lily and supported her family.

Mason's actions, though, demonstrated less swagger than his words. He began appearing in public wearing only shirtsleeves to show he carried no firearms.[123] Mason walked a thin line of portraying normal confidence during those late spring days yet simultaneously demonstrating he wanted no trouble.

Nonetheless, trouble stalked him with a deadly focus beginning a little before 1 a.m. on May 16. That's when three men, one of them carrying a long oblong case, climbed aboard the eastbound SAAP Davy Crockett at the Runge depot. The night train, promoted as "always on time," stopped briefly at Yorktown and Cuero before it arrived at Yoakum a little before 3 a.m. There, the three men disembarked. The traveler carrying the long case roused a hack driver to take him to the Lane Hotel. His two companions followed on foot in the cool night air.

Reassembled at the hotel, the three travelers stirred the proprietor, J. F. Williams, who clerked the desk that night. Williams saw the long case and assumed he was checking in a sales team. Each man signed his name to the register: P. Alexander, San Antonio; M. Arthur, Alice; and William Harris, Cuero. Alexander and Arthur shared Room No. 2, located at the southeast corner of the ground floor; one of them kept the long case with him; Harris took an upstairs room.[124]

Inside Room No. 2, each occupant went to the long case. One man selected a .38-40 Winchester; the other took a similar .44-40[125] out of the long case. Many Texans at the turn of the century used those caliber bullets with soft-nosed tips in older-model Winchester rifles for hunting white-tailed deer. Then the men moved into positions by adjacent windows from which each had a clear view down Lott Street.[126] And they watched and waited.

Activity at the Mason house on the diagonal corner to the Lane Hotel's Room No. 2 started early, just as it did every morning for the feed store owners. Shell was still awaiting breakfast when the clock struck 6:30 a.m. He elected to skip the meal and go open the store.

Mason left the kitchen and walked down the roofed gallery to the house's pantry. He exited a side door and then went out the gate. One yard later, he turned left on Lott Street and strolled south toward May Street and the Mason brothers' business.

The sounds of other local proprietors, also headed to their storefronts, enveloped Mason. Some of the last words Mason would have heard were the town's paperboys hawking the latest editions of Texas newspapers, some of which had arrived on the same Davy Crockett train that carried the three strangers.

Mason had covered in total about twenty-two feet when two, almost simultaneous, rifle shots originating from Room No. 2 shattered the twilight calm. Immediately a third shot echoed through the streets.[127]

Mason dropped to the ground, his body stretching from the street to the gutter. Only the second shot had missed.[128]

Fred and Margaret Mason, in their home just a few dozen yards from the windows of Room No. 2, knew the terrible message those explosive sounds carried. The couple dashed to where Shell lay mortally wounded. Fred carried his brother into his home as Shell's life started slipping away. Dr. S. I. Youngkin arrived within forty-five minutes of the shooting, but could do nothing. Shell died without gaining consciousness ninety minutes after his first step outside his brother's house.

Within the Lane Hotel, panic swept over other guests. Many hotel occupants oddly fled the shelter of their rooms to gather in the lobby.

The occupants of Room No. 2 also acted quickly. They instructed Williams to summon authorities so they could surrender. Williams reached the town's constable who placed the pair, now identified by their true names of Prentice Alexander Newman and Malcolm Arthur Newman, under arrest. Their uncle, William Leckie, who had registered as William Harris, was not included in the arrest and was never mentioned in subsequent legal action.[129]

One account said the Newman brothers appeared before the constable with tears in their eyes. The brothers did issue a short statement: "We are sorry circumstances have forced us to take the steps we have taken." The constable ordered the Newmans confined under guard in their hotel room to await charges.[130]

News of the killing spread rapidly from Yoakum to all other towns in Karnes, Lavaca, and DeWitt counties, and then beyond. Many Texas newspapers ran the story of Mason's ambush the next day. National dailies did too, including *The Washington Post*, which put its report on page one. Some articles mentioned Lily's death as inciting the shooting.[131]

Not all news was accurate. Immediate reports identified Prentice as Pat; however, Pat was the nickname old schoolmates called Arthur. The same account said Prentice operated a gunsmith shop in Fort Worth; again, it was Arthur who repaired guns at his Alice jewelry shop. A reporter erroneously stated that Prentice held many patents on firearm innovations when the only patent either brother had was Prentice's steam engine invention.

Another reporter said Prentice and Arthur both were crack shots. That statement seems obvious since most men who grew up on Texas ranches could shoot expertly. The reporters would later learn, though, that through the Newman brothers' planning, they did not have to be great shots that day; they just had to be patient ones.

Chapter 5
The Unwritten Law

The day after the shooting, May 17, Fred Mason arranged to send his brother's body by rail to the home of their parents, James T. and Rebecca Jane Mason, in Webster County, Missouri. A few days later, the family buried Shell at Pleasant View Cemetery at Elkland, Missouri. After months of spending every available hour together, Lily and Shell were separated for eternity in cemeteries eight hundred miles apart.[132]

The same day, Yoakum law authorities learned that a large contingent of men was headed to their town. The group comprised well-known, longtime area stockmen and merchants who worked the land and conducted business in the area every day. All of them were God-fearing individuals who had known the Newman family all their lives. They watched Prentice and Arthur develop their unique engineering skills. They applauded when Lily, in a white organdy dress, graduated Salome Hospital as a certified nurse.[133] They were among the grateful citizens who contributed two bits each in 1904 to present Lily with a gold watch in appreciation for her health care during the yellow fever outbreak. Now they traveled to Yoakum to support Prentice and Arthur—two of their own.

To these men, Mason was an outsider who had debauched Lily; Mason had arranged the botched abortion; Mason had abandoned Lily in time of need; Mason bore sole responsibility for her disgrace and her demise. Perhaps few men in the group would have sought the same vengeance on Mason if they reversed roles with one of the Newman brothers. Nonetheless, the brothers' deadly action to avenge their sister did not sway these men's support for the grieving Newman family.

Authorities assured Yoakum citizens that they expected no trouble from these twenty men. Just to be sure, though, the authorities brought in other area lawmen.[134]

Lavaca County Attorney W. T. Bagby set the examining trial for 11 a.m. A bit before the hour, guards escorted the brothers to the chambers of Justice of the Peace J. W. Rees. The Newmans, advised by their attorneys, S. C. Lackey of Cuero and A. J. Bell of Karnes County, waived the preliminary hearing and requested bond. Rees set bail at $2,500 for each Newman brother.

Seventeen supporters stepped forward as sureties on the bond. The judge released the brothers with instructions that they appear in Hallettsville for the next session of the Lavaca County grand jury on October 16. Before returning to Runge, the brothers issued an additional statement assuring the public "that the report that had gained circulation that they intended to harm other parties was absolutely without foundation."[135] The words were directed to Dr. Boyd. However, Lavaca County law authorities were not finished with the doctor.

The examining trial marked the beginning of a lengthy legal strategy by the Newmans to stay free. The first step was the brothers' autumn appearance before the grand jury. During that court term, Louis Wagener, foreman of the grand jury, heard testimony and then signed a manslaughter indictment stating that the brothers:

> "...under the immediate influence of sudden passion arising from an adequate cause neither justified nor excused by Law, unlawfully and voluntarily kill and slay E. S. Mason by then and there shooting the said E. S. Mason with a Winchester Rifle."[136]

At arraignment, each brother pled not guilty. Each brother posted $1,000 bond and returned to his home. The Mason family and the county's prosecuting attorneys discovered immediately that securing a conviction would be challenging. In reporting on the indictment, *The Hallettsville New Era* reminded readers that "(Shell) Mason had betrayed the sister of the slayers." Its editor went on:

> "The young men, during their stay here, won the friendship and sympathy of all with whom they came in contact, by reason of their gentlemanly demeanor as well as the extenuating circumstances surrounding their case. This is illustrated by the fact that three members of the grand jury, including the foreman [Wagener], are on their bond."[137]

On the same day, the grand jury indicted Boyd for malpractice in aiding Lily's procurement of an abortion method.

The Newman brothers hired the law firm of Davidson & Bailey of Cuero as defense attorneys. The primary partner, Asbury Bascom Davidson, was elected Texas lieutenant governor before the defense trials had run their course. Davidson also was a personal friend of Arthur's father-in-law, T. J. Lawson.[138]

These attorneys predictably turned to the "unwritten law" as the brothers' defense. The unwritten law had no legal basis in any state or federal statute. Nonetheless, from the nineteenth into the early twentieth centuries, attorneys defending cases involving passion and sex found the legal anomaly highly persuasive with juries.

By the 1900s, the unwritten law defense had developed certain criteria. A defendant who killed an unrelated male had to have done so because the deceased had relations with a wife, an unmarried daughter, or unmarried sister. Defense lawyers employing the strategy sought to make existing law subordinate to personal beliefs on the morality of adultery, seduction, predation, or abortion. When the jury focused on emotion rather than law, then the defense had a chance to gain acquittals for their clients even though a man had lost his life.[139]

In their unwritten law defense, the Newmans' attorneys never disagreed that their clients' actions killed Mason. Instead, the lawyers claimed that the brother who had killed Mason was emotionally impaired after learning the circumstances surrounding Lily's treatment by Mason and her resulting death. That brother pulled the trigger because of temporary insanity.

An integral factor was the brothers' contention that neither had laid eyes on Shell until the moment he left the Masons' house. That claim sidestepped the question of how the brothers knew that Mason's daily routine was to walk to his business at dawn. Or how they knew it was Shell exiting that morning and not his older brother or a servant. Nor did it consider that the Newmans likely had reserved Room No. 2 to gain open lines of shot at dawn. Yet nothing in the scant court records shows that the prosecution ever questioned any of the Newmans' incongruous claims.

When the Newmans' attorneys checked off requirements for an unwritten law defense, they saw all necessary ingredients but one. The attorneys could remedy that deficiency, but the action had dangerous implications to the brothers' fate if the defense failed.

The problem was the initial indictment's charge of manslaughter. Manslaughter's legal definition left open the possibility that one or both Newman brothers still could be convicted even if the jury accepted the unwritten law defense. The alternative was to get the charge changed to murder for an all or nothing verdict. Yet that was a high-risk maneuver since one or both brothers might receive the death penalty if the jury did not accept the unwritten law defense.

The Newmans took the risk and asked the court to change the bill to murder. The Newmans also accepted an equally dangerous but critical tactic to the unwritten law strategy. Arthur went to trial first as the brother who had shot and killed Mason, planning to plead that the act took place in a state of temporary insanity.[140]

In the interim between the indictment and trial, Arthur and his new bride returned to Alice. Within a few months, they moved to Brooks County, where Arthur became a founder and manager of Falfurrias Machine Shops in partnership with cattleman Ed Lasater. The company provided mechanical support to the area's water and oil well drilling companies.[141] Arthur quickly made an impression on the company's clientele by inventing a well drilling tool that perforated casing in the hole. That innovation saved time and money compared to the traditional method of pulling up the well casing, cutting slots in it above ground, then re-fitting the casing in the hole.[142] Arthur reportedly applied for a patent on the process, but, if so, the request likely was rejected because prior art existed.[143]

Prentice, his wife, and their son returned to Fort Worth by May 28.[144] They brought Prentice's parents and their young ward, Ethelyne, with them. All six lived in the boardinghouse on Thirteenth Street in Fort Worth.[145]

At that residence in 1906, Prentice's mother spilled kerosene while lighting a flame. The flame ignited the combustible residue on Mrs. Newman's body. Her severe burns confined her to bed for a long period. That injury affected the schedule of the upcoming trials and impeded her health the rest of her life.[146]

Later in 1906, Prentice left Fort Worth to work as machinist for the R. L. Cameron Auto Company on Commerce Street in Dallas. Newman, his wife, son, parents, and their ward moved into a boardinghouse less than a mile from his job. The new residence was on Akard Street next to where the Adolphus Hotel would be built five years later.[147]

On March 14, 1906, the Newman brothers met in Hallettsville to appear before the Lavaca County District Court. In that session, the grand jury agreed to drop charges of manslaughter and returned a true bill of murder.[148] The Newmans were jailed, the only occasion they served time behind bars, but posted bail on the new charges and received their release in under a week. The court set a trial date for November 12, but the court later granted the Newmans' request for continuance. The court rescheduled Arthur's case for mid-April 1907.

The same district court tempered any relief the Newman brothers gained from evolution of their defense plan when it quashed Boyd's indictment for criminal abortion.[149] Although abortion by drug in Texas was illegal in that decade, the law stated that the person had to "designedly administer" the pharmaceutical to be in violation of the law. The district court determined that Boyd did not do that.[150]

Boyd continued practicing medicine in Yoakum until his death in January 1921.[151] He received no threats from the Newman brothers.

The Mason family anticipated the unwritten law defense. The Masons also knew that community respect for the Newman family prejudiced potential jurors. To counter both concerns, Fred Mason hired his family's own legal team to assist in Arthur's prosecution.[152] The State of Texas v Arthur Newman began in mid-April as scheduled after District Court Judge M. Kennon rejected counsel's plea for dismissal based on temporary insanity.

The judge did consent to a request by the county prosecutor and the Mason attorneys to qualify each prospective juror. The court allowed the prosecution, up to a predetermined limit, to challenge peremptorily a person who answered the following question in the affirmative:

> "If it should develop on a trial of this cause that the defendant shot and killed the deceased, and that he so shot and killed him after he had been informed that deceased had had carnal intercourse with his (defendant's) sister and thereby impregnated her, and that such shooting and killing occurred at first meeting between defendant and deceased thereafter, would that fact so bias your judgment in his favor as that you would not be able to render a fair and impartial verdict in the case?"

The prosecution team quickly used up its allotment of challenges.[153]

After the jury was empaneled on the morning of April 18, a full gallery gathered to watch the trial progress rapidly with "hot" debate. Defense attorneys maintained that Arthur fired from his Winchester both fatal shots that entered Mason's body. The defense also stated that Arthur was temporarily insane at the time of the shooting. As proof, they brought in several former schoolmates who testified that "in the past he (Arthur) had been mentally irresponsible at times."

The prosecution attacked the insanity plea. The prosecutors contended that Mason did not deserve death at Newman's hands based on his behavior toward Lily.[154]

The question went before the jury at 11 a.m.[155] At 1 p.m., jury foreman J. M. Carson Jr. read his handwritten summary of the decision: "We the Jury find the defendant not guilty as charged in inditement (sic)."[156]

Arthur was free, but in reality the verdict appeared never to have been in doubt. The day after his acquittal, *The Hallettsville New Era* stated: "The sentiment of those of our people familiar with the case is reflected by the verdict of the jury."[157]

Over the next days, more Texas newspapers reported on the decision, with one telling their readers that Arthur "has been tried and acquitted on plea of unwritten law and impairment of mental faculties."[158] The first leg of the Newman legal strategy had succeeded.

A free man, Arthur, his wife, and their infant daughter, Lillian Lucille, born October 22, 1907, left Falfurrias in 1908 and moved to Brownsville, Texas. The reason for abandoning a promising partnership with Lasater is unclear. However, that same year, Lasater and Texas Lieutenant Governor Davidson became embroiled in a courtroom dispute through Davidson's prosecution of a Republican Party organizer from Starr County.[159] Davidson already had secured Arthur's acquittal and was still representing Prentice. So Davidson's dispute with Lasater may have strained the business relationship between the cattleman and Arthur, particularly because of Davidson's friendship with

Arthur's father-in-law, T. J. Lawson. Whatever the reason for his departure, Arthur in 1908 took a machinist's job at Lawson's Rio Grande Machine and Repair Shop in Brownsville. From the tip of Texas, Arthur awaited his brother's fate both in the court case and in his professional life.

Chapter 6
Conquest of the Upper Regions

Arthur's acquittal gave Prentice hope. Yet he still had to wait to appear before the court. In the midst of uncertainty, Prentice elected to change positions and locations again in early 1908. This time, he moved south to San Antonio to become machine shop manager of the Alamo Automobile Company owned by G. A. C. Halff.[160]

The company's showroom and machine shop were located over a basement in a building on Losoya Street near the company's namesake. From there, Halff serviced a clientele that included heads of the elite business class in South Texas: architect Atlee B. Ayres and banker T. C. Frost, to name a few.[161] Halff had vision—the kind of entrepreneur with whom Newman identified. When Halff extended an offer to bring Newman into his dynamic new automobile company, Newman accepted. The job also brought him to a city accessible by direct rail to the Lavaca County Court House.

Newman left his wife, son, parents, and Ethelyne at Runge with the Leckies for a few months.[162] Then he moved to San Antonio to begin his job. His family, his father, and Ethelyne joined him in San Antonio before mid-August.[163] His mother remained in Runge, still recuperating from her burns under relatives' care.

San Antonio inspired Newman's entrepreneurship in a way that Fort Worth or Dallas had not. More than location, it was timing. Newman arrived in San Antonio just when the pace of aviation development increased amazingly fast. Although 1908 had started slowly for aviation, the last seven months saw jaw-dropping developments in both America and Europe.[164]

In May, reporters converged on Kitty Hawk, where the Wright brothers conducted a week of motor-powered aeroplane trials observed publicly for the first time. Newspapers fed the world regular reports on the famous brothers' activities and published the first halftone of a Wright plane in flight.[165]

Political and military leaders began to imagine the strategic wartime advantages of a fleet of aeroplanes. In July, the U.S. government purchased a dirigible as well as a Wright brothers' aeroplane for $25,000 to compare the two technologies in military aviation experiments at Fort Myer, Virginia.[166] By September, Orville Wright had answered all questions when he flew his biplane around Fort Myer for fifty-five circles on one day and 57½ circles the next.[167]

Another July landmark, this one occurring over Independence Day, was Glenn Curtiss piloting the first flight to cover a mile in distance.[168] Wilbur Wright surpassed Curtiss' significant milestone in early August when he flew more than two miles at Le Mans in France. Wright's feat also silenced European critics who had referred to the flight pioneers as "'the bluff Wright brothers,' of whom everybody has been talking, but who as yet had not made good."[169]

Newman, though, knew they were making good. Since the Wrights achieved motorized flight at Kitty Hawk in late 1903, he had followed their experiments earnestly, learning as much as he could from available reports on their architecture of a heavier-than-air craft. By the time he moved to San Antonio in 1908, the Wrights' string of successes, complemented by the aeronautical innovations advanced by Curtiss as well as Europe's pioneers including Henri Farman and Charles Voisin, fueled Newman's innovative instincts.[170] The early science of aeronautics espoused by Langley and Maxim from Newman's teenage years had advanced to new plateaus achieved by aviation entrepreneurs of his generation. The more public excitement and national pride grew with each milestone, the more Newman resolved to join the movement. And the possibilities of how to differentiate his approach engrossed his mind.

Newman taught himself the science of flight by analyzing technology cases generated by the maestros of flight. Langley, for instance, had shown him that in aviation even failure had value. He saw that when the Wrights observed Langley's problems with wind in his public attempts at flight, they developed ideas regarding how to avoid similar mistakes. That knowledge, in turn, ultimately helped the Wrights achieve flight in 1903.[171] Newman followed the same process. He resolved to build upon elements of flight where other pioneers, including the Wrights, had succeeded as well as improve upon areas where they had failed.

In November 1908, after the Wright brothers' successful September trial at Fort Myer, Newman began to shape his vision. What started out as an idea quickly would become the first heavier-than-air flying machine ever built in the southwestern United States in the post-Wright brothers era.

To assist him, Newman recruited Bruce Massey, a fellow machinist at the company.[172] As workspace, Newman commandeered the basement under the automobile dealership.

Under Newman's direction, the pair designed an aeroplane generally based on the Wright brothers' plans. Newman adjusted the Wrights' model to fit his studies of airflow, his experiences with motor-driven vehicles, and his personal concept of how a pilot's body would fly an airship.[173]

Although Newman's approach to controlling the airship differed from the Wrights, he had the advantage of knowing about the Wrights' intellectual property that they termed wing warping—the comprehension that if the angle of the biplane's wings could be modified, in order to put to work the power of wind currents to lift one wing higher than the other, then the pilot had command of the aircraft's direction and stability. The Wrights also were the first successful aviation engineers to understand that a pilot's body had to shift in order to maintain altitude or alter the heading of an early aeroplane's flight. The principle was no different from how a rider of a Wright brothers' bicycle guided the vehicle around a curve by shifting weight to one side. To combine both those findings to their advantage, the Wrights built a prototype where the pilot's body movements adjusted the angle of the wings to keep the aircraft level or to enable a turn. As a result of those innovations, the Wrights successfully kept their motorized aircraft aloft at Kitty Hawk for the first time in 1903.[174]

Newman likely built off the Wrights' knowledge, although it is possible he may have developed his own theory of flight after working with his bicycles in the previous decade. Regardless of the source, he and the Wrights followed a similar path regarding aeroplane control.

Although Newman had no formal engineering training, he understood the value of an orderly development process.[175] Part of that process was keeping his project private, at least at first. The few acquaintances he told of his vision serenaded him with lines from "Darius Green and His Flying Machine," a popular poem by J. T. Trowbridge about the folly of man's attempts at flight.[176] As Newman's work with Massey became more focused, only Halff knew the scope of the project, but without total approval.

"I will admit that I have discouraged the boy in every way that I could, thinking he could never build a practical machine," Halff said. Even as a skeptic, though, Halff did not stop Newman from proceeding.[177]

During construction, Newman quickly realized he could not power his first aircraft. He could not transform the explicit knowledge from reading about aviation into the proprietary insight that the Wright brothers had acquired over five years of actual aviation testing with a motor. What Newman could do, though, was make speedy improvements after a rapid series of tests. That approach theoretically would catch up Newman's aeroplane concept to the motorized flight level of the Wrights and other aviation pioneers.[178]

In his aeroplane's first embodiment, Newman built its frame from cypress, a wood that easily bends. He reinforced the cypress connections with angle steel and covered everything with duck canvas. He projected gaining lift when pulled by an automobile traveling at twenty-five miles per hour. To boost that momentum, Newman wanted his aeroplane equipped with bicycle wheels. For expediency with his first attempt, however, he followed the Wright brothers' example on their earliest trials and switched to sleigh skids.[179]

To correct flight in response to the pilot's body—the concept going back to his bicycling days—Newman connected controls to the pilot's seat. No engineering drawings of Newman's architecture exist. However, some idea of his concept is available through the interpretation of a journalist who interviewed Newman just after he had finished building his first machine. The reporter states that Newman equipped his biplane with two rudders installed at the back of the structure. One rudder connected to the pilot's seat. Newman suspended this seat from the biplane's frame and positioned it on a gimbal ring so body shifts in any direction could activate elevation controls and automatically achieve lift or stabilize flight. Newman's system also employed stirrups so the pilot could push off, thus activating the gimbaled seat to initiate or override controls. The other rudder connected to hand gears to provide steering capabilities to the left and right.[180]

A 1905 article written by engineer Robert Esnault-Pelterie in *L'Aérophile*, a well-read French aviation publication, attacked the same problem through an innovation called ailerons that provided an alternative to the Wrights' wing warping.[181] Nor were gimbals new to transportation. They had been used for centuries to stabilize compasses on ships.[182] At the time Newman considered gimbals for aviation, Elmer A. Sperry, an inventor who founded the company that became Sperry Corporation, already used gimbals to develop the first automatic pilot system through his gyroscopic stabilizer apparatus.[183] It is impossible to say how much Esnault-Pelterie's and Sperry's work influenced Newman. Yet Newman acknowledged that he read widely and studied other aviation approaches that he adapted to his theory of flight.[184]

Newman believed his control apparatus differentiated his innovation from other aeroplane architects: "While it (the Newman aeroplane) is on the order of the Wright aeroplanes, with canvas wings, I am of the opinion that it will be more automatic in flying," he predicted.[185]

Momentum stalled temporarily when the court set the next trial date for November 4. However, Newman's attorneys requested a continuance since his mother, a key witness, was still ill. The court granted a delay.

As December neared, Newman planned to test his aeroplane. For location, Newman chose the cavalry post parade grounds at Fort Sam Houston. The publicly accessible site featured two miles of open country.[186]

From the downtown basement, just three miles away, Newman and Massey rushed final construction details to meet Newman's timeline. By Christmas, they had completed all components for a "200-pound biplane aircraft with a spread of sail of about 360 square feet." It was twenty-five feet long and ten feet high and featured thirty-five feet of wingspan.[187] The wings on this first machine mimicked a bird's wings by taking the slight upward dihedral angle that helped control the lateral stability that aviators referred to as roll. Langley had utilized this approach on his early aeroplanes.[188]

Using what he had taught himself about aerodynamics, Newman theorized that each pound of floating surface lifted two pounds of dead weight. The airship's weight plus his 160 pounds equaled a 360-pound payload that was half the maximum 720 pounds he calculated his airship could lift.

On December 30, Newman brought his invention piece by piece out of the basement. He transported the components by trailer to Fort Sam Houston. The winter weather cooperated as temperatures reached seventy degrees while he assembled the first "real flying machine" ever seen in the southwestern United States. Before long, a crowd of interested citizens, including reporters, gathered around him. Newman engaged the crowd, and answered questions as he worked.

Will the aeroplane be motorized?

"It has had absolutely no try-out, but I will certainly know whether it will be more automatic in flying [than the Wright brothers' efforts] and will certainly know whether it will fly or not tomorrow."

What were his goals?

Following a successful test, he would begin construction of a motorized airship immediately.

Can anyone watch the trial?

He knew of no law to prevent such a thing.[189]

After the newspaper report, curious residents gathered the next day on the parade grounds. The sizable crowd included supporters, led by his wife, son, father, and Ethelyne. Cynics also arrived in good numbers, expecting to expose a charlatan. Yet the shocking scale of the innovation showed this was no hoax. Newman's big bird, sitting on skids, featuring dual wings with an

This forty-five-horsepower Stoddard-Dayton automobile provided the propulsion that enabled Newman to achieve history's first heavier-than-air flight in the southwestern U.S. on January 2, 1909, at Fort Sam Houston in San Antonio. The automobile, recognized as the class of the era after winning auto races all over the Midwest, belonged to Newman's boss, G.A.C. Halff of San Antonio. Lorraine Owens Family Papers.

almost twelve-yard span, kept doubters quiet.

The day's sky, though, was "heavy, murky." When Newman postponed the planned trial because of weather, he displeased the doubters. But Newman paid no attention.

"I am in no hurry for the trial," Newman said. "While I do not think there is any particular danger in going up with it, I certainly am going to see that everything is in shipshape before I take any chances."

When asked about the cynics, Newman said:

> "Many people do not believe I have the real thing, but I expect to show them within the next few days that I have. It is always the way with anything new. The Wright brothers and every other searcher after ways of conquering rapid transit have had the same ridicule, the same questions as to their ability that now confront me, and such things do not worry me the least bit. I have been immensely interested in the aeroplane ever since the first appearance and long before, and I have worked faithfully in conquering the problem [of flight]."[190]

With friends, including his father, guarding the aeroplane, Newman let the project rest on New Year's Eve. Then on New Year's Day 1909, his thirty-eighth birthday, he had to postpone his first test because of an unnamed part that he could not readily procure in local hardware stores.[191]

On January 2, though, Newman arrived eager to fly. Two hundred San Antonio residents joined him, watching every move as he went about his checklist. Newman carried on, unfazed by battling emotions in the crowd of supporters and detractors. He checked and double-checked every detail of his machine.

Finally, the inspection ended. The crowd's anticipation grew as Newman secured one end of a three-eighths-inch Manila rope to the aircraft and the other end to a light-bodied automobile.[192] Sixty-five years later Ethelyne remembered the crowd emotions well. She wrote, "The air plane flight in San Antonio was very exciting and of course viewed with fear."[193]

Newman was the least concerned of all, it seems. He climbed aboard, taking his seat on what a journalist dubbed the "fighting deck of the new air ship."[194] Newman signaled the driver to begin acceleration to launch the aeroplane into the air. The crowd members mentally prepared themselves to be the first Texans ever to see man fly, an event that until that day only occurred in dreams.

The driver revved the auto's engine. And nothing.

Catcalls and laughter reached Newman, but he remained unruffled. His assessment was that the aircraft was too heavy for the light-bodied automobile. Like any good entrepreneur, Newman had a backup plan. He sent word to his boss, and Halff, an experienced pleasure driver, consented to tow the airship with his much heavier forty-five-horsepower Stoddard-Dayton automobile.

Halff later said he agreed to participate just to humor Newman. In his heart, he believed the whole effort was doomed. He said he hoped "to give Newman one of the roughest sleigh rides he ever heard of."

Despite skepticism, Halff performed expertly. He secured a towline to his Stoddard-Dayton and drove the automobile forward. The moving aircraft, twenty yards out, remained earthbound. When Halff saw the speedometer hit the thirty miles per hour tick, though, he felt a change in the rope's tension.

Newman felt the lift too as his invention left the ground and continued to rise. He used his gimbaled seat to level out the aeroplane as the crowd cheered the most exceptional technological achievement any of them ever had witnessed.

Newman then made the specific body movement that dropped the tail to gain elevation, and the airship shot up vertically. The aircraft zoomed over the Stoddard-Dayton, and from Halff's perspective it looked to be flying at a height of about fifty feet. Newman estimated he achieved about seventy feet in altitude.

Newman caught his breath and "realized the great joy that surged through him, because the product of his brain really flew." He leveled the aircraft once again and cruised parallel to the ground. Unexpectedly, the tow rope broke, sending a loud snap across the parade grounds. The crowd watched nervously as the now untethered aeroplane again rose vertically. Some spectators said they were certain the aircraft would turn a top-over somersault preliminary to a crash dive, but Newman again regained control. He leveled the aircraft slightly, and brought the nose down. He almost had his aircraft in for a landing when the right wing dipped, hit the ground, and shattered.

The aircraft slid unrestrained until its momentum ceased. The crowd rushed to check Newman's condition. What they found, according to a reporter, was a pilot who was "white of face, but smiling bravely at the people, still seated in his chair and not even so much as jolted."[195] As Newman left his seat, a bit bruised in one hip due to a pair of pliers he had left in his back pocket, the reporter noted Newman's flushed face.[196] The reporter attributed the emotion not to the narrow escape but to the applause of two hundred persons.

Newman wanted to repeat the trial that day. His assessment showed, however, that he could not readily repair the wing. He also concluded that he needed a stronger tow rope. The first test of the Newman aeroplane was over.

"I am greatly elated over the outcome of my first trial of the flying machine," Newman said. "I suppose it was the most successful initial test ever made of any aeroplane. The rise came readily when the required momentum was reached, and the ascent was high enough to prove it will fly."

Halff appeared sold as well. Newman's trial "convinced me today that he can at least build one that can fly, and I begin to believe in him.... When the rope broke I thought there would be a tragedy, but the machine lit with scarcely a jar to the occupant," he said.

Newman's mind, though, was already moving toward the next iteration of his innovation:

> *"Of course, it is readily understood that these first tests are rarely ever productive of any results at all, and I felt as if I had made prodigious strides toward the conquering of the upper regions already. I will keep on trying until I know that it is not only possible, but practicable to fly in the air."*

Newman made history on the second day of 1909 as the first person in the southwestern United States to know "how it feels to be a bird." He said he would keep the public informed of when his next test would occur.[197]

Newman would keep his promise. At that moment, though, even he did not realize it would be a public three hundred miles south.

Chapter 7
An Aeroplane of Practical Value

*A**eronautics*, an early twentieth century monthly magazine published by the Aeronautical Society of America, ran a news piece in March 1909 about a startling development in Texas—an uncharted aviation frontier.

The article described Newman's achievements at Fort Sam Houston sixty days earlier. "Mr. Newman is a practical man, and his work, no doubt, will be of value," *Aeronautics'* report stated. Although Newman's success was with a towed flight, the correspondent added that it was done "with the idea of obtaining data as to the power required for the motor machines now being built." It said Newman's future attempts would be with an aeroplane powered by a fifty-horsepower motor "said to approximate that of the Wright Brothers."

Throughout his career, Newman used periodicals such as *Aeronautics*, *Flight International*, and *The Automobile* to gain knowledge of the activities and progress of aviation pioneers in the U.S. and Europe—the Wrights, Farman, Voisin, Louis Blériot, and Curtiss. Absorbing these innovators' concepts inspired Newman to generate creative ideas for his aeroplane.[198]

Yet Newman also used these same publications to spread knowledge of his accomplishments. And almost anything Newman did in 1909 was news simply because he was pioneering aeronautics in a new geographic area. The Newman airship in San Antonio was only the fourth distinct aeroplane architecture yet built that actually had flown in the United States.[199] Since no one, certainly not magazine editors, knew from where the next inflection point was coming in aviation technology, they could not ignore new entrants in the field. Editors had to associate Newman's name with aviation pioneers even if his only accomplishment was with a glider.

By the time the *Aeronautics* article reached readers, Newman truly owned aviation's first-mover advantage in the entire southwestern United States. Yet the paradox of being a first-mover was that unless Newman achieved motorized flight before anyone else, no regional advantage actually existed. His legacy as a leader of aviation technology's growing momentum relied on results.

Within hours after his successful test at Fort Sam Houston, Newman performed a post-mortem to leverage his advantage and plan a second test. He concluded that he had learned more about the science of aeronautics from the minutes-long flight than he had from years of studying other pioneers' accomplishments. Newman said principles underlying aerodynamics became clearer in his mind.

The brief flight also revealed a number of construction modifications that he needed in his next aeroplane. The improvements, he added, would move him closer to attempting motorized flight.[200]

An equally vital step was to secure funding to finance further efforts. To interest investors, Newman had to build a better aeroplane than the Wright brothers, who already had achieved flight. Newman's objective was to popularize aeronautics through innovations that made it "safer to operate an aeroplane than it is to run an automobile."

In essence, Newman wanted to make flying so automatic that anyone could take off, fly, and land a Newman aeroplane. He said: "What I am trying to do is to give the machine a greater degree of utility than it now has. As long as the aeroplane needs an expert to operate it, its practical value will remain small."

A starting point to that goal, Newman said, was reducing costs per aeroplane operation. The thorny problem aviation engineers of Newman's era faced was a high likelihood of losing their creation after a single flight, regardless of how successful it had been. Cypress wood frames covered with canvas broke apart at landing. The magnitude of the issue for aeroplane entrepreneurs in early 1909 is proportionally the same a century later for commercial space enterprises. If the aeroplane cannot be reused, just as if the rocket booster survives only one launch, then operational costs cannot be controlled and flight output is stymied.

Newman's solution was to use lightweight angle steel throughout the framework to strengthen cypress wood connections and make the structure more durable at landing. If Newman reached his goal, that modification would achieve economies of scale by spreading costs over multiple flights per aeroplane.

Finally, Newman sent notice to potential investors that this was no lark. He was committed to turning his innovation into an economic reality.

"There is no use fooling around with a scientific toy. What I am trying to get at is something practical—something useful. I fail to see any reason why I should not

succeed in this. The whole problem is governed by well known mechanical and physical laws."[201]

Newman's analysis, printed in a San Antonio newspaper, served the same function as a business plan. His findings advised investors that he could solve difficult challenges that prevented aeroplanes from becoming mainstream transportation vehicles. These proprietary innovations as low-cost, common-sense improvements could add value to a financial stake in his project. He knew what competitors offered, and he had differentiated his innovation from other aviation entrepreneurs.

As likely investors, Halff referred him to several technology enthusiasts within the San Antonio elite.[202] One potential target, the wealthy Dr. Frederick J. Fielding, had founded the San Antonio Aero Club that registered thirty members. Newman had become the club's secretary-treasurer the same year he moved to San Antonio.[203] Most of Halff's other potential investors belonged to the club. Newman, though, found no interest from Fielding or anyone else in this group, perhaps because in early 1909 Fielding believed balloon technology was more sustainable than aeroplanes.

The rejection frustrated Newman's urgent need to leverage first-mover status. More seriously, it obligated him to scramble for funding outside of San Antonio just when he needed to prepare for his March 29 murder trial.

Almost overnight, though, Brownsville emerged as an unexpected champion of Newman's technology thanks to Prentice's brother, Arthur. After the successful test at Fort Sam Houston, Arthur touted his brother's aviation accomplishments to the Brownsville Chamber of Commerce.

Arthur's timing was superb. Since 1904, Valley landowners had witnessed an explosion in land prices thanks to irrigation technology made viable after completion of the SLB&M Railway.[204] In five years, dryland jumped in value from $1 per acre to between $40 to $100 per acre and irrigated land increased to between $60 and $150 per acre.[205] To further that growth, the chamber, land developers, irrigation companies, and SLB&M Railroad saw mutual benefits in inviting teams of Midwestern dryland farmers to see the benefits of farming irrigated lower Rio Grande Valley croplands.[206]

The chamber had never considered aviation as an added selling hook, but as soon as its leaders heard Arthur's story, some far-sighted chamber members "believed a 'bird-man' would prove a good drawing card to lure more of these prospective land buyers."[207] After all, positive perception of the Valley's dynamism and modernity could grow through a strategic partnership with a Texas-bred aviation innovator whose goal was to surpass the Wrights and Curtiss in aeroplane technology.

The chamber asked Arthur to invite Prentice to relocate to the Valley, build a Brownsville aeroplane, and turn the region into an aviation incubator.

Arthur Newman, seated, and Prentice Newman in 1909. George Banker Owens Collection (MGC 1167-GBOC), Midwest Genealogy Center, Mid-Continent Public Library, Independence, Missouri.

Prentice responded that the effort would take a minimum of $2,500. Arthur quickly replied that in Brownsville "he had been encouraged to believe that the enterprise could be financed." With that statement, Brownsville moved decisively while San Antonio hesitated.

By January 14, Newman arrived by train to pitch his concept to Brownsville investors.[208] During his presentation, Newman mobilized the group with his enterprise vision. He pointed out two hundred San Antonio witnesses already had observed his initial aeroplane gain flight at half the speed previously thought necessary. He said that the real-world test was evidence that his engineering ability could make possible a commercially viable aeroplane built in Brownsville. Newman predicted that his next aeroplane would exceed the Wright brothers' then-existing record of a single aircraft flying continuously for more than two hours and ten minutes.

Newman also disclosed his engineering design for a Brownsville aeroplane. Every point of his message was to promote his innovation's "automatic" stability. His creation would be built similar to a Wright brothers' biplane with a major differentiation—his focus on the pilot's automatic controls. He explained how the Brownsville aeroplane would rely on a pilot's body shifts to manipulate controls connected to the gimbaled seat. Those controls made automatic navigation adjustments of stability and direction. Newman also predicted he would locate the center of gravity lower in his next creation compared to existing aeroplanes. This latter engineering change, he said, further would promote stability.

As to scale, he described an impressive structure for investors who had never seen an aeroplane:

- **Length:** thirty feet
- **Wings:** two eight-foot by ten-foot wings parallel to each other and four-and-a-half feet apart on each side
- **Frame:** angle iron and cypress wood
- **Wrapping:** canvas
- **Power:** a sixty-five-horsepower engine
- **Thrust:** two propellers
- **Total weight:** 210 pounds
- **Takeoffs and landings:** wheels rather than skids
- **Capacity:** two persons

The buzz in the group was who would occupy the second seat. Newman cleverly suggested a contest to identify his passenger.

Newman established a tight timetable for when his funders could see return on investment. Newman said he could begin construction "very shortly." The prototype, he estimated, would be built eight weeks after he began.

A diverse array of Brownsville's professionals and entrepreneurs constituted the chamber-organized group. They were attorneys, a judge, bankers, insurance agents, realtors, investors, merchants, druggists, farmers, and an automobile dealer who doubled as the town's undertaker.[209] Of that group, Newman's pitch mobilized thirty-four persons.

The group organized the venture under the name of Brownsville Aeroplane Company with subscribers for an announced capitalization of $6,000.[210] The company appointed Thos. R. Tumlinson, a Brownsville realtor, as acting trustee.[211]

As pledged, Newman went right to work. Two days later, Newman traveled to Houston to buy parts.[212] On February 1, he traveled to San Antonio for additional purchases. During that stop, Newman gave a San Antonio reporter an interview that praised the newly formed Brownsville group for its confidence. His comments sent a subtle message to his San Antonio Aero Club colleagues:

"I have had all possible co-operation from the people of Brownsville in my undertaking. Thomas R. Tomlinson (sic) *and J. E. Head* [George J. Head, a Brownsville druggist] *raised the money for the company in less than two days. There is no doubt in my mind I will succeed in building an aeroplane of practical value."*[213]

Besides being the intermediary who brought his brother's aviation expertise to Brownsville, Arthur also provided a second important element. As machinist in his father-in-law's Rio Grande Machine and Repair Shop, Arthur offered Prentice skilled machine shop services essential to designing and building the Brownsville Newman Flyers. Photo by Robert Runyon, RUN03220, RRC, DBCAH, The University of Texas at Austin.

Newman chose the rice mill, located where the Reynaldo G. Garza-Filemon B. Vela United States Courthouse is today, for building his Brownsville aeroplane. The mill had opened just five years before, but closed after the Rio Grande Valley's brief failed experiment in rice production ended. Photo by Robert Runyon, RUN08786, RRC, DBCAH, The University of Texas at Austin.

When Newman returned to the lower Rio Grande Valley to launch his venture, he found Brownsville had embraced his project with enthusiasm. Before he had built a single component of the Brownsville aeroplane, its citizens wanted to pit Newman against the Wright brothers and Curtiss in a commemoration of the first running of Robert Fulton's steamboat. Competing aeroplanes would retrace the steamboat's route by air over the Hudson River from New York City to Albany. The winner of *The New York World*-sponsored contest would take home $10,000.

"Just wait until Brownsville's air-ship, which is now building, makes its first flight, and you will see some more world's records shattered," wrote the editor of the *Brownsville Daily Herald*. "Wilbur Wright can then take a back seat."[214]

Newman's design elements for his second iteration meant the Brownsville aeroplane would be twenty percent longer than his San Antonio creation. That scale required a manufacturing facility larger than the San Antonio basement Newman used previously. The investor group requisitioned the abandoned Merchant & Planters Rice Milling Company just north of the city center for his purposes.

Newman's engineering plan also called for the aeroplane's motor to actuate propulsion. His familiarity with automobile manufacturers gave him confidence a leading player could build an aeroplane motor. He contacted Adams-Farwell in Dubuque, Iowa, about a sixty-horsepower engine with four revolving cylinders rather than a turning crank. Newman, who might have been specifying a rotary engine for his aeroplane, believed the gyratory cylinder action would further stabilize the aeroplane. He asked that the engine, usually weighing about 250 pounds, be made lighter.

Newman toyed with the idea of traveling to Dubuque to oversee the motor's construction, but his tight development schedule made that journey impossible. With a March 29 court date looming, his professional priority became an airborne Brownsville prototype to prove his competency to investors and the Brownsville public.

On February 19, with the Adams-Farwell motor still months from delivery, Newman completed the aeroplane's frame at the rice mill. As he wrapped the structure in canvas, he proposed a public exhibition of the aeroplane sans engine the following week.[215]

Chapter 8
An Honest, Moral Man

On December 4, 1908, the day after Nora Young Runyon's death, the weather in northeastern Kentucky shifted to windy and wet, the ground turned to mud, and snowstorms threatened. At 2 p.m. on this gloomy day, Runyon buried his wife at Catlettsburg Cemetery. Then he vacated their home. He stored all household goods—bedding, silverware, dishes and kitchenware, furniture, Nora's and William's clothes, and Nora's jewelry—at a friend's residence. Father and son the same night moved in with Nora's parents at Hampton City. It was a rapid chain of actions that Runyon could not have imagined just forty-eight hours earlier.

At the end of the week, Runyon left William with the Youngs and rented a room at Mrs. O. L. Lark's boardinghouse. Runyon devoted the next six weeks to planning his and William's lives.

For advice, Runyon consulted with several family members in Kentucky and West Virginia. His most impactful meeting occurred on December 13 when he traveled by train to Williamson, West Virginia, to meet with his Uncle Harry and Aunt Ella Lawson. To them, Runyon expressed interest in leaving his Appalachian roots and starting a new life in the Southwest. He found encouragement from the Lawsons. Their son, Lafayette, also was considering moving to Texas to work in dentistry. Following that meeting, later correspondence indicates Runyon may have paid a courtesy call to the N&W rail yard to see old train colleagues before returning to Catlettsburg by rail.[216]

Runyon also anticipated great uncertainty in an unknown future, so he wrote a will on December 23. He spent Christmas Day away from family, staying at a private boardinghouse in Lexington. Then he returned to Boyd

County for the last time as a resident. Over the first two weeks of January, he penned a legal document concerning William's care to leave with the Youngs, and packed a substantial quantity of personal belongings for an implausible odyssey to Texas.

His typed diary states:

"On January the 19th A.D. 1909, I departed for the Southwest and left Catlettsburg at 1:15 p.m. on #3, over the C. & O. Ry."

His first stop was Cincinnati, Ohio, a layover that provided a physical and mental escape from the sadness of Catlettsburg. The night of his arrival, he went to the Lyric Theatre to see actress Gertrude Hoffman perform her celebrated Salome dance in a performance of *The Mimic World*. The next morning, he toured the city, and, in the afternoon, attended a vaudeville matinee at the Columbia Theatre. He took in a burlesque show at the People's Theatre the next day, but by nightfall he was in berth No. 10 on Pullman Car Numidia aboard the southbound Illinois Central Railway.[217]

The train arrived at New Orleans' Union Station late on January 22. Runyon checked into Hotel Richelieu, in that year located near the station at Rampart and Howard Streets.[218] Over the weekend, he enjoyed local food and continued to catch up on entertainment. At New Orleans' Greenwall Theatre, Runyon took in *Mardi Gras Beauties*, a show that had recently toured Ohio to good reviews. He then headed to the Crescent Theatre to see *The Time, The Place and The Girl*, a musical comedy about a sanitarium in the Virginia mountains.

The most lasting impression Runyon gained from New Orleans was the variety of the city's unique vegetation. Runyon took streetcars to Audubon Park and City Park and walked both grounds with his Kodak, carefully recording the exposures and distances of photographs he took of evergreen tree groves and City Park's lagoon. He closed the day by visiting "the five cent shows."[219]

Runyon left New Orleans via the Southern Pacific Railroad on January 24 at 11:55 a.m. and arrived at Houston's train station just before midnight. He spent the night at Hotel Brazos, but secured lodging the next morning in Mrs. Phillips' boardinghouse at 1716 Texas Avenue. Runyon devoted the rest of the day to moving the many possessions he brought with him from the depot's baggage storage to his room.

On Thursday and Friday mornings, Runyon looked for work, but also took photographs whenever possible. On Friday afternoon he climbed aboard the Santa Fe Railway and traveled twenty-five miles south of Houston to Algoa. He noted the day as "very windy and cloudy." For the first time, he saw oranges and grapefruits growing on trees. His exposure record shows he had difficulty photographing them as the images came out "slightly out of focus" and others "slight moved because of the wind." He rated his exposures as "all fair."[220]

By February 1, Runyon found work. He had responded to an address in a classified advertisement for a "Young man wanted for news service" that led him to the Gulf Coast News and Hotel Company office in Houston. The company provided foodservice, curios, and sundries on trains and at depots under contract with the SLB&M Railway and other railways. Runyon would discover that this news butch position was undemanding: the uniformed young man hawked fruit, newspapers, and cigars to onboard passengers. The company ran the same want ad on a regular basis, indicating turnover for the low-level position was high. Ideal or not, Runyon applied at just the right time to get assigned to the Brownsville route.

Although the SLB&M Robstown-Brownsville leg had run since 1904, the line opened the entire route from Houston just thirteen months before. And, on January 31, a few days after Runyon's arrival, SLB&M had begun an additional night train service to South Texas. This night train became Runyon's first assignment for Gulf Coast News. The route left after dark from Houston and terminated at Brownsville in late morning of the next day. On return, the northbound train departed Brownsville at 4:30 in the afternoon and arrived in Houston before 8 a.m. the following day.[221]

Runyon's previous railroad experience provided him quick acceptance among other rail workers in Houston. Just before his first rail service, he went February 7 with colleagues on a duck hunting trip to Morgan's Point at the junction of the San Jacinto River and Buffalo Bayou. There, he took photos of his acquaintances and the spot's prominent oyster reef and took his first recorded photograph of cactus. By day's end, he saved one exposure on his film for his first journey south.

Runyon's initial day of employment on the SLB&M train came on February 9. Darkness settled soon after departure for night train passengers, so Runyon could not see much of the new landscape for several hours. But by the time the train departed its Kingsville stop at 7:05 a.m., he had four and a half hours to view completely new vistas as the train traveled toward the Rio Grande. He saw the land's appearance change as thorny mesquite, huisache, acacia, guajillo, and nopal began to dominate the countryside. Then, as the train entered the lower Rio Grande Valley, newly cleared farmland indicated the commercial changes brought to the southern tip of Texas by the railroad. Closer to Brownsville, Runyon had his first views of palms—both the native *palma de micharos* (*Sabal texana*) as well as *Washingtonia robusta*, a larger palm species introduced to the lower Rio Grande Valley from the western coast of Mexico. When he disembarked from the train at its terminal stop, he would have experienced a medley of culturally hybridized scenes—human, architectural, and linguistic—and smelled the unique and sometimes noxious odors of a border trade town.

With Pullman conductor J. A. Gregg guiding him on this first visit, Runyon took off for Mexico. They walked through the depot's palm-laden garden toward a boardwalk within view of the Rio Grande. The pair took the ferry across the river, where Runyon captured his first of thousands of historic scenes he would take in his lifetime of South Texas and northern Mexico.

Runyon finished the roll of film in his camera with a shot of his companion, Gregg. The remainder of the day he took photos of sights in Matamoros that he had never before imagined: the piperos; the panteón antiguo; and, after returning to Brownsville, photos of the train depot.

Once he had the shots developed in Houston, he rated his photography efforts as "fair." He needed more practice combining light, exposure, and structure to achieve a high-quality image.[222]

Runyon began making the run to Brownsville on a regular basis. On one trip, Runyon discovered he had a *paisano* in Brownsville. William B. Cox, also a native of the Appalachian region, had come to hunt fortune with his youngest son, Norvin, and other acquaintances about a year before. Cox's other son, Ira, remained in West Virginia, where he worked as a call boy on the N&W Railway in Williamson. Ira either knew Runyon when Runyon worked for the railroad or he met Runyon when he traveled to Williamson for the day just before leaving for Texas in early 1909.

Runyon and William Cox connected several times when Runyon's southbound leg terminated in Brownsville. Cox noted those meetings in an April 27, 1909, letter to Ira:

> "Bob Runnions [Runyon] *is here, running on the train as news boy. He comes to see me often. He remembers you. He worked in the* [Williamson railroad] *yard some time ago."*[223]

As an adventurer, Cox's circle of acquaintances in Texas and Mexico would grow soon to include P. A. Newman as well.

The more trips Runyon made between Brownsville and Houston, the more the terrain, culture, people, and towns of Brownsville and Matamoros showed infinitely more promise than Houston as a home for him and William. In Brownsville, he believed they could jointly pick up life again as a family.

Yet Runyon knew he could not yet be a good father to his young son if he traveled constantly. He was also keenly aware that William needed a mother. His travel schedule gave little time to socialize in Houston even though he acknowledged eligible single women lived in his boardinghouse.[224] So he picked up correspondence with a few candidates back in Kentucky.

Fannie Short, a young woman who worked in Huntington, West Virginia, for a fruits and vegetables wholesaler, was one of the chosen. Runyon's letters to Fannie included photographs and gifts, such as opals, that he bought in the exotic markets of Mexico. In letters, typed on company letterhead, Fannie suggested that she would welcome expanding the friendship:

> "I ahve (sic) received postals from you occasionally, and certainly do appreciate your remembering me. The scenery is all new to me, but I only wish I was there to look at it in reality, instead of looking at it on postals. However, if that cant (sic) be, will have to put up with the Next Best."[225]

Another of Runyon's female friends stated her intentions more bluntly. Ada Spears, writing from Catlettsburg in June 1909, chided Runyon for not being more aggressive despite being a recent widower.

> "You are being awfully true to your little Ky widow [Runyon's late wife], aren't you? I don't want you to be so true as all that. Have a good time and you can love me all you want too. I wont (sic) object to being loved just so you love me true.... I will be down real soon and we will go in bathing in the gulf. Wont (sic) we have one good time. You telegraph me a ticket and I will come and spend a week or ten days. You can entertain me as your sister."[226]

Although she added that she was just kidding, fate intervened on Runyon's behalf before he could discover whether Ada would make good. An auspicious meeting with the very young Evelyn French of Fort Worth just about the time of Ada's letter immediately changed Runyon's perspective.

Evelyn's father, Marcus French, was principal owner of the French-Webb Live Stock Commission Company, an order buying firm that occupied bottom-floor offices at the west end of the Exchange Building at the Fort Worth Stockyards.[227] French's company effected sales of calves from Texas ranchers directly to Armour & Company and Swift & Company, major beef packers that had plants at the stockyards. French also was an avid outdoorsman who hunted wild game along the Texas and Pacific Railway from Thursday to Monday morning almost every week.[228]

When he traveled to South Texas, French was able to combine focuses—acquiring calves and hunting—by doing business with ranchers like Captain John B. Armstrong and then taking time to hunt the Armstrong Ranch's 50,000 brush-filled acres between Kingsville and Raymondville.[229]

French's wife, Anna, and daughter, Evelyn, often came along too. Anna was related to the Tandy family of Bosque County, Texas, that in 1900 had acquired land near the Resaca del Rancho Viejo at Olmito just north of Brownsville.[230]

In the Valley, the Frenches sometimes stayed in a green bungalow on Tandy land near the SLB&M tracks and sometimes they stayed at the San Carlos Hotel in Brownsville.[231] They took the trip so frequently that Evelyn jokingly referred to the route as the "Slow train through the Swamps of the Rio Grande Valley."[232]

One of their trips south greatly impacted Runyon. It took place around June 10, when Anna and Evelyn, then fifteen and a high school student, traveled to Olmito to christen the Tandys' new *resaca* home. The ladies departed Fort Worth for Houston, where they changed to the SLB&M train. Runyon, just shy of his twenty-eighth birthday and in his fourth month of employment, worked the train.

Runyon struck up conversation with mother and daughter en route to Brownsville. From that chance meeting, Evelyn, almost half Runyon's age, became his focus for the next year. Within days of their encounter, he invited Evelyn on a tour of Matamoros, an offer she declined because of the Tandys' extended social schedule over the next month that included sailing and bathing in the Gulf.[233] Rapidly, though, the friendship grew through exchange of letters and postals supplemented by occasional meetings in Brownsville. Whenever possible, at least in the first weeks, they tried to time the train's passing by the green bungalow to wave at each other as Runyon made the regular transit between Houston and Brownsville.[234]

Coincidence or not, Runyon, soon after meeting Evelyn, resigned from the Kentucky State Guard on June 12. The guard accepted his request and honorably discharged him from service "by reason of removal from state." Runyon had resolved to make Texas his home.[235]

Despite their age differences, Evelyn's parents never discouraged her friendship with Runyon. Just two weeks after their first meeting, Evelyn wrote:

> "I can truly say that I have never seen a young man better looking or truer than you. My mother thinks more of you than any young man she has ever met and I can truly say the same."[236]

Two weeks after that letter, the relationship had progressed to where Evelyn established her principles:

> "So you will see I am strictly Temperate and I am happy to know that smoking cigars is your only indulgence in dissipation, that is all my Father ever does is just to smoke cigars."[237]

Just days after sending that letter, Evelyn expressed surprise and urged caution when Runyon sent her a serious token of his feelings by mail:

> "I feel it quite an <u>honor</u> for your <u>Dear</u> friend to ask me and no one else to wear your Diamond ring but I feel perhaps <u>it</u> is best that we should wait until we get more acquainted and as we grow to know each other better for I feel that is too <u>great</u> and <u>sacred</u> to be in haste as I have always felt towards you as no one else who I can depend as <u>my true friend</u>."[238]

In his correspondence, as he related stories about his frustrations, accomplishments and ambitions, Runyon impressed Evelyn with his drive and principles:

> "I am glad to know you are an honest, moral man and I thought that of you after I met you, but you know it is just with us the one way or the other. Now don't think, I think you are bragging on yourself but I like to hear and to know you are honest with the world and making an honest living."[239]

As the letter exchange continued, and after Evelyn kept the ring, Runyon laid out his expectations of the relationship. She sensed his disapproval when she attended social activities with boys her age. She replied:

> *"Dear Bob, you can rest assured the other boys I go with are few and far between and they can't even get near to the heart that beats for you. They are only friends for you are the one I think of all through the day and dream of at nights."*[240]

Evelyn's increasingly frequent written defenses indicated that the long-distance courtship was starting to collapse. It was not the development that Runyon had hoped to see. He appeared exceedingly lonely after months of traveling within the eastern part of Texas and certainly desired to establish a more stable life. His solution was to make changes in his life, both professionally and personally.

To his Gulf Coast News bosses, Runyon floated new business opportunities using his photographs to increase the company's postcard sales revenue. He and his superiors corresponded about the concept through mail addressed to him at the Brownsville depot. When expected letters did not arrive, Runyon grew suspicious. He accused C. Woer, the manager of the Gulf Coast News' lunch room at the Brownsville depot, of stealing the post.

His bosses investigated and found merit in Runyon's complaint. On September 1, the Gulf Coast News replaced Woer with J. Hanning, who headed up the company's restaurant at Valley Junction, Texas, on the I&GN Railroad.[241] That transfer did not last long. By September's end, the company's superintendent traveled from San Antonio to Brownsville "to take out some of the knots into which the station lunch counter has been tied and turn it over to a new man."[242]

In early October, federal authorities arrested Woer for secreting and embezzling Runyon's correspondence "with a design to obstruct the correspondence and to pry into the secrets of said addressee of said letters."[243] The charge was later dismissed for lack of sufficient testimony.[244] However, Woer was gone for good.

That same month, the "new man" for Gulf Coast News turned out to be the person who initiated the imbroglio. Runyon accepted the lunch room manager position at the Brownsville depot without hesitation.

The abrupt change in Runyon's life and his move to Brownsville surprised Evelyn, his most regular correspondent. "Well I never was so surprised when I read in your letter you had gone to B__ to stay," she wrote, "that beats all[;] well you are far away now sure enough."[245]

In letters to friends, Runyon expressed happiness with the change. The monotony of traveling back and forth from Houston to Brownsville no longer interested him. He had become enamored with the geography, the winter climate, and people on both sides of the Rio Grande. Brownsville was his home.

Edyth Christie, a young woman friend in Kentucky, had held out hope that Runyon would return. When Runyon's new job ended that possibility, she resigned herself to moving with her family to Indiana. Her letter, sent shortly after Runyon's relocation in Brownsville, reveals how much he had grown to appreciate borderlands culture:

> "I dislike to think of leaving Lexington but I hope to be as well pleased with the Hoosiers as you are with the Mexicans. Well I shall postpone my wedding and await your 'Whispers of Love,' for I do not want to be too hasty with my decisions. It certainly seems strange for me to be writing such dope but of course you understand just what I am referring to."[246]

Ensconced in his new position by late October, Runyon immersed himself in duties that included managing daily inventories of foodservice items from cocoa to cooked ham as well as sundries like cigars.[247] In addition to lunch room duties, Runyon also managed and sold necessities and curios to passengers who came through the depot. A big demand item that particularly enthused him was postcards.[248]

Runyon's next goal was to reunite with his son. Runyon advised his bosses almost immediately that he would take extended travel to Kentucky in early summer 1910 to move William and all their possessions to Brownsville. As a first step to making William a good home, he accepted Evelyn's standing invitation to visit the French family in Fort Worth. He chose early January 1910 while she was still on her Christmas break from high school.[249]

The events promised interesting dynamics as not one of Evelyn's more than forty existing letters indicated she was aware Runyon was a widower or that he had a son ten years her junior. What Runyon did make clear to Evelyn was that he had other female friends.

In his first few months in Brownsville, Runyon lodged at Mrs. Kate Leahy's boardinghouse and hotel. Half-French and half-Irish, Mrs. Leahy was the widow of Michael Leahy, an Eighth Cavalry veteran once stationed at Fort Brown. An acquaintance described her personality as a "tongue like a razor, Irish wit, French élan, has a host of friends and is highly respected by both Mexicans and Americans."[250]

Mrs. Leahy's hotel, located near Fort Brown at the corner of Elizabeth and East Fourteenth Street, had gained national attention in 1906 after it was sprayed by bullets allegedly fired by black soldiers stationed at Fort Brown in the event called The Brownsville Affray.[251] Although she believed the black soldiers did the shooting, she also became disgusted by the federal investigation that led to the soldiers' dishonorable discharges. She complained to authorities that after the event the black soldiers "were treated outrageously, insulted and imposed upon in every imaginable way."[252]

As landlady, Mrs. Leahy ran a lively establishment. At least once after Runyon's stay at her house, Mrs. Leahy, then about thirty-nine years old, hosted Runyon at a dinner. After it, he went out with the "girls" in Brownsville.

He explained the evening to Evelyn by remarking how lonely life had become for him in Texas. To that news, Evelyn simply replied: "I don't see why you don't go more often for then you would not be so lonesome. What's in life if you don't go and mix some."[253]

At the same time, Runyon made sure his Kentucky female friends knew about Evelyn. By this time, his female correspondents bluntly expressed their feelings when he mentioned his relationship with the young Fort Worth girl. In one letter, Fannie Short responded:

> You so make me feel awfully jealous when you say you guess you will have to wait for the little school girl. You see I told you would get a girl out in Texas, and then, naturally, forget the Kentucky girls. Still, it is better to have someone to go with than go by oneself, isn't it?"[254]

In October 1909, Runyon rented a small cottage from R. L. Ginn, another railroad man, at 1104 E. St. Charles in Brownsville, just across the street from the depot where he worked. From this leased residence, he began to study how to advance professionally in his new region.

He immediately took Spanish from a tutor. By April 1910, he also signed up for Spanish lessons by mail from the International Correspondence School in Scranton, Pennsylvania.[255]

Runyon concurrently renewed his desire to advance his photography skills through accelerated practice. He took more landscape views of Brownsville and Matamoros. Plants, especially subtropical species new to him, comprised many of his exposures. He took fields of sugarcane and pastures with yucca as well as individual papaya, lemon, and Texas ebony trees. He also shot palms—both *Sabal texana* and *Washingtonia robusta*.

He integrated into film processing through self-education. Runyon converted space in his cramped new residence to make his darkroom. This new competency allowed him to correct exposure errors and salvage some poorly lit photographs. As a result, he began rating his photos progressively better, stating more were "good" than "fair" and dropping the "bad" rating altogether.[256]

Runyon's investment of time and money in photography set him on the path to the professional status he desired. That same investment of money, study, and practice would be a gateway to multiple other aspirations yet to emerge within him.

Chapter 9
Mr. P. A. Newman, Texas

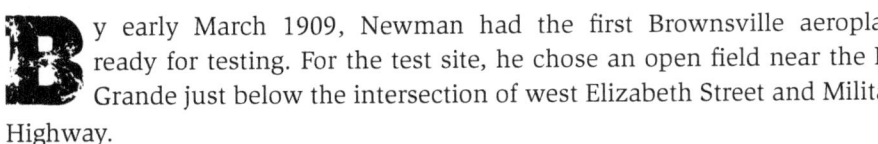y early March 1909, Newman had the first Brownsville aeroplane ready for testing. For the test site, he chose an open field near the Rio Grande just below the intersection of west Elizabeth Street and Military Highway.

Many Brownsville residents showed up on March 5 to watch Newman move the aircraft from the rice mill to the test location. For those who couldn't make the event, a reporter wrote a lengthy non-technical description (page 72) that included a caveat: "…it is a frail looking craft, and there are probably few people who would trust themselves to ride in it on level ground over a smooth road to say nothing of taking a soar skyward in it."

The article's caution had no impact on acting trustee Tumlinson. He claimed he would occupy the passenger seat when Newman took off.[257] However, that never happened.

On Saturday, March 6, another large crowd gathered early, expecting to constitute the second group of Texans ever to observe a heavier-than-air machine take flight in Texas skies. The hours dragged by as Newman readied his craft for an announced 4:30 p.m. takeoff.

Finally, at 8 p.m., Newman told his helpers to cut the machine loose from its moorings and hitch the rope to the automobile. Newman climbed in the pilot seat, and signaled his driver to start. The aeroplane just skated along, never lifting above the ground. Much of the crowd had already departed, and Newman disappointed stragglers when he told them to return on Monday.[258]

Newman's instincts suggested that insufficient horsepower again kept him from achieving flight. He had solved that problem at Fort Sam Houston by calling in a forty-five-horsepower Stoddard-Dayton Touring Car. So, on Monday, he sought to add more horsepower—literally and mechanically—to his next attempt.

Another large crowd and a breezier Monday than expected met Newman when he arrived at the test site. The crowd he wanted, and the weather was no deterrent. He hitched the airship's tow rope to an automobile powered with a four-cylinder engine. He also commissioned four horses that spectators had ridden to the field, using lariats to secure each horse to the aeroplane. The combination of mechanical and actual horsepower pulled the aeroplane a full city block, but again it failed to leave the ground.[259]

Newman's two setbacks, though disappointing, had not doused the public's enthusiasm for his venture. Residents up and down the Gulf Coast hungered for his success. And the regional excitement, even without aviation success, was exactly the public notice that Brownsville Chamber of Commerce leaders had envisioned when they invited Newman.

As *The Corpus Christi Caller* editor wrote:

> "A gentleman by the name of Prentice Newman has constructed an air-ship at Brownsville today. Should it be a success, the people of Brownsville will feel like flying to Corpus Christi about every other day to take a swim in our bay."

The editors of the *Brownsville Herald* responded that Corpus Christi had the right idea, but the wrong location.

> "As for swimming in Corpus Christi bay, of course, that is fine, especially for those who have never known the pleasures of surf bathing. It must be said, however, that the bay is rather a tame attraction for those who have so near at (h)and such splendid surf bathing as that of Tarpon Beach, which is Brownsville's favorite seaside resort."[260]

Newman opted for a quick, non-publicized test-run for his next attempt—the first time he had not opened his efforts to scrutiny by all comers. He later stated that he conducted the private test to not impose on "human patience further." Perhaps he just needed to measure his status before he went to Hallettsville for trial the following week. Whatever the reason, on March 22, Newman's non-motorized airship took flight and reached an altitude, by his estimation, of forty feet. A handful of passers-by witnessed the flight and some of them stated Newman had ascended sixty feet. All witnesses agreed that he held the airship level for a brief time before descending under control and landing smoothly.

Newman was elated. He predicted future aviation milestones once he received the motor and propellers, all of which were on order. He then took the aeroplane to storage at the rice mill before boarding the SLB&M train that would connect with SAAP below San Antonio to take him to Hallettsville.

As he traveled, news of his accomplishment spread widely and rapidly, although the follow-ups greatly exaggerated his accomplishments. The most ludicrous report datelined Galveston came from *The Sun* of New York. It reported that on March 24 Newman flew his plane for thirty minutes at an altitude of 150 feet and covered twelve miles of prairie. It said Newman could have kept the aircraft in the air longer except some of the machinery was a "little stiff." The apocryphal report was front page news of that day's edition. A month later, the same report appeared in *Flight International* out of the United Kingdom, just in its first year of publication but already a respected aeronautical news weekly. [261]

Newspapers in Washington, D.C., and Baltimore covered the flight as well, probably through information provided by the same Galveston correspondent. The eastern papers' reports varied a bit by giving Newman an honorary title of professor, jargon used to recognize innovative cleverness in that era. Both papers also played loosely with facts. They said Newman controlled the aeroplane for a thirty-minute flight that rose to about 130 feet and circled an area of approximately ten miles.

The Washington paper ran Newman's report next to an article announcing a Wright brothers' aviation exhibition in Rome, Italy. The juxtaposition, combined with over-reporting Newman's achievement, for that moment gave his name equal standing with the pioneer Wrights. [262]

All reports omitted the fact that the Newman aeroplane miraculously achieved its fictional dozen or so miles of flying without power. Yet all the articles correctly advised the public that the aeroplane was Newman's invention and was based on the Wright brothers' model.

Newman's long trip to the Lavaca County Court House resulted in another request for continuance on March 29. A physician attested that Arthur was too sick to travel. The court granted Newman's request for postponement. [263]

Newman returned to the Valley in a professional quandary. He had earned international recognition as the pioneer aviator in the southwestern United States because of his successful San Antonio flight in January. The recent alleged exaggerated success in Brownsville added to his expanding fame. A person in Paris, France, once sent him a fan letter that was addressed simply "Mr. P. A. Newman, Texas," and the U.S. Post Office delivered it to him in Brownsville. [264]

Yet acclaim meant nothing unless Newman took his aeroplane concept from mind to the marketplace. By early April, he was no further along than when he left San Antonio in early January. The calendar quickly became Newman's biggest enemy as his investment group placed more demanding requirements on his engineering time to moderate the risk of money pledged to the innovation.

The investors, who had not fully met their financial obligations to Newman, became concerned about existing and potential competition. By early spring 1909, they watched the Wright brothers roll up success after success in Europe and the U.S. with a motorized airship. Now millionaires across the United States had become enthralled about the new industry. Word spread in early February that E. H. R. (Ned) Green of Dallas, president of the Texas-Midland Railroad Company, had ordered a Wright brothers-manufactured aeroplane. Green planned to fly it around the State Fair of Texas fairgrounds in late October 1909.[265] J. W. Oman, an Ohio native, had filled San Antonio's aviation entrepreneurship gap left by Newman's relocation to Brownsville. By May 1909, Oman had organized the Aerial Navigation Company to build an aeroplane. Word was that Oman signed up more than thirty San Antonio investors with a reported capitalization of $5 million.[266]

Even San Antonio physician Dr. Adolph Herff planned to fly that same year with a plane he was building in Boerne, Texas.[267] Herff's father, Dr. Ferdinand Von Herff, a German native who became a pioneer Texas physician, in 1863 had invested in the allegedly successful airship of Jacob B. Brodbeck of Gillespie County, Texas. According to legend, Brodbeck's airship, powered by helical springs, flew either at Luckenbach or near San Pedro Springs in San Antonio.[268]

Still, it was one thing for singletons to chase aeronautical notice. More threatening to the investors' goal of making the Rio Grande Valley an aviation center was the growing number of lucrative aeroplane racing competitions cropping up across the nation. These races, often featuring a Wright brothers plane, offered healthy prize money as well as national publicity for the participating aeronautical companies. Without a functional craft, however, Brownsville investors could not compete or generate publicity. So, during April and May, the Brownsville group held investor meetings to discuss how to get involved.

Newman by that time had cancelled his order with Adams-Farwell, but had not ordered a replacement. The treasurer announced that the company had enough investor subscriptions to buy the engine and propellers as soon as a third-party factory built them. The group directed the treasurer to assess sixty-five percent of the pledged subscriptions to make the purchase.

The stockholders then ordered Newman to pick up the pace.[269]

Newman already had been invited to showcase his airship against Green's Wright brothers plane and Oman's entry during San Antonio's International Fair in the fall.[270] The stockholders agreed he should participate.

Then the investors added additional pressure. They directed Newman to showcase his innovation at Brownsville's three-day Fourth of July extravaganza. The investors wanted Newman to circle the Fort Brown parade grounds three times in a motorized Brownsville Aeroplane Company aircraft during the holiday celebration.[271]

That instruction left Newman less than forty-five days to do something never accomplished south of Kitty Hawk—achieve flight in a powered heavier-than-air machine. The board meeting that day taught him a lesson about outside funding: Daily focus shifted abruptly from perfecting technology to achieving return on investment. He had to get a product, any product, to market.[272] Newman now stared into a fast-closing window driven by others' expectations. He had lost control of his innovation's development pace.

The consequences of his ramped-up schedule were mounting bills and cash flow issues. To deal with finances, the stockholders called a meeting to discuss purchases. Most subscribers had not contributed the promised funds. And, perhaps to avoid getting bothered for their shares, many stockholders found reasons to be absent from the discussion that evening. The company's chairman appointed a committee that included Newman to determine how to move forward.[273] After that report, the stockholders agreed to incorporate and to issue six hundred shares of stock at ten dollars each. The investors also appointed a board of directors that included Newman. However, no record exists with the Texas secretary of state that the company registered as a corporate entity.

With the promise of new funding behind him, Newman ordered a forty-horsepower, eight-cylinder motor from the Herring-Curtiss Company of New York, one of the first companies to build motors specifically for aviation. Its principal, Glenn Curtiss, known for his record-breaking flight records, was an aviation innovator. Curtiss and his partner, August Herring, had begun building powerful, lightweight aviation engines. At the time of Newman's order, Herring-Curtiss Company had been in operation a brief sixty days.[274]

While Newman awaited delivery, he sought to revitalize his investors with another successful flight of his prototype. He had spent a month in the rice mill adjusting his aeroplane. He strengthened the central frame of the structure yet reportedly had dropped the overall weight by a hundred pounds.[275] For motor power, he recruited the seventy-horsepower automobile and driving services of wealthy Lon C. Hill, an attorney and a real estate developer whose accomplishments included co-founding the cities of Harlingen, Mercedes, and McAllen.[276]

On May 29, a Saturday of the Memorial Day weekend, the test in west Brownsville attracted a throng of spectators who arrived in carriages and automobiles. After repairing a broken wooden strut between a set of parallel wings, Newman tied a 150-foot rope from the airship to Hill's powerful vehicle. Newman climbed in the pilot's seat, waited as people cleared the course, then gave Hill the signal to go.

A hundred yards out, the aircraft veered off course just as it began to rise. Within seconds, the right wing collided with thorny brush on the side of the field. The unexpected resistance broke the tow rope. The untethered aeroplane skittered into the *mezquital* before shuddering to a stop.

The aeroplane, battered and beaten, matched Newman's mood even though he again escaped unhurt.[277] As he watched the crowd disperse, he felt for the first time after a failure that his investors and the public were deserting him.

"Brownsville's Air Navigator,"
Brownsville Daily Herald, March 6, 1909, 8.

"...The main frame of the machine is made of angle iron, thin, light pieces that give the least possible weight. The main frame proper is about nine feet high and twelve feet long by four feet wide at the bottom, tapering towards the top to a width of four inches. This frame is mounted on a double pair of bicycle wheels, two in front and two behind. The frame is made to tilt from front to back, when starting on its flight.

"Extending nineteen feet on either side of the main frame are the wings, double deckers, eight and a half feet wide. The framework of the wings is of wood and the covering canvass (sic). On top of the main frame, standing upright is the 'fin,' three feet high and twenty-six feet long, designed to keep the vessel in an upright position when in the air. In the rear are two rudders and the 'tail,' the former designed to guide the ship through the air, and the latter to regulate its upward and downward course. The rudders are 3x6 feet and the tail is 5x12 feet with three sections about three feet apart.

"The entire mechanism is controlled from the driver's seat in the front of the main frame. Beside the driver's seat, is another for a passenger and behind the seats is a place for the 50-horse power gasoline motor that is to be installed to propel the machine. The motor has not yet arrived and the flight today will be made merely to test the buoyancy of the machine. With the motor, will be two propellers, eight feet in diameter and having capacity of 450 revolutions per minute. These are intended to move the machine through the air.

"The outside dimensions of the airplane are 32x40 feet, the greater dimension being its breadth from tip to tip of the wings. The other dimension is from the front of the main frame to the tip of the tail. The entire canvass (sic) area is 814 feet, about two and a half times that of the air ship built at San Antonio."

Chapter 10
Home of a Successful Aeroplane

Newman dissected all previous tests to identify externalities that thwarted efforts to become airborne without a motor. His analysis pointed to two deficiencies: lack of experienced drivers and poor choice of test location.

On Sunday, May 30, Newman carried an open letter to the *Brownsville Daily Herald* news room. It was generally directed to Rio Grande Valley citizens, but more pointedly to his investors. Newman had four weeks before the anticipated delivery date of the Herring-Curtiss motor. Once it arrived, he would have no more than ninety-six hours to install it and test the powered aeroplane before July 4, when investors expected him to fly multiple loops around the Fort Brown parade grounds. In the interim, he felt compelled to prove his engineering competence and the airworthiness of his aeroplane architecture to the public and his investors. His letter appeared in the next day's newspaper.

> To The Public: It is with regret I have several times had the public interested (Especially the stockholders of the Brownsville Aeroplane Co.) to witness an aeroplane flight, only to disappoint them.
>
> These trials, as is probably known by most people, are simply to conform to a contract to show the stockholders that the aeroplane, at a pre-determined speed, is capable of lifting its own weight and to show stability while in flight before installing its own motors. Depending as it has on outside conditions which, with one exception, have been very unfavorable, it has been handicapped by lack of speed or power in the automobiles towing it and by insufficient space in which to operate so large a machine not under the control of its own power. Unless an aeroplane is sufficiently accelerated from the start or attains the proper speed in a limited space it is in danger of destruction by being dragged into the brush.

Notwithstanding the misfortunes met with, I intend to give the aeroplane another trial and you can rest assured that at this trial it will go up and that you will see one of the best exhibition aeroplane flights ever shown in Texas. I know exactly what the machine will do under proper conditions and I intend this time to make every condition favorable.

In his missive, he would make good on this guarantee "promptly at 4:30, Tuesday afternoon, June 1st."

With a damaged airship to repair and not even twenty-four hours after the letter's publication to fulfill his pledge, Newman had no time to scout for a better site. He would again use the west Brownsville location. Newman did make a driver change. He chose Curtis Everson, a fellow machinist, to pull the aeroplane with his forty-five-horsepower Pierce-Arrow automobile. Everson's knowledge of an automobile's mechanical power made him a better choice than the pleasure drivers Newman used for previous tests. Everson's responsibility was to attain and maintain the required speed so the towed aeroplane lifted off the ground. [278]

Newman moved the renovated aeroplane to the exhibition site on schedule. The morning sky on Tuesday, June 1, broke clear, but with headwinds that gusted twelve to fifteen miles per hour. An optimistic crowd watched Newman work throughout the day.

At 4:30 p.m. Everson began towing the aeroplane, secured to his automobile with a 180-foot-long, three-quarter-inch rope. Newman cut short a first attempt and instructed Everson to increase acceleration.

A second try followed. Between 150 and 200 feet from the starting point, with the automobile reaching eight miles per hour, Newman's aeroplane lifted off the ground. At ten to twelve miles per hour, the aeroplane became airborne. At twenty-five miles an hour, to the spectators' delight, the aeroplane smoothly climbed to an altitude estimated at seventy-five feet.

In flight, Newman showed complete control of his machine, guiding its travel over a half mile and reaching a peak altitude estimated at between ninety and 130 feet. The afternoon gusts had no effect on the aeroplane's stability when airborne. As the looming *monte* at the edge of the navigable course forced Everson to pull up the Pierce-Arrow and release the tether, Newman flew the aircraft with its own momentum for another three hundred feet, swung it to one side to miss trees, and then brought the aircraft in for landing. At contact with the ground, one wheel hit a small stand of brush and broke off, but that was a minor setback.

"As gently and as easily as a bird, the large air-craft came back to earth, alighting without a jar," a reporter wrote.

For the first time in Brownsville, Newman had achieved flight in a publicly announced exhibition. Spectators, including Brownsville Aeroplane Company stockholders, were elated. Newman received a spontaneous three cheers, and the newspaper celebrated his accomplishment the following day in an editorial entitled "Brownsville Is Proud." It said faith had to be restored in Newman, "who has worked so persistently in many disappointments and the discouragement of a doubting public." The editor predicted that this successful flight would bring Newman fame and shower attention on Brownsville, "which has the honor of being the first southern town to be the home of a successful aeroplane."[279]

Attention did come. *The Automobile*, a national weekly auto enthusiasts' magazine that carried aeronautical news, ran a report on Newman's success in its June 17 issue. Its lead read: "From Brownsville, Texas, comes a story of the successful trial trip of the first aeroplane constructed in the Lone Star State."[280]

Newman's stockholders convened the day after his successful flight. In addition to his assignment to fly around the Fort Brown parade grounds, they added more ambitious plans. Some spirited directors reiterated their desire for Newman to go head to head against the Wrights, Curtiss, and other leading aviators of the day in *The New York World*'s racing competition over the Hudson River. Brownsville once again was giddy with aviation fever.[281]

Two days later, Newman recorded another successful test, again with Everson driving the automobile. All previous attempts were made into a headwind, a condition Newman preferred to aid ascent. On this test, Newman confronted crossing winds that he initially feared might adversely impact stability. Nonetheless, the Newman aeroplane flew a quarter mile and again landed smoothly. This success marked a significant milestone for the innovation: Newman's aeroplane could take off, cruise, and land without optimum conditions.[282]

Luckily for Newman's legacy, Charles Gilhousen had recently moved his family to Brownsville from Keokuk, Iowa. In the next decade, Gilhousen would gain notoriety from his New York and New Jersey studios as a photographer of nude beautiful young women. Today, the Metropolitan Museum of Art in New York holds twenty-three Gilhousen nudes as "significant works of art" in its collection.[283]

In 1909, however, Gilhousen was simply a new Brownsville resident with a camera who had set up a portrait studio in a Brownsville bank building. Runyon, who did not yet consider himself a professional photographer, even had Gilhousen take his portrait soon after he came to the borderlands (page 3).[284]

At this exhibition, Gilhousen captured striking action shots of Newman's aircraft in the air. Gilhousen overwrote his name and date on the negatives, and developed several prints on postcard-sized paper. The next day, he sold these postcards through shops around Brownsville.[285] For the first time, the Newman machine in action had visual proof.

Portrait photographer Charles Gilhousen captured this action scene of the Newman aeroplane at takeoff on June 3, 1909. Brownsville Historical Association.

Gilhousen's second photograph provided a unique rear view of the Newman Brownsville aeroplane in flight. Lorraine Owens Family Papers.

Newman said later that confidence in his mechanical abilities left him little doubt success would follow. The missing ingredients were motorized tests and facing his charges for the murder of Shell Mason. When those were resolved, his mind could focus totally on aviation.

Chapter 11
Success, Innovation and Freedom

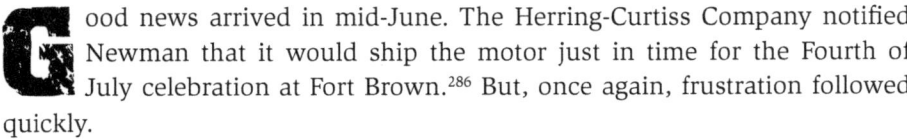ood news arrived in mid-June. The Herring-Curtiss Company notified Newman that it would ship the motor just in time for the Fourth of July celebration at Fort Brown.[286] But, once again, frustration followed quickly.

When the long-awaited motor did arrive, it was too late. Around-the-clock effort could not produce a fully operational motorized aircraft by the Fourth of July holiday. Nonetheless, Newman promised some form of an air show during the holiday at a different location.

Newman selected a site five miles from town toward Point Isabel.[287] The site likely was near Loma Alta on what was known locally as the Jackass Prairie, the coastal flats between Brownsville and Point Isabel. The Rio Grande Railroad Company, a narrow gauge line that ran from its passenger depot on Eleventh Street in east Brownsville to Point Isabel, scheduled a special car, probably to the line's most western section house called Mesquite Station. The car would transport the large number of spectators expected to attend because of Newman's recent successful exhibitions.[288]

Early on the morning of June 30, though, a storm moved into the lower Rio Grande Valley. From daylight to midafternoon, rain came down in torrents and high winds buffeted the towering palms. Between three and ten inches of rain fell, flooding many locations. By evening, the outlying areas, including Newman's test site, stood in twelve to eighteen inches of water.[289]

Newman's assessment the next morning found that the storm slightly damaged one of the biplane's wings. He could make the repair quickly. What he could do nothing about was the water-soaked ground. A soggy field meant the aeroplane could not achieve desired speed for flight under its own power, by being pulled by any automobile, or a combination of the two. He postponed the exhibition until conditions improved, ending the city's persistent hopes for a history-making Fourth of July in the sky.[290]

As with every other setback, Newman went back to work on the aeroplane to secure connections and tinker with improvements. Reports indicate this was the period when he mounted the engine in front of the pilot rather than keep it behind as in his original plans.[291] He also retained the dihedral angle for his parallel wings. Both changes were different than the Wrights' design, who at the time kept their wings flat and positioned the engine alongside the pilot.

Newman's mistake this time was not moving the structure back to the rice mill. A severe hurricane came ashore just south of Matamoros on July 21. Brownsville proper suffered light wind damage, yet flooding again was severe and widespread.[292]

On August 1, Newman, already twice hit by deluges in the same season, again chose to attempt flight near the Mesquite Station

On the next day, a Monday, Newman conducted a private test of the motorized aeroplane at the new location. The airship achieved full speed and skimmed along the ground in what he assessed as an attempt to rise. He shut the motor down rather than ascend at that time, although he said he would attempt flight on Friday of that week.[293] Spectators and stockholders planned an automobile caravan to the Mesquite Station site to watch.[294]

On Friday, though, he cancelled the test. He was dissatisfied with the motor's performance and said he would not attempt flight until all conditions were optimum.[295] He proposed to try on Monday, August 9, yet on that day the new motor failed to turn over. While Newman worked on it, a late summer shower swept over the site, again making the ground too soggy for a test.[296]

The continued weather challenges quickly began to dampen public expectations of seeing a Brownsville aeroplane success of any level. When the newspaper published its short piece on the engine failure, the story ran just below an advertisement from the Electric Theater in downtown Brownsville. The theater's feature film was a movie of the Wright brothers' recent achievements in France.[297] For citizens of Brownsville, the juxtaposition of those two articles starkly contrasted Newman's failures against the amazing success of the world's leading aviation pioneers. Seemingly insurmountable separation had occurred between Newman and the Wright brothers.

The newspaper would soon inform its readers of an amazing August feat by Frenchman Louis Blériot in flying a monoplane from Les Baraque near Calais, France, to Dover Castle in England.[298] Blériot flew twenty-three miles over the English Channel and landed in England in just twenty minutes; Newman's longest successful flight had occurred in a blink of the eye, without a motor, over a distance of less than 880 yards, and with problems before every takeoff and after every landing.

News stories about Newman once merited twenty column inches on the front page of the *Brownsville Daily Herald*. Syndicated services often spread the stories throughout the state and sometimes the nation and world. After July 4, his news received an inch of coverage buried in the "Local Items" of the middle pages of the local newspaper. Newman's once revolutionary technology had been outpaced by the aviation world around him; the citizens of the lower Rio Grande Valley concurrently lost interest in seeing local history made at Newman's pace.

Even more worrisome was stockholders' lost confidence in Newman's capacity to catch up to aviation's leaders. No investor again mentioned pitting Newman's aeroplane against the Wright brothers' inventions.

Newman, though, possessed unflagging faith in his engineering abilities. He believed in his vision for commercializing flight, and he devised different combinations to help him catch up to the leaders.

On August 14 at Mesquite, Newman planned to fly but failed again. Over the weekend, he made changes to the motor, removing what he considered defective magnetos. To replace its steel magnets, which generate and then discharge electricity to the fuel mixture at the right time and in proper order for each engine cylinder to generate power, Newman turned to a battery for power generation and a commutator to distribute the electrical charge more reliably. He tested the newly configured system on Thursday, August 19, and scheduled a public test for the next day.

On Friday, a few spectators arrived in automobiles to watch Newman's now familiar pre-test procedure. Although Newman wanted his aeroplane to lift off and fly by its own power, on that day he augmented the new motor with acceleration from an automobile driven by Andres Cueto, a local merchant.[299]

No one knew what to expect from Newman's constant tinkering. What the few spectators and Newman experienced, however, was vindication for the patience they had invested in the project during 1909. On that day, those spectators witnessed aviation history even though it was fatefully brief.

In the morning hours, just after securing the tow line to the automobile, Newman climbed into the "prow" of the aeroplane. He directed his crew to release the aeroplane from the wires that secured it to the ground, and he started the engine. Cueto's automobile pulled the aeroplane, but the airship's motor propulsion allowed Newman's craft to overtake and pass the vehicle, the tow rope cast off in transition.

Then the aeroplane left the ground and flew briefly under its own power. No photograph exists of Newman's accomplishment. Fortunately, a reporter was on site and chronicled the achievement for the afternoon edition. Yet what historic first comes without controversy?

In the article, the journalist credited the ascent to a sudden gust of wind that "struck the wings full in front and the bi-plane was raised fully six feet from the earth." That phrase raises the question: Was it wind or the motor that lifted the aeroplane?

Yet the same reporter also wrote that he had seen powered flight. He wrote: "That the Newman bi-plane will move through the air under its own power was demonstrated this morning at Mesquite." Later in the news report, he added: "The trial was considered successful as it is believed to have demonstrated that the machine will move under its own power."

Certainly, the spectators left that day believing with their eyes and ears that the motor had powered the flight. They saw the aircraft leave the ground, accompanied by the sound of a functioning motor. While it had propulsion, they watched the aeroplane fly. Years later, Newman estimated it had flown about one hundred yards under its own power. Within seconds, though, the crowd heard the motor cut out and the turning propeller blades go silent due to what Newman diagnosed as a malfunctioning connection. When the whirring subsided, the crowd saw gravity take over, bringing the aeroplane down in a rough landing that destroyed one wheel.[300]

Newman could have put the controversy to rest with a second test, but the damaged wheel grounded the aeroplane. Still, for the next two decades, reporters recognized Newman as the first pilot of both an unpowered and powered heavier-than-air machine in the southwestern U.S. One account, published in the late 1920s when the world's passenger aviation technology was growing exponentially, stated that Brownsville "claims the first motor-driven flights in the Southwest" with credit to Newman "as the builder of the ship that flew here."[301]

Before the next week had ended, another tropical storm came in from the Gulf of Mexico over the mouth of the Rio Grande. First accounts said heavy winds took the airship, still staked in the open, fifty feet from its moorings and left it "a twisted shapeless mass." Later assessment said the wreckage was limited to just the Newman aeroplane wings. Nonetheless, the damage was severe enough to call in the Brownsville Aeroplane Company stockholders who authorized the aeroplane's repair. The official statement was that the next test, which stockholders fully expected to be successful, would take place in a couple of weeks.[302]

Yet their announcement was not in concert with Newman's plans. He moved the aeroplane back to the rice mill to protect it from wind and rain. Likely influenced by Blériot's recent monoplane successes in Europe, Newman made revolutionary changes. Newman also may have introduced elements of Santos-Dumont's experiments with a single-pilot monoplane featuring dihedral wings after reading about those tests in the same April issue of *Flight Illustrated* that had reported Newman's successful but exaggerated flight over the brush in west Brownsville in late March.[303] Such influences persuaded Newman to drop the concept of the biplane, and start building the first monoplane in the United States.

Newman rightly theorized that an aeroplane could achieve lift from single fixed wings powered by its own motor just as efficiently as it could with dual parallel wings.[304] He also desired a more airworthy machine, and losing half of the parallel wings on each side meant a lighter aeroplane. The monoplane's wing spread was thirty-four feet.[305] He constructed each wing out of new components, employing a light wire in place of the old cypress wood frame connected with angle iron of his earlier iterations.[306] Newman used the same light wire for the tail, a vital element of his novel steering mechanism, drastically decreasing the tail's size at the same time.[307] One report stated that his original tail was the equivalent of a two-story building laid on its side so scaling down its size greatly reduced the amount of wood and canvas wrapping required. Newman later admitted, however, that his tail modification was a significant error in engineering judgment.

Newman planned to seek a patent for the single wings once he had proved that the innovation aided flight. No record exists that he filed, and by the time his single-wing iteration had been constructed several other inventors already had applied for monoplane patents in the U.S. Yet Newman always believed he was the first American aviation engineer actually to construct a sophisticated single-wing innovation for transportation in the post-Wright brothers era.[308] *The New York Times* recognized that claim without qualification in Newman's 1964 obituary.[309]

As Newman completed his changes, he moved toward another motorized test before October ended. The autumn, however, proved a whirlwind in the Newman family's lives. On August 30, his brother, Arthur, who still provided vital machinist assistance, and his wife, Lucy, had a baby girl, Gladys. On September 17, Newman and his wife, Pearl, welcomed their second child, Lillian.[310]

Prentice as defendant and Arthur as a witness also still had to travel to Hallettsville for Prentice's next court appearance in early November.

The court date and the test date eventually converged when Prentice set the next exhibition for October 29 two days before he would leave for Hallettsville. As was his custom, Prentice invited the public as well as stockholders to observe the test. This time, he returned to the west Brownsville location that he had earlier criticized as a poor location.

Rumors of his radical modifications plus news of his brief success with a motor had created a renewed buzz in the region. Word also spread that Newman planned to use just the aeroplane's motor to achieve lift. Several automobiles of spectators showed up at the test site.

Newman was unable to get airborne on his first attempt. Everyone noted, though, that the monoplane achieved notably high speed and seemed ready to rise, although it could not sustain momentum. Hope pervaded the field for two subsequent afternoon attempts, but motor and battery issues cropped up. By day's end, the crowd went home frustrated once again.

The next trial took place the following day at 10:30 a.m. This time, Newman's monoplane reached forty miles per hour, twice as fast as the speed achieved on his successful short motorized hop in late August. It also was faster than Newman had ever traveled with any airship, and his vision and reactions did not adjust. Just as lift should have occurred, Newman approached ubiquitous brush at the perimeter of the course. One propeller blade shattered on a branch, ending that test and any chance that Newman would try again.[311]

Before leaving for Hallettsville the next morning, October 31, Newman announced he would hold another exhibition in a day or two. He likely expected the court to grant his attorneys' request for another delay.

Newman's attorneys filed the case's motion for continuance with the Lavaca County District Court. The defense claimed that there was no certainty all called witnesses could appear in the upcoming court term. Absence of these witnesses, they said, would injure Newman's case.

The court refused the petition.[312]

Newman stood before the jury on a charge of murder early on the morning of November 5, ending four and a half years of uncertainty. Testimony showed that Arthur admitted to the shooting, but he had been found not guilty by reason of temporary insanity in an earlier jury trial. The defense admitted that Prentice was present in the room when Arthur shot and killed Mason. His lawyers did not attempt to portray his actions as being of unsound mind. The unanswered question before the jury was whether Prentice was an accomplice in the murder.

Late that evening, news leaked out that the jury was hung at six for conviction and six for acquittal, but the tally may have been a red herring. A cynical reporter at a local newspaper wrote that the half voting for conviction did so only to receive lodging for the night at county expense rather than travel home after rendering a late-hour acquittal. Indeed, the jury voted 12-0 to acquit Newman in the first poll on the morning of November 6.

Texas' pioneering aviator was free.[313]

The court action made state-wide papers, but the *Brownsville Daily Herald* was the only newspaper to identify Newman as "inventor of aeroplane,"[314] an accurate statement for the borderlands.

Newman, no longer burdened by uncertainty about his future, returned to the Valley after a week's absence. He immediately resolved to test his new innovation. He decided again to abandon the west Brownsville test site "on account of there being so much brush along the road side as to render it very difficult to maneuver his machine." This time, he transported his smaller and lighter aeroplane to Loma Alta. A hundred-yard road led to the top of the *loma*, which at thirty-eight feet high dominated the flat coastal landscape. Newman's plan was to position his airship at the top of the road, start the motor, and then have gravity augment the motor's speed to achieve lift. The approach emulated the same gravitational strategy the Wrights had used with good results at Kill Devil Hills at Kitty Hawk nine years earlier.

Newman announced the public test at Loma Alta for early Thanksgiving week. His advisory earned a three-inch boxed article at the bottom of page two of the Brownsville newspaper.[315] That test likely did not take place as a minor rewrite of the same announcement ran in the newspaper on December 3. To this one, the editor wryly added: "The Brownsville airship, which heretofore has been entirely too fond of Mother Earth to leave her bosom, except when given an impetus (by an) automobile, will make another attempt."[316] No record exists to indicate whether the latter test occurred.

A couple of days later, the *Brownsville Daily Herald* ran a humorous filler titled "Wouldn't Go Up" at the bottom of a column. Even if the editor was responsible for its creation, any Newman investor could have been the source:

"With one exception, everything I've put money into has gone up in the air."
"What was the exception?"
"An airship."[317]

The year that had been one of ups and downs for Newman kept coming with disruptions into the last month. Even as it appeared that his professional dreams were coming to an end, his personal nightmares continued. On December 11, Newman and his wife, Pearl, learned her father, T. S. Williams, committed suicide early that morning at his home in Cuero.[318] No further mention of Newman's activities with a Brownsville aeroplane exist after that date.

In retrospective articles that appeared two decades later, Newman said he did repair the aeroplane after the propeller damage and did test it. He faulted his revised tail design as lacking needed size to lift the aeroplane. He likely could have re-engineered that component, but stockholders stopped further funding. Newman never again flew his creation nor did he try to build another.

Architecture aside, he blamed insufficient funding for his lack of success. With a higher investment, he said he would have purchased a sixty-three-horsepower motor, as he first intended, instead of the forty-horsepower motor. In reality, he probably could have used a few more assistant engineers as well.[319]

All first-mover advantages Newman once held in Texas and the Southwest were irretrievably taken away in Houston on February 18, 1910, when

Frenchman Louis Paulhan made the state's first sustained powered flight at an exhibition seen by hundreds of Texans. L. L. Walker, not Newman, is the first Texan credited with sustained motorized flight. He did so nine months after Paulhan, also in Houston.[320]

From a performance standpoint, Paulhan and Walker indisputably made history. From an innovation standpoint, however, a boundless difference exists between these two men and Newman. Paulhan flew a Farman aeroplane and Walker flew one designed by Blériot. Of the three, only Newman flew an aeroplane that he had imagined, created, constructed, innovated, and flew. Newman's year-long string of creativity and flight achievement raises him closer to the lofty heights of the Wright brothers as an aviation innovator rather than just a pioneer pilot. Certainly, he was far less successful than the Wrights, but no less ambitious, imaginative, and enthusiastic. In fact, one reporter, who was a contemporary to all the pioneer aviators, stated in 1930, when aviation technology was progressing rapidly, that Newman's designs were more revolutionary than the Wrights'. He said Newman "had correct ideas and his planes of that day more nearly correspond to present-day planes than did those of the Wright brothers."[321]

There is no question that Newman was the first person in the southwestern United States to achieve multiple aviation milestones in the post-Wright brothers' Kitty Hawk era. On January 2, 1909, at the Fort Sam Houston parade grounds in San Antonio, he made the first successful heavier-than-air flight in the Southwest. Then, less than nine months later, on August 20, 1909, on the coastal plains of Cameron County, Texas, he became the first person anywhere south of Kitty Hawk, North Carolina, to fly an aeroplane under motorized power. And a few weeks after that, in Brownsville, he constructed America's first monoplane, although it never took flight.

There are no markers recognizing these accomplishments, but visitors to Brownsville still can visit the location where Newman imagined and then built important parts of that history. The old rice mill is gone, but its footprint is now occupied by the Reynaldo G. Garza-Filemon B. Vela United States Courthouse.

Still, Newman's dreams had to end. When they did, he fell back on his machinist skills and automobile expertise to earn a living. His mind continued to innovate, but on a less grand scale as he moved on to his next challenge—taming the terrain of northeastern Mexico.

Chapter 12
Brownsville Boom Timber

Brownsville and Matamoros, twin towns on the Rio Grande, did not appeal to everyone who traveled to the tip of Texas. You might include someone who had spent twenty-seven years in eastern Kentucky and West Virginia, someone unfamiliar with the smells, sights, sounds, and customs generated by connected border towns, among the persons who found living on *la frontera* objectionable. Yet Runyon experienced only excitement at his new home's potential, and he was not reluctant to tell family and friends of his content.

Evelyn told him it was no surprise. "Of course you like Texas for she is the Grandest Old State in the Union."[322] Fannie Short realized his intentions by his second summer in Brownsville: "Presume you are so smitten with Texas that you will make your future home there. Will you not?"[323]

It was true. Runyon eagerly boasted of Brownsville's and Matamoros' bounty. In the borderlands, Runyon took unique photographic scenes to make postals to send to his Kentucky and West Virginia acquaintances.[324] Sometimes he sent friends and relatives packages of Valley-grown citrus, mangoes, or curios he had bought in Mexico. *Huaraches* became a popular item among relatives.

His correspondents in turn sent him news of friends and relatives in Boyd County, Kentucky, and Mingo and Logan Counties, West Virginia. Sometimes, they sent him pawpaws, a tree fruit of which he was fond.

On November 23, 1910, Runyon sent a package to W. J. Lampton, a Kentucky colonel who once had edited a newspaper in Ashland, the town adjacent to Runyon's hometown in Catlettsburg. Lampton, at the time living in

New York City, was a satirical poet with a national audience. Lampton caught Runyon's attention after a relative sent a clipping from *The Catlettsburg Tribune* with Lampton's opinion on the value of postcards for advertising. Runyon's package showed Lampton how he did just that with his postcards to promote his new borderlands home. Runyon's accompanying letter said:

> *"...these are my own makeup and are original. I made the photographs and had the cards made from them and have twenty other new view subjects in print now, will send you a sample of each as soon as I have them. I was born and reared in Catlettsburg and still love the old town, but I am now a citizen of Brownsville, Texas, and could never be induced to return to the east. We have here the best climate and the most progressive small town in the United States."*

After viewing that package, Lampton branded Runyon as part of "the Brownsville Boom and Bust Society for the propagation and profit of Brownsville, Texas." Lampton forwarded his and Runyon's comments to *The Catlettsburg Tribune* editors, who published them. In them, Lampton said Runyon was "not only an artist but an advertiser as well and naturally he (Runyon) is successful in business and that he does not want to go back to the old town of his birth is a loss to Catlettsburg." Yet Lampton also said Runyon's advancement was a credit to Old Kentucky: "Catlettsburg may feel that however prosperous Brownsville be, not a little came by way of what Catlettsburg contributed." The newspaper editors ran Lampton's piece under the heading: "Brownsville Borrows Some Boom Timber From Catlettsburg."[325]

Runyon owned up to his reputation as resolute borderlands timber during 1910 by investing in several Cameron County properties and buying his rent house.[326] Still, being separated from his son, relatives, and longtime friends wore on his spirit. Even while complimenting Brownsville, he bemoaned his solitude in correspondence to family and to friends. Beginning in January 1910, Runyon acted to overcome that loneliness.

He traveled by rail to Fort Worth just after New Year's Day to discuss the future with Evelyn. There, he plainly laid out his feelings and plans. Within a week of his return, Evelyn wrote Runyon:

> *"...I really did not know you cared for me so and then again I would not for all the world do anything that you would think the less of me. I am so glad you had the chance to come up so we could know each other better."*[327]

Runyon had thought about this meeting for quite a while. He previously had disclosed his intentions to Edyth Christie in Kentucky. She sent a rapid reply, although it did not reach Runyon until he had returned from Fort Worth:

> "Well things seem rather suspicious. You have bought a cottage and then journeyed to Ft. Worth. I think it wise for me to cancel some of my correspondents (sic). Do you? Do not be too hasty in christening it 'Bachelor's Hall' for I think you can find a more appropriate name. I can suggest a few viz. 'The Queen's Palace,' 'The Cottage of the Future Queen' or Ft. Worth would be quite suitable."[328]

In the following months, though, his Fort Worth meeting with Evelyn had a result opposite of what he intended. The correspondence continued through January and February, but in March Evelyn added as an aside. "I am getting quite popular here of late (a-hem). I have a date almost for every night & after noon."

Runyon wrote back and asked for a return of the diamond ring he had sent her. She mailed it to Brownsville, commenting on the curtness of his letter. She said, "I did not know I had turned you down as you term it as you and I are the truest of friends and I have never had the chance."[329]

Runyon, though, refused to let that squabble end the relationship. He asked his favorite cousin, Julia Ford, to intercede from Kentucky. He told Julia of his plans, and asked her to contact Evelyn on his behalf. Julia sent an introductory postcard to Evelyn, but she also urged caution to Runyon, especially since his main objective in romancing Evelyn seemed to be to secure a good mother for William.

"Now Robert, I should like to see you marry and make a home for that dear little boy, but look long before you leap. Be sure that she will take his mother's place and do the right thing by him. You know it is a trying thing for a young girl to be a stepmother. Don't think me harsh, I am only anxious that your future home, be a bright one."[330]

Later in the year, the strains in his relationship with Evelyn showed no improvement. So, Runyon turned to a backup plan. Shortly before departing, perhaps more in jest than in conviction, he told friends he wanted to find a marriage prospect during his extended visit to Kentucky.

Fannie, with a gem of a run-on sentence, said she would assist:

"Yes I will do my best to help you get a wife when you come back to Kentucky, that is if you really want one, and I should think that would be Easy as there seem to be so many on the market, but then one does not always want what they can easily obtain, and I have heard that in a case of this kind that the pursuit is greater than the winning but as to that I can't say, as I do not know, but anyway I'll lend a helping hand, and do my best. Ha! Ha!"[331]

On June 20, Evelyn came to the Valley and she, some friends, and Runyon went out for the day. Runyon took several photographs that he listed in his exposure records as "comps –Eve y su amegas (sic)." Yet he also penned a cryptic, melancholy, unfinished comment in the same record: "*muy triste todo el día. Porque si...* (very sad all day. Because if...)"[332] It was clear he and Evelyn had drifted apart.

Runyon left for Catlettsburg in mid-July on a six-week visit.[333] He retrieved William, now six years old, in time to enroll him in first grade in Brownsville that autumn. He did not travel through Fort Worth as he told Evelyn he would. She penned a letter on August 2 to Runyon in Catlettsburg, but by the time it arrived he and William had already left Kentucky. The letter was forwarded

A Thoroughbred (Texas Long Horn) Brownsville, Tex.
Copyright by R. Runyon, 1910.

Among Runyon's earliest lower Rio Grande Valley postcards was a Texas Longhorn steer whose extended hooves indicated that the animal had been pen-raised for some time. Nonetheless, the image received good response back in Appalachia from persons who thought the legendary breed was extinct. Photo by Robert Runyon from author's collection.

to his P.O. Box 11 in Brownsville. A few postals, but no later letters between them, exist. Still, he and Evelyn saw each other occasionally, at least through the summer of 1911, when she visited her Tandy relatives.

His son's presence in Brownsville, though, vastly changed Runyon's outlook for the better. William started elementary school just a few weeks after moving to Brownsville. Runyon suddenly had to keep two lives on schedule. Each day he combined his job as lunch room manager with duties as the father of a low first-grade student at St. Joseph's College.[334]

William's arrival also inspired Runyon to devote more time to his camera, both for personal use and for added income through the railroad. As he built his photography catalogue, he re-pitched his idea to his bosses to market a Runyon line of postcards through the Gulf Coast News-managed depots.

Runyon's daughter, Amali, said that despite the photography advancements he made, her father always felt he had to learn more to master the art. One example occurred before Runyon left for Kentucky when he entered an Eastman Kodak contest to compare his work with other photographers. By June 1, Kodak returned Runyon's entries because they did not meet the contest's requirements for class of prints. The company, though, added valuable comments:

"As to the quality of the negatives from a technical standpoint they are undoubtedly good as are many of the prints submitted. A few are a trifle dark, due to slight overexposure of the paper, but that may be readily remedied."[335]

By October 27, though, Runyon felt he had improved enough to send several photographs to C. U. Williams Photograph Company to convert into postcards, or to use that company's proprietary term, "photoettes."[336] From the beginning, Runyon showed a keen interest in intellectual property protection. He advised Williams that he did not want unauthorized copies made of his work. The company told Runyon that it would "give you protection on the photos that you sent us, and will publish them for you, and no one else." He also contracted through the Elite Postcard Company, Incorporated, for three thousand postcards of one subject at a price of $6.50 a thousand.[337]

Runyon that same year projected enough demand for his postals that he turned to a volume postcard specialist, Tom Jones Art Publishing Company in Cincinnati. In the twelve months from December 1910 to November 1911, Runyon ordered and received 37,500 cards from the Jones company.[338]

He sent his San Antonio bosses proposals typed on Gulf Coast News letterhead listing his growing portfolio.[339] His initiative paid off as he had a standing order of ten thousand cards from Gulf Coast News by March 1911.[340]

Intellectual property protection continued to worry him as his orders increased through Tom Jones and Curt Teich, another volume postcard printer. Jones personally wrote Runyon to recommend that he not copyright the images. Jones said: "It would cost $1 each, and as I will not make these cards for others, it will not be necessary to have them copyrighted on my account."[341] Nonetheless, Runyon dutifully filed for protection with the copyright office at the Library of Congress on all images for which he anticipated commercial returns. Each protected postcard carried "copyright Robert Runyon" or "©R. Runyon." This practice, initiated early in his career, proved a wise strategy in later years against unauthorized use of his original work.

Another challenge Runyon quickly encountered was slim profit margins on individual postcards. Runyon's solution was to encourage customers to buy postcards in sets to generate higher return through volume turnover. As early as January 1911, he promoted package sales to friends and relatives.[342] He initially turned to a ready-made card filing system produced by Holder Manufacturing Company of Albany, New York. Runyon manually inserted his postcards to create serial scenes of landscapes or bullfight action, his most popular photo series.[343] Later, he eliminated the labor by commercially printing his cards in sets.

By May 1911, though, Runyon became exhausted at his pace and told his bosses he needed a sabbatical. He took leave on May 25 ostensibly for health reasons, but his correspondence records show that on June 12 he

Runyon's custom folders featured sixteen postcard-sized photographs printed on fifty-pound enamel, in color two-sides, and tipped into a color cover printed on card stock. This version folded accordion-style into a mail-ready package. Even that early, Runyon emphasized the region's native flora on many sets. Photo by Robert Runyon from author's collection.

Runyon promoted his line of postcards for sale through the Gulf Coast News lunch room after becoming its manager. His portfolio included every good exposure from the day he arrived in Houston in January 1909 to his most recent exposures. Runyon had captured this shot of the cockpit, or palenque, in Matamoros on January 16, 1910. Photo by Robert Runyon from author's collection.

Runyon understood national U.S. interest in unique photographs from Mexico. His postcard images offered through the Gulf Coast News lunch room included this rear-view shot in Matamoros of Casa Mata, a casemate, the construction of which dated from the Mexican War. He took this exposure on February 8, 1910. Photo by Robert Runyon from author's collection.

inquired about a photographer's position with H. G. Zimmerman & Company of Chicago, Illinois, a postcard printer.[344]

In July, Runyon considered competing with Gulf Coast News. He probed the possibility of representing the news and curio interests of the Rio Grande Railway Company that on February 1 had taken over operations of the Rio Grande Railroad Company.[345] Runyon validated the opportunity by contacting the same vendors who supplied the Gulf Coast News lunch room. But that supply strategy ran into multiple complications. For instance, Rueckheim Bros. & Eckstein of Chicago, makers of Cracker Jack®, told him to buy through Gulf Coast News. Although Runyon eventually received some vendor pledges, by October he had given up the idea and was back on the Gulf Coast News payroll.[346]

During 1911, Runyon accelerated his self-instruction that included extensive correspondence with experts to gain new photography techniques. He inserted technical questions requiring an answer whenever he mailed catalog requests to suppliers like Bausch and Lomb Optical Company. On December 18, he enrolled in a correspondence course offered by The Bissell Colleges-Illinois College of Photography in Effington, Illinois. He ordered its *Complete Self-Instructing Library of Practical Photography* for $12 on Bissell's installment plan at $2 per month. The course entitled him to one year of advice and criticism from the American School of Art and Photography.

His focus on improvement steadily earned him wider recognition for his photography talents. Lower Rio Grande Valley residents began to ask for "the photographer in Brownsville" to order postcards, to contract for photography on assignment and to seek local film processing, for which Runyon promised guaranteed work and prompt delivery.[347]

Runyon also used his growing reputation to generate new postcard sales whenever possible, even while managing the lunch room. In October, Runyon reminded Gulf Coast News executives that Midwestern farmers were headed to the Valley. "The season is almost here for the Homeseekers and you will want Postcards and I have the cards to sell," Runyon said. At the time, he had on order one hundred thousand postcards, including the "Bull Fight cards that I have that will sell like hot cakes."[348]

His earlier leave of absence, though, was for a reason. He needed new challenges. By the last quarter of 1911, Runyon's crash courses in self-education had given him the confidence to say he was a professional photographer. He also had become proficient in Spanish even if he always spoke it with a Kentucky accent. So, he resigned his lunch room position at the first of 1912 and committed to photography full-time.

His first entrepreneurial project was to photograph the riding and roping, the parade, and the prize-winning fruits and vegetables at the January 1912

Midwinter Fair in Brownsville. The *Brownsville Herald* editor praised Runyon's camera expertise. The short blurb the day after the rodeo said:

> **Good Pictures**—*Several fine postcard pictures of yesterday's riding and roping contest have been made by Robert Runyon. The pictures do credit to Mr. Runyon's skill as a photographer.* [349]

Soon Runyon launched a full-service business. His multiple services available to Rio Grande Valley residents included:

- **Postcards:** "'Runyon's Original' local view postcards a specialty, wholesale prices quoted on request."
- **Bull Fight Postcards:** "The best descriptive colored bull fight postcards on the market, also bull books and other bull fighting paraphernalia."
- **Commercial Photography:** "The most up to date equipment in the Rio Grand (sic) Valley; work excellent and prices reasonable. Always a nice line of photographs for sale."
- **Kodak Finishing:** "All work first class in every respect and guaranteed permanent; prompt delivery and prices low enough."
- **Enlarging and Copying:** "All work carefully executed on the finest material and satisfaction guaranteed."
- **Lantern Slides:** "Without question the best work in the Southwest, prompt delivery and prices reasonable." [350]

Runyon was not the only photographer competing for business in Brownsville, but the small, tight-knit group maintained a collegial relationship with the new entrant. Gilhousen already had moved away by 1912, but another well-respected professional, Miguel Morales, asked Runyon to serve in his wedding party in November 1912. [351]

The changes Runyon had withstood in just three years had borne fruit. His new business showed promise, and his son was at his side, also enjoying his new life in the borderlands. But Runyon still lacked what he had sought almost since he arrived in Texas—a wife.

Chapter 13
'Será Bien Recibido'

Every Sunday, young *matamorenses* congregated at Plaza Hidalgo, the Matamoros square known originally as Plaza de Armas. In the early twentieth century, many participants came from families whose roots in northeastern Mexico went back 150 years to the region's establishment as Nuevo Santander by Spanish explorer José de Escandón.

Since Matamoros' settlement as a villa in the last quarter of the 1700s, just thirty miles from the Gulf of Mexico, it attracted businessmen, entrepreneurs, and adventurers of many nationalities who came to seek profit from trade offered by a viable sea port. Later, after the Mexican War, establishment of the international border added to the commercial attraction. These aliens were Italian, Irish, Scottish, and French, and some of them married into older established families, most of whom by then carried a bit of Indian genetics mixed with Spanish blood of the founders. The multicultural influence made Matamoros, even into the early twentieth century, a predominantly Spanish New World villa featuring an unmistakably cosmopolitan accent.[352]

Through the decades, the villa's founding families' traditions and culture remained largely unchanged. In the early twentieth century, even as revolution threatened their country, the city's youth continued to gather at Plaza Hidalgo on Sunday to perform the ancient courtship ritual called the *paseo*. The rules of this legacy from Spain required unmarried young women and their chaperones to stroll in one direction as eligible young men walked in the other. Its function was a prelude to formal introductions.[353]

One day in August 1912, Runyon, either knowingly or by circumstances, elected to participate in that tradition. Earlier that morning, he stepped out

Runyon took this photograph of a skiff headed to Mexico probably around 1910 when the first International Bridge opened. The Matamoros crossing point of Santa Cruz might have been named with two purposes—in honor of the Holy Cross itself and in hopes that each skiff passage resulted in a safe crossing. Photo by Robert Runyon, RFP, DBCAH, The University of Texas at Austin.

of his cottage, walked past the railway station where he had worked until recently, and strolled through the park adjacent to the depot.

A block away, at the corner of Levee and Twelfth Streets, right where the Blue Bird Saloon and Maltby's print shop faced each other, Runyon stepped on to what he called the "Old Board Walk." The wooden avenue, eight feet wide and twelve inches high, provided a dry pedestrian path that curved down two blocks to St. Francis Street and the boarding point for the ferry to Matamoros.

Along the path, Runyon passed the eight hundred-square-foot building that belonged to Don Emilio Forto, a native Spaniard and former Brownsville mayor who built the Old Board Walk before the arrival of the railroad. Forto, who also owned the property where the ferry terminated on the American side, served as ferry supervisor. A bit further down was John Viano's piano store; the photographic studio of A. Holms, one of Runyon's photography colleagues; the C. Galbert Curio Store, billed as "The Homeseeker's Headquarters;" and, finally, a long building that housed fruit and curio vendors, many of whom lived with their families in the same structure. Where the Old Board Walk ended at the Rio Grande, the Immigration Office occupied the east side and U.S. Customs operated from the facing side. Customs officers stayed busy as they assessed and collected duty on almost all merchandise that came into the U.S. from Mexico in those years.

At the ferry, Runyon boarded a skiff. Before bridges were built across the Rio Grande, these skiffs offered water transportation twenty-four hours a day to and from Santa Cruz, the Matamoros landing point. Runyon, who had long experience with river crossings from growing up at the confluence of the Ohio and Big Sandy rivers between Kentucky and West Virginia, always admired the Rio Grande skiffmen's skill and strength. It was no simple task to handle waterborne vessels always filled to capacity with passengers at every crossing—a testament to the lively commerce between Matamoros and Brownsville.

If the river span was more than twenty feet or so, then the ferry passage was quick. However, at high water levels, passengers experienced a completely different crossing. It not only covered up to five hundred feet, but also required the skiffman to cope with swift and dangerous currents.

The skiffman used great strength to push the heavy raft off the bank, and then row it upriver parallel to either shore for about a hundred feet. Then he would turn the skiff and head directly to the stationary floating platform at Santa Cruz or Brownsville where passengers disembarked. Sometimes, the skiff would end up a bit below the platform, but the skiffman took advantage of the river's eddy, always strongest near the banks, to row back upstream before tying up.

Even after Brownsville built the International Bridge in 1910, Runyon preferred to use the ferry to cross to Mexico several times a week to take photographs or visit the *yerberías*. Not until 1928, when the second Gateway Bridge connected the two cities, did the ferry system become obsolete.

On every trip to Matamoros, after passing through Mexican Customs, Runyon proceeded to the mule-powered public cars that carried passengers to the plaza at a reasonable cost over a narrow-gauge rail.

Years later, Runyon fondly remembered this travel routine. He said: "The mule drawn car, for the first half mile, passed through a shady lane of beautiful Alamo [cottonwood] trees, which gave shade to both sides of the mule cars."[354]

Compare his description to that of an English journalist who used the same transportation during the same years: "[We] jogged...in a filthy streetcar drawn by one wretched mule, through the long-street of Matamoros, the desolation of the once flourishing city lay upon our spirits like lead."[355]

Those different perspectives of the same mundane travel mode in the same location indicate just how deeply the geography, customs, and culture of Mexico had entranced Runyon.

But back to this particular day. Runyon may have traveled to Matamoros with the intent of taking bullfight photographs, but that afternoon he decided to linger at Plaza Hidalgo.

During those same hours, twenty-year-old Amelia Leonor Medrano Longoria, accompanied by a chaperone, walked to the plaza from her home just two blocks away.[356] Perhaps she came hoping to meet Runyon. William, by then known in Brownsville and Matamoros as Willie, believed Amelia previously had observed his father through her home garden's barred gates on the many days Runyon walked past them to the nearby *corrida de toros*.[357]

But whether planned or not, random or not, it was a lucky day for both. At this paseo, the young Matamoros señorita caught Runyon's eye as their paths rotated in opposite directions and their fates merged.

Amelia was a true child of Matamoros. She was the daughter of José Telésforo Medrano Montalvo and Felipa Longoria Longoria. Those surnames placed her among those matamorenses whose ancestry stretched back to Spanish pioneers who built northeastern Mexico two centuries before.

On her mother's maternal and paternal sides, Amelia descended from an established family of soldiers and ranchers. Mitochondrial DNA tests on her son Delbert show that Amelia's maternal line also had Indian blood, a heritage that by early 1900 she shared with the vast majority of the sons and daughters of the original families who settled Tamaulipas.[358]

In 1767, Amelia's maternal fifth-great grandparents, José Matías Longoria and María de Hinojosa, received a land grant from the Spanish Crown. Their allotment, *Porción* 93, was located north of the Rio Grande in today's Starr County. The grant made Amelia's Longoria ancestors some of the first Europeans to own Texas land.[359]

On her father's side, Amelia descended from a long line of merchants and public servants. In the 1820s, her great-grandfather, Cayetano Medrano, a merchant, served as *síndico procurador* for the Matamoros *ayuntamiento*.

In 1826, the same year that the Tamaulipas government christened the villa Matamoros, the ayuntamiento directed Don Cayetano to survey the region north of the Rio Grande and divide it into the common land called *ejidos*. The action was a preliminary step in Matamoros' never-executed plan to unite its holdings across the river. Don Cayetano's survey established boundaries that twenty-two years later would become the streets of the original site of Brownsville under the city's Anglo founder, Charles Stillman.[360]

Don Cayetano and his wife, Doña María Teresa Gutíerrez, had ten children, including Amelia's grandfather, José María Medrano, born in 1812.[361]

As a businessman, José María co-owned a meat packing plant at the Mexican port of Bagdad, east of Matamoros, where he frequently came in contact with a wide range of people.[362] Through commerce, he respected the principles of the United States and its businessmen. When it came time for his son, José Telésforo, to continue his education, José María chose to send him to the eastern U.S.

In 1864, José Telésforo, then about sixteen, and five other young men from Matamoros, took ocean passage from Bagdad to New Orleans and then to New York, a distance of about 2,500 miles. From there, they made a short trip by land to enroll at Seton Hall College, a new Catholic school at South Orange, New Jersey. Over the next three years, other young men from Matamoros and

The constant activity at Matamoros' beautiful Plaza Hidalgo made it one of Runyon's favorite photography locations over the years. The bullfight ring was close by and the Plaza also was where he met his future wife, Amelia, who lived with her family just two blocks away. Photo by Robert Runyon, RFP, DBCAH, The University of Texas at Austin.

The mule-drawn cars took passengers from Mexican Customs to Plaza Hidalgo in the city center. Runyon later remembered that the "fares were reasonable and the car service was considered good at that time." Photo by Robert Runyon, RFP, DBCAH, The University of Texas at Austin.

Runyon made it a regular practice to photograph action scenes at the corrida de toros in Matamoros. He recorded his first bullfight exposures as early as March 1910 around the time he moved permanently to Brownsville. Throughout his photography career, Runyon found great demand among all market segments for these action postcards. Photo by Robert Runyon, RFP, DBCAH, The University of Texas at Austin.

Brownsville would join them, including Medrano's younger friend, eight-year-old Daniel Yturria,

The young Mexican men found that they traded one complicated place for another. During their education, Medrano and his schoolmates witnessed America's national fatigue as the Civil War drew on, the nation's relief after Appomattox, and the deep sorrow at the assassination of President Abraham Lincoln. Years later, Medrano told an interviewer he was in New York City on April 15, 1865, the day Lincoln was murdered. He remembered well the "excitement attending that catastrophe."[363]

Medrano and his fellow matamorenses did not experience war firsthand from New Jersey. Ironically, though, while they were attending Seton Hall, the Civil War's last battle took place in May 1865 at Palmito Ranch in southeastern Cameron County, just twenty miles from their Matamoros homes.[364]

What they did experience firsthand at Seton Hall was the sprouting seeds of America's pastime. Base ball, as it was then spelled, had grown in popularity in northeastern U.S. colleges before and during Civil War years. While attending Seton Hall for three years, Medrano and several of his schoolmates apparently closely observed the play of Seton Hall's Alert Base Ball Club as it competed in "match games" from New Jersey to New York.

After graduation, the Seton Hall boys returned home and organized el Union Base Ball Club de Matamoros—a unit that sports historians recognize as the first organized Latin American baseball team in history—with at least one fellow matamorense who had attended St. John's College at Fordham, New York, also during Civil War years. Historians also recognize the first recorded game by an organized Hispanic team when el Union played the Rio Grande Club at Fort Brown on Christmas Day 1868. The official box score lists Medrano as history's first Hispanic winning pitcher in the 49 to 32 slugfest.[365]

After finishing school, José Telésforo worked briefly for Daniel Yturria's father, Francisco, in his Brownsville mercantile business before starting his own store in Matamoros.[366]

Runyon knew none of this when he first saw Amelia. Yet his good fortune that day not only was to meet a beautiful señorita, but one whose father compensated for Runyon's unfamiliarity with borderlands culture. If anyone in Matamoros understood the customs of different parts of the United States, it was José T. Medrano.

Over the decades, Runyon's meeting with Amelia at the paseo proved wondrous in multiple ways. Not only did he encounter the female companion for whom he longed, one he would marry, who would become a stepmother for his son and mother to their own children, but he also gained validation into the lives and culture of both South Texas and northeastern Mexico.

Those two regions played huge roles in his personal, professional, and economic fortunes for the remainder of his life.

The courtship started Labor Day, the Monday after Runyon's initial paseo experience. Runyon took advantage of the holiday to write Amelia for permission to see her again. He asked a friend to translate his thoughts into Spanish so the grammar was correct. Then he transferred his friend's typewritten page to stationery by longhand and sent the handwritten version to Amelia.

She responded on September 3, 1912, sending her handwritten letter to Runyon in Spanish:[367]

> *"Recibí su muy correcta y atenta carta en la que me indica si podremos hablar alguna vez? y en contestación diré a Ud. que in la Plaza podrá Usted hacerle pues será bien recibido."*
>
> ("I received your very proper and polite letter in which you indicate to me that you would like to talk again? And in answer, I will tell you that in the Plaza, if you should make it, you will be well received.")

The pace of the weekly paseo, though, was a painful courting process for an American who lacked cultural ties to the young woman he wanted to romance. It also was tedious for an entrepreneur who worked seven days a week to build his business. Limited to infrequent encounters, Runyon soon believed Amelia was losing interest.

Perhaps Amelia felt the same for she apparently sent him an encouraging message that elicited his quick response. On October 3, 1912, Runyon indicated a desire to escalate their budding romance. He proposed a more formal courtship to replace the weekly promenade in the plaza.[368]

This time, he typed the note on his commercial photography letterhead to prove to Amelia that he was a business owner. This letter in English said (punctuation as written):

> *"I am in receipt of your short note and was very glad indeed to receive it. I wrote you a letter the other day but afterwards decided to not send it, because I had not seen you for so long, I thought that you may not care to receive it.,*
>
> *"With your permission and at your convenience, I will be pleased to call to see you. If this meets your approval and the approval of your parents, why you can write me or tell me when to come.,*
>
> *"Thanking you for past courtesies and hopeing* (sic) *to see you at shorter intervals, I am as ever your true friend."*

Amelia turned Runyon's letter over to her father for his permission. On October 10, 1912, Medrano responded with a handwritten English letter to Runyon that relayed the same message that Amelia had sent previously in Spanish:

> *"Answering your letter of the 3rd and having consulted the opinion of all the family: We are in good disposition to accept your pretensions, so that you will be well received—whenever you wish to visit the house."*[369]

The following day, Runyon replied to Medrano with a short note that ended: "I desire to further assure you of my earnest sincerity and beleive (sic) that you will not be disappointed in me."[370]

Runyon asked Carlos Calderoni, an acquaintance from Brownsville, to interpret during the formal introduction. They crossed the river and went to the Medrano home and introduced Runyon to José T. Medrano. That formality opened the way for Runyon to visit Amelia[371] on his regular trips to Matamoros for photographs.

Business, though, made his trips less regular than he liked. Willie helped overcome that obstacle. He had become fluent in Spanish and comfortable with the culture on both sides of the Rio Grande. When Runyon was busy but needed to communicate with Amelia, he sent Willie across on the ferry with a note. After delivering it, Willie returned to Runyon with Amelia's response.

In a matter of months, Runyon asked Amelia to marry him. The proposal marked the culmination of an improbable courtship between a Kentucky entrepreneur and a Mexican señorita. And it was a romance that could progress only because of an Old Board Walk, a twenty-four-hour ferry, a centuries-old ritual, a dutiful son, and a Seton Hall-educated Mexican patriarch.

Chapter 14
Mortal Duel, Bloody Battle

In 1913, when Mexico's three-year-old Revolution had come to Tamaulipas, Newman and Runyon were proven entrepreneurs in the lower Rio Grande Valley and in Mexico. By then, both men had embraced life fully on both sides of the Rio Grande. They felt and welcomed the constant Gulf breeze. They found beauty in the subtropical vegetation and the varied geography from sea level at the coast to the flat prairie land in the middle to the hilly terrain in the upper Valley with its mirror image south of the river. They absorbed the language, the culture, the people, and the cuisine unique to the borderlands. And now they lived life not as newcomers but as natives.

Uniquely, each man mixed within the combustible internal affairs of Mexico without taking sides. They each accepted assignments from government Federals as well as revolutionary Constitutionalists. Each man considered Mexico's politics to be Mexico's business. It would be a practice that would serve both well from 1913 until almost 1920. It also was a time when the two entrepreneurs' fortunes linked for a brief period—a time marked by exciting, always violent, events surrounding the Mexican Revolution and the Texas bandit wars.

Immediately after suspending all aviation activities, Newman focused his engineering skills on his automotive clientele. Initially, Newman's primary income came from working as a machinist for Hinkley & Batz, a firm that advertised itself as "the best equipped automobile shop in the Valley." Newman's name had enough brand identification that the company's ads featured "P. A. Newman" in display type "with Hinkley & Batz" in a smaller point size. The ad listed Newman's specialties as "repairs Automobiles, Gasoline Engines, all kinds of machinery, Centrifugal Pumps and Gasoline Engines for sale."[372]

The automotive world respected Newman's name because of his aviation fame. His reputation as an innovator plus his well-regarded technical expertise as a machinist brought him opportunities beyond just automobile repair from both sides of the border. In June 1911, he constructed an agricultural irrigation system in Mexico.[373] In the early 1920s, he turned his attention to developing a new rotary drill for the lower Rio Grande Valley's oil industry.[374]

Yet it would be automobile transportation in Mexico that would define his career in the post-aviation years.

Newman's mother had died in 1910 in Brownsville and was buried in Runge. Newman's father and Ethelyne returned from the funeral to Brownsville to live with him, Pearl, their son, P. A. Jr., and daughter, Lillian, in a rent house on west St. Charles Street. By 1912, Newman had launched his own garage business on Eighth Street between St. Charles and Levee Streets, just to the south of his rented home. At this location, Newman added chauffeur services to his commercial offering.

The French word chauffeur initially described a person who stoked the fire in steam engines to keep early automobiles running before introduction of internal combustion engines.[375] The word's context later expanded to mean a hired driver. Newman operated in the transitional phase of those two definitions. His chauffeuring competency was as a machinist who could keep automobiles running on South Texas wagon paths and northeastern Mexico senderos. When early automobiles broke down, as they often did, he fixed them. Driving for hire was merely a feature to that primary maintenance service.

The first automobiles had come to both Brownsville and Ciudad Victoria, the capital of Tamaulipas, just in 1910.[376] For years after that, an automobile remained a unique sight anywhere in Tamaulipas because byways were suitable only for transport powered by a hoofed animal. The choices for navigable paths in Tamaulipas shocked an English journalist in 1913. He wrote:

> "As for roads through this wilderness, well, to put it plainly, there are none. There are merely rough trails, sometimes quite difficult to find. They run through marshes, through rivers, down steep "arroyos" (ravines) and up the other side... They set you ploughing through deep sand, or floundering in mud up to the axles of your wheels. They are so narrow that you have be perpetually on guard against thorny switches tearing hands and face. As for their ruts, I shall not describe them, for no one would believe me."[377]

Conditions were not much better north of the Rio Grande. Not until 1921 did motorists enjoy the first hard-surfaced road from Brownsville to Harlingen. Yet the American side advanced rapidly after that.[378] Mexican travelers saw painfully slower road construction progress. In 1924, Tamaulipas was one of just three Mexican states that had no highways or roads considered suitable for automobiles.³⁷⁹ Even though efforts to construct a highway from the border to the capital began in 1928, by Depression years the entire route was described as "only rutty dirty lanes." Not until 1944 did the city of Brownsville help the Mexican government link Matamoros to Ciudad Victoria by a paved highway.³⁸⁰

For decades, rail was the only mechanical overland option to travel from Matamoros to Ciudad Victoria or the busy port of Tampico. Passengers took a branch railway line on the Mexican National Railway from Matamoros to Monterrey. From Monterrey, the passengers transferred to the División de Monterrey, a continuation from Torreón, that took them to the state's capital city and then Tampico.³⁸¹ The risk factor of the trip, if indeed the trains even ran in the first place, depended on whether the traveler experienced track problems, equipment issues, bandits, or all three.

Newman offered a substitute when he trailblazed an automobile route to the south that took passengers from Matamoros through the old village of San Fernando to Ciudad Victoria. An early automobile could make respectable time over the ninety miles of flat coastal plains between Matamoros and San Fernando. Between San Fernando and Ciudad Victoria, though, the *monte* reigned thick, with mesquite and the ever-present nopal impeding rapid travel. Broad rivers that originate in the mountains to the west and flow to the Gulf, including the Conchos and El Purificación, crossed the route multiple times.³⁸² An automobile chauffeur had to ford all rivers as no bridges existed to handle motor traffic. Farther south, the traveler maneuvered over broken land, routing around masses of small mountains that loom on both sides. Then, as the traveler made a slight ascent, the view of Ciudad Victoria at the eastern foot of the scenic Sierra Madre Oriental marked the end of two hundred miles of navigation. Later, Newman extended his route to Tampico to the south and Monterrey to the west.

On twenty-first century paved roads and river-spanning bridges, the trip takes a good four hours. In the early 1900s, it took an automobile chauffeur three to four days of skilled driving. It could take much longer if travelers ran into grazing livestock herds, sinkholes, troops, or bandits. An occasional heavy rain could shut down dirt paths for days.

Despite these difficulties, the risk to life and schedule had its rewards. With a chauffeur like Newman, the trip was quicker than train, carriage, or horseback travel even without marked roads. The expediency value of Newman's automobile services first attracted affluent civilians and, later, government officials and military leaders.

One of Newman's first automobile assignments into Mexico occurred in November 1912. He was hired to transport by automobile a group of St. Louis businessmen on a hunting excursion to the mountainous area around Ciudad Victoria.

A vice president of the Frisco Railroad hosted the party from St. Louis to Brownsville in his private rail car, a sign of the prestige of the participants that included executives in the railroad, brewing, banking, and oil industries. In Brownsville, the Frisco representative parked his private car and the group loaded into three automobiles to travel into Mexico. Newman's fellow drivers on the trip included one of his bosses at Hinkley & Batz as well as Frank Cushman Pierce, a Brownsville attorney and historian.

Ten days into the trip, Newman's convoy arrived at Abasolo, about seventy-five miles northeast of Ciudad Victoria. There, a member of the party who had tired of adventure discovered the Mexican National Railway passed through that village. That meant he could abandon the automobile trek, take the train to Monterrey, and head home to St. Louis through Laredo. His angst proved contagious as his colleagues decided they too had experienced enough automobile travel. They unanimously decided to depart with him. The group wired instructions to Brownsville for the private car to meet them in Monterrey. From there, they planned a luxury ride home to St. Louis to put their travel hardships through Tamaulipas behind them.[383]

The decision meant Newman and his fellow chauffeurs had to deadhead the vehicles to Brownsville from deep in Tamaulipas. Still, it was a beneficial exercise. Once Newman returned, he had as much knowledge as anyone alive on navigating an automobile from Brownsville to the center of Tamaulipas. He would only get more experienced after that trip.

Within months after his return, the Mexican Revolution entered Tamaulipas. In early 1913, Venustiano Carranza, the *primer jefe* of the revolutionaries, had refused to recognize the legitimacy of President Victoriano Huerta. Huerta had led a coup that ended with the assassination of democratically elected President Francisco I. Madero. In the Plan de Guadalupe, issued in March, Carranza fundamentally created military opposition to Huerta through formation of the Constitutionalist army.

As part of his military strategy, he turned his focus on the vital state of Tamaulipas. He directed his subordinate, General Lucio Blanco, to take Matamoros from Federal forces, the first efforts of which Blanco launched by April 1913.[384]

The revolutionaries' threat necessitated counter action by Federal officers. Most travel between posts was taken by rail, by horseback, or *por la carreta*. Yet Newman's recent automotive foray deep into Tamaulipas provided a new travel alternative, and the Federals took advantage of his expertise.

In February 1913, Newman accepted an assignment to drive Federal Lieutenant Colonel Falcón B. de la Peña to San Fernando. De la Peña's orders were to take command of the hundred-man garrison quartered in that village.[385]

On all American automobiles manufactured before 1915, the driver's wheel was on the right side of the vehicle, a legacy from coachmen who traditionally drove horse-drawn wagons from that seat.[386] So, Newman manned the right-side driver's position, and de la Peña, armed with a loaded .30-30 Winchester rifle, sat in back, just behind Newman's left shoulder.

At evening twilight, a few miles outside San Fernando, Newman had to repair a flat tire. As he patched the puncture, seven Federal soldiers on horseback approached the automobile, among them a captain who served as the garrison's interim commander. De la Peña identified himself as their new commanding officer and ordered the group's captain to return his men to San Fernando and prepare dinner. De la Peña said he and Newman would follow once the tire had been repaired.

The captain might have been drunk and resentful about being replaced by de la Peña, yet the lieutenant colonel chose to deal with it later. Or, perhaps, in the brief time they talked, the captain hid both his inebriation and resentment. Regardless, de la Peña's orders set in motion strange actions by his subordinate.

After Newman had fixed the flat, he drove only a short distance when he had to slow down. In the distance, Newman counted six men on horseback facing the vehicle but stationary. As the seventh horse approached, de la Peña and Newman saw it carried the captain with pistol drawn.

Newman pulled up and cut the engine as the drunk captain reined in his horse just to Newman's left. De la Peña ordered his subordinate to holster his pistol, but that command led to angry words between them. Newman then decided to listen to the discussion from outside the automobile.

Before further words were said, the captain fired his pistol at de la Peña. The crack of the shot startled his horse and it abruptly shifted to the captain's left, altering the angle of fire on his following shot.

Newman hit the ground as bullets came from both directions. He later estimated that de la Peña and the captain exchanged two shots each. By the time he looked up, the drunk captain lay dead, just off the sendero, the victim of the lieutenant colonel's truer aim.

Further up, the detachment held its position, neither aiding their captain nor coming to their new commander's defense. De la Peña ordered them to return to San Fernando. It was a head start the soldiers used wisely to make amends for their inaction. The moment Newman drove the car into the village, pealing of church bells and cheers heralded the lieutenant colonel's arrival.

Inside the villa, Newman inspected his automobile. The first bullet hole ran to left of the driver's seat in line with where de la Peña sat, somehow missing the officer. The entrance and exit path of the second bullet was off the mark for de la Peña, but would have gone through Newman's chest. Exiting promptly had saved his life.

Newman waited ninety minutes but heard no further mention of the incident in the village. Then he headed back to Brownsville despite the late hour. When he passed the site of the gunfight, the captain's body lay undisturbed in the dust, a scene of death in the Mexican soil that Newman would see often during the coming months.[387] As to de la Peña, before the year had ended, he too would die. He was killed in a battle against Constitutionalist forces either in Coahuila or Chihuahua.[388]

Runyon's assimilation into Mexican culture came later than Newman's and in more discrete stages. While Newman was a native Texan who had lived on the border as a teenager, Runyon arrived in the lower Rio Grande Valley from Kentucky as an adult with no knowledge of the Texas brush country or Old Mexico other than stories he had heard. Before Runyon could assimilate, he had to learn Spanish and participate in the culture's customs. He started gradually, but moved to total immersion because of a rapid chain of events that collided with his life after mid-1913.

The first trigger took place about April 21, when Blanco arrived in Burgos, Tamaulipas, with 250 men and a plan to grow his brigade much larger. Blanco, full of dynamism as a military leader, had directed his troops to victory in several battles since spearheading the Constitutionalist cause. He was a good military strategist.

From Burgos, Blanco quickly assessed the region through visits to sectors held by the Constitutionalist army. He and his troops traveled to Méndez on April 23, then to San Fernando on April 25, and then to Santander Jiménez through April 27. While Blanco was in Jiménez, General J. Agustín Castro's Twenty-First Rural Corps, led by Captain Miguel Navarrete, attacked Federal troops at Ciudad Victoria. The government forces repulsed the revolutionaries, but suffered key officer casualties. In exchange, the Constitutionalists gained strategic knowledge on Federal defenses when the time came to attack the capital city again.[389]

On April 30, Blanco met Castro at El Encinal near Santander Jiménez. An interesting aspect of that meeting is that Castro arrived in an automobile. It was among the first times a military leader in the northeast used such technology. No evidence exists that Newman was the driver. However, Newman's chauffeur business would benefit from Castro's trend-setting transportation mode.[390]

Blanco left that meeting with momentum. His troop count had grown to seven hundred men as popular support for his presence in northeastern Mexico had strengthened each week since his arrival. Amelia Medrano's family members were among the converts. That conversion became another valuable trigger for Runyon.

Eight years earlier in Matamoros, Amelia's older sister, Leocadia Eduviges Medrano Longoria, known to family as Cayita, had married Francisco (Pancho) González Villarreal, a Matamoros shoe shop owner who supported the revolution. González Villarreal persuaded Amelia and Cayita's brother, José Cecilio Medrano Longoria, also to join the Constitutionalist cause.

Amelia and Cayita were close despite being twelve years apart in age. As sisters, they attended the *bailes* at the Casino Matamorense, a private social club, and the *tardeadas* at Hacienda Las Rusias, just south of Matamoros.[391]

Runyon already had taken many photographs of Federal troops on his frequent trips to Matamoros to visit Amelia or to conduct other business. Yet Amelia's closeness to Cayita also brought Runyon within González Villarreal's influence. The two men soon forged a friendship that lasted until González Villarreal's death in 1942. Their relationship grew through mutual respect for each man's character, business acumen, and professionalism. When it became clear Blanco's attack on Matamoros was certain, González Villarreal and Runyon began to collaborate.

Blanco took Reynosa first on May 10, both to cover his rear guard in case Federal reinforcements came from the west, as well as to close an escape route for government troops once he attacked Matamoros.[392]

On June 1, Blanco, by then fit for battle with one thousand cavalrymen and squads of sappers and dynamiters, established his vanguard at Las Rusias. The Federals' failure to respond to this occupation near their headquarters indicated the weak state of the government's position. In reality, the Federals were badly outnumbered with only five hundred soldiers and a smattering of Rurales, the law enforcement force that patrolled Mexico's countryside, constituting all available fighters for an entrenched battle. For additional defense, citizens faithful to the existing government organized a militia headed by twenty-three-year-old erstwhile outlaw Antonio Echazaretta, and another headed by his brother, Hilario. They also mobilized La Defensa Social, a separate volunteer group of armed citizens directed by the city's mayor, Dr. Miguel F. Barragán.

Even if the Federals had recruited more defenders, the government lacked weapons. For what few arms they had, Federal army representatives crossed the Rio Grande to acquire ten thousand rifle cartridges from Brownsville merchants. The Federal troops' sole armament larger than rifles and pistols was a repurposed ancient cannon that Matamoros city leaders had displayed in the plaza to commemorate war with the United States seven decades earlier.

Still, having access to any ammunition or weapon sources was a slight advantage for the Federals. The Constitutionalists, also without ample arms, could not buy ammunition across the border because the U.S. government did not recognize the revolutionaries. The Constitutionalists' primary advantage turned out to be larger troop numbers.[393]

Federal leaders sought to buoy local spirits with rumors that government reinforcements were en route from Monterrey.[394] Nonetheless, desertions and defections dissipated sparse ranks as the Federals awaited Blanco's inevitable attack.

That action came the morning of June 3, when Constitutionalists fired on the city. Home-grown confederates, among them González Villarreal, supported the regulars.[395]

The crux of the bloody battle lasted about nine hours. The resistance ended altogether early the next morning. During the combat, Brownsville residents, including Runyon, monitored the battle from the opposite bank. Runyon said sounds of gunfire kept spectators abreast of the pace of the fighting. Still, neither he nor any of the other Americans saw any actual combat take place from their vantage point.[396]

The fortunes of battle, though, became evident when steady streams of Federal soldiers and government supporters began to cross the bridge into Brownsville to seek medical aid and sanctuary.

Many of the Federal leaders escaped, including Antonio and Hilario Echazaretta. Antonio was caught about nine miles southeast of Matamoros two days later, one of sixty prisoners taken by Blanco's forces.[397] Blanco had led an impressive victory that established the strategic link in northeastern Mexico for carrying out the Constitutionalist strategy in the coming months of the revolution.

Runyon rode the ferry to Matamoros early the following day and for days thereafter to take photographs. The town's population took time to return to a normal routine in the battle's aftermath, so Runyon had numerous opportunities to work with González Villarreal to access engagement sites and photograph effects of the momentous battle.

Runyon observed numerous executions as subordinate officers within the Constitutionalist ranks took it on themselves to punish Federal soldiers and sympathizers before Blanco halted their actions. Some executions took place at the Casa Mata, the ancient casemate Runyon knew well from his first days in Matamoros.[398]

Other executions—the most notorious of which was Antonio Echazaretta—took place at a public square that later would become Matamoros' famed Mercado Juárez. Runyon took a photograph just before the firing squad received the order to fire.

Echazaretta and his brother, Hilario, had lived briefly in Brownsville and they had friends across the Rio Grande. Sympathizers said Echazaretta had valiantly led the local militia as a young volunteer and, even when condemned, went to his execution with gallantry. For those reasons, his death evoked widespread regret and criticism from Mexicans and Texans alike who respected his valor.

In life, though, Echazaretta had been outside the law. In the February before the battle, seventy men, allegedly led by Antonio and Hilario

Echazaretta, had plundered and looted along the Rio Grande about twenty-five miles from Matamoros. The gang robbed ranchers, storekeepers, and even a single woman trying to escape. They stole thousands of dollars in cash and merchandise, and they killed or ran off cattle and horses in their raids. Lack of action against the Echazarettas by the Federal garrison in Matamoros angered many matamorenses.[399] Those outraged citizens found justice in the action of Blanco's troops in the days following the Battle of Matamoros. A few weeks after Anthony's execution, Blanco's forces near Monterrey captured Hilario with other Federal forces on a train. The Constitutionalists executed Hilario on the spot.[400]

Upon returning to his Brownsville studio, Runyon developed his photos and sent prints to news syndicates and newspapers so Americans could see the totality of the Constitutionalist Army's momentous victory in Matamoros. He also printed many images in copyrighted postcards that the public purchased and mailed around the world.

The Battle of Matamoros gave his postcard business a significant boost. A newspaper article in *The Brownsville Sentinel* on October 28, 1913, reported Runyon over the last twenty-four months had sold more than four hundred thousand postcards including battle scenes and local views.[401] It was a massive leap in four years from the news butch selling postcards on the railroad to a war photojournalist creating them. Yet it was just the first of many leaps to come in Runyon's polymathic lifetime.

After the Battle of Matamoros, Runyon took this photograph of the Federals' sole heavy weapon, which was pulled into duty after spending decades in the Plaza as a memento of the Mexican War. Runyon's caption reads: "Federal Canon, Only Shot Once before being captured by the Rebels." Photo by Robert Runyon from author's collection.

Friends made last minute identifications of local Federal supporters killed in the battle. Blanco's soldiers had stacked the bodies amid cordwood, then drenched all with oil and lit the pyres. Photo by Robert Runyon, RFP, DBCAH, The University of Texas at Austin.

Some historians claim the Constitutionalists selected the execution site for Antonio Echazaretta, captured leader of the Matamoros militia, for Runyon's benefit because of the location's favorable light. Runyon years later acknowledged that the majority of other executions he witnessed took place at Casa Mata. Photo by Robert Runyon, RUN00261, RRC, DBCAH, The University of Texas at Austin.

Chapter 15
Los Compañeros de Viaje

ess than a month after the Constitutionalists took command of strategic Matamoros, Runyon returned to that heroic city for another momentous event in his life. It was time to marry Amelia.

As a Mexican citizen, Amelia had to be married in a civil ceremony. As a Roman Catholic, she could only marry another Roman Catholic in a religious ceremony that included Mass. The Medrano family scheduled the civil event for July 3, 1913, and the religious ceremony the next day.

Runyon was baptized into the Church a few weeks before the ceremonies, in time to allow for the Banns of Marriage, probably at the Catedral Nuestra Señora del Refugio on Plaza Hidalgo near the Medrano home. Although the generations of priests who served the cathedral kept assiduous records of baptisms for centuries, little documentation exists for 1913, indicating the turmoil of revolutionary times.

The village's civil records show they married at 8 p.m. on July 3 at the Medrano residence. Runyon asked González Villarreal to serve as witness.[402] For the Catholic Church ceremony the next day at the Catedral, Runyon brought over his best man, Ernest Givens, a Brownsville salesman. And for the wedding celebration at the Medrano home, he brought his camera.

Runyon took several photographs during the day. For wedding shots that included him as groom, Runyon positioned the camera on a tripod so someone else could operate the shutter.[403]

For the honeymoon, Runyon, Amelia, and Willie traveled to Kentucky, retracing the same route by rail through Houston and New Orleans that Runyon had taken to Texas four years earlier.

Left: To record his July 4, 1913, marriage to Amelia in Matamoros, Runyon set his camera on a tripod so someone else could operate the shutter and capture the proper pose for an Edwardian era wedding. It appears to have been taken at Plaza Hidalgo across from the Catedral where the ceremony was held. Right: Amelia Medrano Longoria de Runyon as a young bride in the garden of her parents' home in Matamoros. RFP, DBCAH, The University of Texas at Austin.

In Kentucky and West Virginia, Amelia enchanted the Runyon/Lawson clan, many of whom took up decades-long correspondence with her or made a trip to the Rio Grande Valley to visit the Runyon family. Amelia also learned recipes for Runyon's favorite foods from his years growing up in eastern Kentucky.

The new cooking methods were no issue as Amelia already was as skilled using an indoor stove as she was cooking over mesquite coals *a la parrilla*. Her background was the cuisine of northeastern Mexico influenced by techniques from her mother's well-used 1893 first Mexican edition of *El Libro de Cocina* by noted French chef Jules Gouffé.[404]

Amelia's varied menu for her new husband featured dishes that made northeastern Mexico a culinary wonder to persons who enjoy robust meats and local produce and herbs: *caldo* every day, along with alternating meals of *carne guisada, carne asada, chiles rellenos, rosbif,* and *tamales* as entrees. Her sides included salads, in-season vegetables, *sopa de fideo* or *arroz mexicana, frijoles,* and frequent slices of *aguacate* or *pawa,* all served with fresh *tortillas*

Runyon on August 30, 1913, captured the drama of a momentous event in Mexican history as a diverse assembly of farmers, mounted troops and observers watched General Lucio Blanco (seated with white tie) sign a land redistribution proclamation. The location was Hacienda Los Borregos, a 73,000-acre agricultural operation near Matamoros that had been confiscated by the Constitutionalists. Photo by Robert Runyon from author's collection.

de maíz heated not on a *comal* but directly on the gas stove pilot. After her Kentucky cooking lessons, Amelia added corn meal mush, fried chicken, and other Southern delicacies to her recipe portfolio.[405]

By mid-August, the Runyons began adjusting to life in Brownsville as a family of three in Runyon's small home by the depot. In a matter of days after returning, though, Amelia's family influence brought Runyon a unique job assignment in Mexico, one that would be a predictor of the social change that revolution meant to Mexico.

With González Villarreal's assistance, Runyon was among journalists on August 30 invited to Hacienda Los Borregos near Matamoros. Runyon's assignment was to capture on film implementation of an idea circulating among the Constitutionalist brain trust. As it turned out, that idea would become a landmark event in Mexico's history.

The hacienda was a large farming and ranching operation owned by Félix Díaz, a loyalist to Mexican President Huerta, whom the revolutionaries sought to overthrow, and nephew of the country's former dictator, Porfirio Díaz. Tenant farmers worked the hacienda's land, but tenancy was a hard life. A farmer growing crops in the historically semi-dry climate of northeastern Mexico had to deal with frequent drought, excessively high temperatures, and periodic tropical storms or hurricanes. The revolution made conditions worse as both the Federals and the Constitutionalists requisitioned available harvests to nourish competing armies. The abnormal demand disrupted the market networks for locally produced food and grains. Farming was a brutal way to make a living in 1913 Tamaulipas.

Blanco's chief of staff, Francisco Múgica, who later gained a reputation as a radical socialist under the administration of President Lázaro Cárdenas, had floated a concept to empower the Los Borregos tenant farmers. Blanco gave substance to Múgica's ideal when he confiscated Díaz's land and distributed it to the farmers, giving each a portion proportional to family size.[406]

Runyon photographed that event as the exchange became official. When the images appeared in newspapers, Blanco's folk-hero status grew even stronger among his supporters.

For persons on both sides of the border who opposed redistribution of private land, though, Runyon's photographs sparked concern. Among that group was Carranza, who long had been at odds with Blanco over the latter's failure to carry out orders. The primer jefe may have agreed with land redistribution in principle, but Blanco erred in acting before consulting his superior. Historians, however, dispute whether the agrarian reform or Blanco's chronic insubordination ultimately spurred Carranza to react.[407] Regardless of the reason, soon after Los Borregos, Carranza transferred Blanco to the western theater of the Revolution.

In Blanco's place, Carranza turned over the strategy for Tamaulipas to General Pablo González. H. Matamoros became the Constitutionalists' regional headquarters under command of Carranza's brother, General Jesús Carranza.

González immediately set his sights on controlling the state by attacking Ciudad Victoria. On November 4, his troops focused on Estación Garza Valdéz near Villagrán and destroyed trains and tracks. On November 6, the revolutionaries incited skirmishes with Federal troops defending the capital city to test again the government's defenses.

Two days later, Generals González and Jesús Carranza gathered subordinates in Jiménez to plan final troop mobilization before marching on the capital. By nightfall, they positioned forces about fifty miles north of Ciudad Victoria at Padilla and Güémez. González Villarreal, recently promoted to captain in the Constitutionalist Army, and Amelia's older brother, José Cecilio Medrano, were among the revolutionary troops concentrating in those locations.[408] With all population centers north of Ciudad Victoria now in Constitutionalist control, the generals convened again on November 13 in Güémez and implemented their plan. That day, the Constitutionalists began bombarding Ciudad Victoria from the hills surrounding the city with two batteries of fourteen machine guns and eight cannon.

Carranza, accompanied by his aide, Lieutenant Colonel Luciano Decuir Latiolait, a resident of Veracruz, returned to Matamoros by automobile on November 13 to manage communications from the region's strategic command center. They arrived at 2 a.m. on November 14.[409]

González's troops assaulted the capital at 7:30 a.m. on November 16. They attacked the Federals' defensive position established at the Santuario De Nuestra Señora De Guadalupe, just as church bells called brave faithful to Sunday Mass.

Eyewitnesses claimed that Federal troop numbers defending the city did not exceed eight hundred men. In addition, the Federals had support of another one thousand untrained citizens serving in La Defensa Social. Other contemporary reports stated that the Constitutionalists vastly outnumbered the defenders with González having five thousand troops committed by his various generals to the battle, with 2,500 additional men available if needed. Leading Mexican Revolution historian Dr. Joe Lee Janssens states, however, that González and the Federal commander each probably entered the battle with just half the men that the historical accounts alleged.[410]

The Federals and loyal citizens gave up ground slowly on Sunday and into Monday even while suffering large losses in bloody battles at outer locations, including defensive stands near the hacienda called Las Virgenes and the city's panteón. By Monday evening, though, Federal commander General Antonio Rábago advised the citizens' group that he could no longer hold the city. A few hours after midnight, he withdrew his troops to the south. At daybreak the next morning, the revolutionaries expelled the remaining Federals from their bunkers at the Santuario and rang the bells of victory.

As the Constitutionalists entered the city for which they had battled for forty-nine hours, they saw that their bombing, combined with what the fleeing Federals purposefully destroyed, had significantly damaged the state government's infrastructure. Many buildings had been shelled and burned, among them the state's archives with more than a century of deeds and other historical documents forever lost. The battle damage also destroyed the penitentiary, although the Federals already had released and pressed into service many criminals.[411]

González dispatched Generals Antonio Villarreal and Francisco Murguía after the fleeing Federals, who were trailed by a large contingent of civilian city leaders and their families who also had evacuated. On the path to Tula, the Constitutionalists located the Federal troops. Before the Constitutionalist troops attacked, the Federal officers abandoned their forces and rode away. The leaderless government forces were routed.[412]

Once the Constitutionalists controlled the capital, one of González's priorities was to reconnect telegraph communications between Ciudad Victoria and Matamoros. Runyon's brothers-in-law, Medrano and González Villarreal, were among the first to communicate with Matamoros after the lines had been restored. They sent a telegram to José Telésforo Medrano, who shared that message with local newspapers. It told borderlands residents that "all quiet in Victoria and that the effects of the battle are being cleared away."[413]

Indeed, González quickly set about bringing calm to the capital city. He ordered the dead buried in mass graves or stacked and burned. His troops also gathered captured arms to be sent to Matamoros and refitted for future use. González formed a new state government with General Luís Caballero, a native of the state, as governor. The takeover reportedly had few executions and only sparse drunkenness among the victors. Looting was minimal at the smaller stores as those owners had supported the Constitutionalist cause. The larger storekeepers who backed Huerta and the Federals, though, suffered intense scrutiny. The Carrancistas plundered their inventories, and each large shop owner seemed fated for execution.

Newman and Runyon played an important role over the following days in chronicling the Battle of Ciudad Victoria. But it was the fortunes of Lieutenant Colonel Decuir, who at the end of 1913 was a man in too much hurry, that scripted Newman's and Runyon's actions.

Decuir was a native of New Orleans, born of Cajun parents, around 1879. At the age of four, his family moved to the state of Veracruz and settled in the villa of Papantla. On March 20, 1907, at Puebla, he married Cristina Dondé Valdés and they had two children.[414] By 1910, Decuir had joined a core of other Veracruzanos in support of Madero and the revolutionaries.

Decuir found his way to northeastern Mexico by 1913. After the Battle of Matamoros, in the same month of Runyon's wedding in Matamoros, General González ordered Decuir and Heriberto Jara, a leader of Veracruz's revolutionaries, to cross to Brownsville and privately purchase arms for Blanco without raising U.S. concerns.[415] In August, both men crossed again at Eagle Pass, Texas. Decuir's documents on the latter trip stated his occupation as lawyer.[416] After successfully completing both missions, Decuir was assigned to Blanco's brigade and, after Blanco's transfer, to the command of Jesús Carranza under whom Decuir rose to the rank of lieutenant colonel.

On November 20, two days after the capital's fall, Carranza ordered Decuir to organize a convoy that would deliver 3,300 rounds of ammunition and several subordinate officers to González at Ciudad Victoria. González needed the ammunition and reinforcements to fend off an expected Federal counterattack. Tradition says that Major Raúl Gárate, a teenage native of Tamaulipas, was the convoy's second-in-command.[417]

Runyon, perhaps at the suggestion of González Villarreal, was invited to participate in the convoy. A couple of American newspapers ran short blurbs that announced Runyon was embedded in the convoy and would provide photographs for coverage of the Battle of Ciudad Victoria upon his return. So Runyon had known he would be a part of the mission for some time before it actually left.[418]

In one of Runyon's initial photographs of his coverage of the Battle of Ciudad Victoria, he organized the six convoy automobiles in a staggered line with all passengers and most chauffeurs seated. However, Newman, who throughout the mission drove the automobile in which Runyon rode, stands with his rifle at far left, his foot rested on the hub of the front wheel. Photo by Robert Runyon, RUN00060, RRC, DBCAH, The University of Texas at Austin.

Runyon photographed the Constitutionalist convoy's officers and a few chauffeurs partaking of galletas *and coffee provided by the family living in the* jacal *during a rest stop on the trip south to Ciudad Victoria. Newman is in the front row, second from right. The seated officer staring directly at the camera, front row center, is likely Lieutenant Colonel Luciano Decuir Latiolait, the Constitutionalist convoy's ill-fated commanding officer.* Photo by Robert Runyon, RUN00065, RRC, DBCAH, The University of Texas at Austin.

With no bridges yet built to handle automobile traffic, every river, including the broad Conchos and La Purificación, had to be forded one automobile at a time by the convoy. Runyon captured this crossing of a convoy vehicle with assistance from two mounted Constitutionalists with trailing revolutionaries ready to push if needed. Photo by Robert Runyon, RUN00052, RRC, DBCAH, The University of Texas at Austin.

This convoy was the most unique military supply wagon train in Mexico's history. The Carrancista command had become fascinated with automobile technology after Castro's chauffeured arrival at El Encinal a few months prior. After that meeting, Runyon had photographed Blanco standing next to one of the rare vehicles at Las Rusias around the time of the Battle of Matamoros.[419] Observers fully expected Blanco, before his transfer, to travel to Ciudad Victoria by automobile for the attack. Yet it was Decuir who ultimately was chosen to fulfill that prediction.[420]

Newman's engineering reputation made him an essential chauffeur to transport the critical park of artillery and officer replacements. Another driver was Curtis Everson, Newman's colleague from his days experimenting with the aeroplane.[421] In all, Decuir organized a convoy of six American automobiles, each with a Brownsville driver.[422]

The convoy left Matamoros just after midnight on November 21. From the outset, Runyon and his camera equipment rode in Newman's vehicle. The travelers followed dirt roads south all night, making their first stop soon after sunrise at a *jacal*. Runyon took advantage of that morning break to begin his photographic record.

Consistent with every photograph Runyon took—even those during coffee breaks—is that each subject holds a Winchester or Mauser rifle, with bandoliers full of cartridges always in reach. That persistent armed readiness indicates how seriously the convoy considered the threat of Federal troops headed their way.

The convoy members spent the night probably at the garrison in San Fernando. The next day they headed toward Santander Jiménez. After passing through the village, though, nightfall approached. Decuir kept the convoy advancing as he wanted to make Padilla before halting.

En route, a harried Constitutionalist telegraph operator named Ramos met the group. Ramos lacked a functioning telegraph yet he had to alert the Constitutionalist command that two thousand Federal troops had been sent to retake the capital. Ramos had ridden his horse hard for thirty miles, and the animal had given out a few miles up the road. Ramos was now afoot, hoping to locate a working telegraph at Jiménez.[423]

The nearness of the Federals was news many in the convoy did not want to hear. They urged Decuir to halt for the night and wait for developments. He compromised by riding alone on horseback to check on conditions in Padilla even though his subordinates protested his actions.

In the hour before midnight, Decuir neared sentries who guarded Padilla's perimeter as part of General González's vanguard. The sentries eyed Decuir suspiciously when he reined in his horse to allow the passing of several ambulance wagons headed to Matamoros with wounded soldiers from the recent battle.

Once Decuir could advance, he approached the guard post, where a sentry requested the *santo y seña*. Decuir either did not know the watchword or he did not hear the challenge. The lieutenant colonel reportedly said "paisano" to the guard and rode past the checkpoint.[424]

At that point, something went terribly wrong. Less than seventy-two hours later, Stanley Morton, Everson's employee and one of the other drivers, said he understood that Decuir and the sentry each believed the other to be a Federal. Morton said that instead of giving the countersign, Decuir "whipped up his horse and started ahead" as he exchanged fire with the sentry. What is certain is that the sentry indeed did take aim, his shots alerting a nearby picket, who also fired at the lieutenant colonel. Five bullets hit Decuir, and he died at 2 a.m. His haste cost him his life.

Decuir's body was returned by buggy the next day to Santander Jiménez, where he was buried in an individual grave at the panteón. The death report described him as a native of Veracruz, married, with an occupation as a *capitalista*. The title may have indicated that DeCuir had a business to which he would have returned after the war.[425]

The convoy personnel heard the news of Decuir's death about the time another rumor reached them that Federal troops had captured Güemez, the village the convoy had to pass through between Padilla and Ciudad Victoria. Gárate was now in command. He was advised to spend the night at nearby Hacienda de Dolores, where the park of artillery would be secure. Gárate accepted the advice and bivouacked the convoy at Dolores. The convoy likely spent the next night there also as the investigation into Decuir's shooting held up further movement.

Upon awakening on a gray, overcast November 25 morning, Runyon and Newman learned that nothing had changed in the overnight hours to quell the convoy members' anxiety. Persistent rumors still spread that the Federals were nigh. Ultimately, Gárate ordered the convoy to return to Matamoros.

As entrepreneurs, Runyon and Newman disagreed with that decision. Runyon could not earn money from the trip if he did not send out battle photographs of Ciudad Victoria to multiple newspapers. Newman needed to finish the job he was hired to perform. So, these two *compañeros de viaje* bound their fortunes together for a while longer and elected to make the high-risk journey from Padilla to Ciudad Victoria.

Before they split off from the main convoy, Runyon and Newman hired bodyguards from the pool of Carrancistas in the area. It had to have been a difficult sell. All travelers headed to Ciudad Victoria would face consequences if they encountered the Federals. Newman and Runyon likely would have been inconvenienced but unharmed because of their nationality, their professions, and their neutral position in the revolution. The two Mexicans, though, would

Los Compañeros de Viaje

Soon after Runyon and Newman became the only participants committed to completing the mission after the untimely death of Lieutenant Colonel Decuir, Runyon took this candid shot of Newman and their two hired Carrancista bodyguards as a slice-of-life memento of wartime Mexico. Today this photograph, perhaps the only images ever captured of either revolutionary soldier, displays two brave men from Mexico willing to share huge risks with two Texas entrepreneurs. Photo by Robert Runyon, RUN00062, RRC, DBCAH, The University of Texas at Austin.

have been shot. Despite the risk, Newman and Runyon, using "some effort" and probably money, convinced two men to guard them on the trip.[426] The four travelers carried Winchester and Mauser rifles, ammunition, and camera equipment, and one of the revolutionary soldiers had at least one bottle of tequila.

Runyon and Newman also requisitioned a different automobile. Years after the event, Runyon had told his son, Delbert, that he and Newman left their Model T Ford in Ciudad Victoria and returned to Matamoros without it.[427] However, it appears the Ford already had worn out. The *compañeros de viaje* advanced to the capital that morning in a Cole "30," a five-person touring car with a four-cylinder, thirty-horsepower engine.

The trip took hours to cover the fifty miles to the capital. As they drove, each man watched the monte for movement and prayed not to be intercepted. Somewhere along the way, the bodyguards' apprehension turned to anxiety, and they convinced Newman to stop the vehicle.

Their fear inexplicably turned to panic and the two soldiers began firing wildly at unseen enemy in the brush. When shooting ended, Runyon discovered a single casualty of the barrage. One of the nervous soldiers had shot the sights off his comrade's rifle.

Throughout the trip, no one for a moment forgot the region roiled with revolution. Yet at some point they stopped for a photograph of *los compañeros de viaje*, almost as if they were on a holiday jaunt. Upon reaching Ciudad Victoria, they parted ways and Newman and Runyon began their work in earnest.

In the center of the city, Runyon and Newman headed to the main plaza, where they viewed the bombing devastation. They learned that the Constitutionalists had destroyed the state building where the Federals had made a stand. Runyon and Newman affirmed that all vital records stored in that beautiful building, once the pride of Tamaulipas, were destroyed. The fires that gutted the government buildings had jumped to the roofs of many jacales surrounding the city center, devastating the city's poorer residents. Yet close-by buildings, including the governor's residence, stood largely untouched by the bombardment, perhaps by plan so the Constitutionalists could immediately govern. [428]

On November 26, Runyon and Newman finished their assignments and started back to Matamoros, carrying a wounded man with them. The pair had been gone at least two days longer than originally intended. Recent rains had turned barely existent roads muddy, but Newman made good time on the return.[429]

Runyon and Newman crossed into Brownsville late on November 28 and the next day conducted interviews with both the *Brownsville Herald* and *The Brownsville Sentinel*. They told of Decuir's tragic shooting. They reported the capital's condition as good and improving. They said there was no doubt the Ejército Constitucionalista was in control of the region and that government troops had been sorely demoralized. Runyon estimated that approximately five hundred Federal soldiers had been killed in the battle.

Runyon developed his images rapidly and sent prints of the battle's impact to newspapers. Because local interest was high, Runyon told *The Brownsville Sentinel* that he would show his photographs in a public lantern slide exhibition at The Dreamland Theatre. At 9:30 a.m. on December 1, he hung a three-by-ten white banner with red and black letters that said: "TO-NIGHT Scenes from the BATTLE OF VICTORIA" in front of the theater.[430] Adults paid ten cents and children five cents to see Runyon's "Extra Special" magic lantern presentation followed by two two-reel silent features.[431]

By December 3, Runyon's photos had made page one of the *San Antonio Express* and the *Houston Post*. He put clippings of each article into his string book.[432]

Los Compañeros de Viaje   123

Runyon and Newman's first stop in Ciudad Victoria was the hillocks near Hacienda Las Vírgenes, a site of initial heavy fighting in the recent battle. Newman stands on top of the facing building, second from left. Photo by Robert Runyon, RFP, DBCAH, The University of Texas at Austin.

The panteón near Ciudad Victoria, a site of heavy conflict, was another early stop made by Runyon and Newman. This photograph became one of Runyon's postcards. Photo by Robert Runyon, RUN00269, RRC, DBCAH, The University of Texas at Austin.

Prisoners that Runyon and Newman saw in Ciudad Victoria included Federal soldiers as well as the city's larger storekeepers. Most of the individuals in Runyon's photograph later were executed. Yet Runyon persuaded Constitutionalist leaders to spare one storekeeper's life. Runyon had met the man on an earlier trip to the state capital a few years before the revolution entered Tamaulipas. Photo by Robert Runyon, RUN00251, RRC, DBCAH, The University of Texas at Austin.

Yet the one negative from this trip that provided photographic proof of Runyon and Newman's collaboration, the one that embodied the importance of their daring on this long and anxiety-driven trip, the photograph of *los compañeros de viaje*, never became a print nor ever was published in newspapers or postcards. Runyon relegated this glass plate negative to storage in a wooden cigar box that lay on the dust-laden shelf of his smaller photography studio for seventy-five years.

Now, more than a century after the photograph was taken, we can view it as more than just the snapshot in time it probably was. It is a historical photograph of transition in the entrepreneurial careers of Newman and Runyon—two men whose science and technology accomplishments, unique innovations, and knowledge creation, in indiscernible, minuscule, yet pervasive ways, underflow life still in the twenty-first century lower Rio Grande Valley.

Chapter 16
The Revolution in Monterrey

Newman's next two driving engagements returned him to Ciudad Victoria, just days after the battle. On his second trip that departed December 10, it is likely he chauffered another Veracruzano revolutionary chief, General Gabriel Gavira. Primer jefe Carranza had instructed his brother in Matamoros to assist Gavira by providing him an automobile to travel to Ciudad Victoria during the same dates as Newman's travel.[433]

Newman returned to Brownsville on December 14 with updated news of a capital city under a new Constitutionalist government. To the relief of borderlands residents who had family members in Victoria, Newman reported the city had regained its routine. He said commerce had picked up, food supply chains were functioning, and citizens were again productive. He also shared intelligence on the Constitutionalist Army's strategy, saying the next step was likely attacking Tampico.[434] Newman's trip seemed routine, but it showed U.S. intelligence interests he mixed effectively within inner circles of the Mexican revolutionary hierarchy.

Although Newman made other trips into Mexico, 1914 was a complicated year for him. On January 23, 1914, Newman's father died in Brownsville and was buried in Runge. Later that year, Newman and a partner, E. Fernandez, began Texas Auto Sales Supply Company. Newman advertised his garage as the "Best Equipment Shop in the Southwest," with "Complicated Work a Specialty." His services included autogenous welding and iron, bronze, and aluminum casting.[435] During 1914, Newman also developed an automobile radiator anti-leak solution that doubled as an antifreeze. In a *Popular Mechanics* advertisement, he offered readers a "large sample" of "Newman's Perfection Radiator Compound" for twenty cents.[436] And on July 4, he and Pearl had their last child, Thomas Cline.[437]

Runyon, meanwhile, used 1914 to continue working with the Constitutionalist leadership. González Villarreal remained a strong advocate within the revolutionary brain trust for the use of Runyon's publicity skills. Runyon's postcards of Mexican Revolution scenes had received wide distribution, thanks in part to advertising in national publications that included *Popular Mechanics* and *Modern Electrics and Mechanics*. He offered readers six postcard "Pictures of leaders, piles of dead, soldiers executed, cremation and other real war scenes" for just a quarter.[438] In one such ad, he told prospective customers "I have some remarkable pictures."[439]

On March 14, 1914, the Constitutionalist command ordered its chief of trains, Ciudadano Eleuterio Reyna, to issue a rail pass to *"Roberto Runyón"* for round-trip travel between Matamoros and Monterrey.[440] In reality, uninterrupted train travel between the two cities was not possible since Blanco's Constitutionalist forces had destroyed many rail sections to disrupt Federal traffic between the two cities. Nonetheless, the pass gave Runyon official status with Constitutionalist forces in both Tamaulipas and Nuevo León.

On March 27, 1914, Runyon and Amelia welcomed their first child, Lillian.[441] A few days later, González Villareal helped lead revolutionary forces in an attack on Tampico.

The following week, Runyon used his rail pass to travel to Monterrey, the capital of Nuevo León and a city under attack as part of González's northern campaign. That same week, President Woodrow Wilson ordered U.S. marines to invade Veracruz. That order, which occurred while Runyon was entrained, would complicate the Battle of Monterrey upon his arrival.

This assignment was different than his coverage of Matamoros and Ciudad Victoria. In Monterrey, Runyon took photographs during the actual battle rather than after the conflict. Challenges inherent with war zone photography cropped up quickly when he had to truncate his rail travel. A blown-up bridge forced him to detrain at Los Ramones, a village under Constitutionalist control about fifty miles from Monterrey.[442]

He had brief disruption, though. The Constitutionalist troops with whom Runyon camped at Los Ramones worked to get him to the front line. The immediate commander provided Runyon with a buggy, a mule, a driver, and guards. He believed the Constitutionalist leadership extended him privileges he never would have received with a U.S. military unit going into battle.

Upon reaching the fighting in Monterrey, Runyon developed a different plan for documenting the conflict on film (the words in parentheses are the reporter's editorial aside):

Runyon watched the final assault against the Federals at Palacio de Obispado, the see of the bishop of Monterrey that was constructed in the late Eighteenth Century. In the aftermath, he took this photograph. Photo by Robert Runyon, RFP, DBCAH, The University of Texas at Austin.

Empty Shells used by a Federal Cannon at Monterrey.

This photograph gives an idea of the shelling Constitutionalists withstood while storming the Palacio in the final assault. Yet Runyon noted that even though the Federals rained shrapnel on the attacking revolutionaries, they used only solid-iron projectiles that inflicted much less damage on the revolutionaries than would have a direct hit from a percussion-detonated bomb. Photo by Robert Runyon, RUN00237, RRC, DBCAH, The University of Texas at Austin.

"I at once started photographing the battle scenes. I did not find it practical to make photographs during the attack. One bullet through my machine (Runyon did not mention the possibility of one bullet through him) would have spoiled all my chances to take the photographs. The Mexicans in that part of the country know very little about guns and they would have been very likely to fire upon me directly thinking I was putting up some new kind of machine gun if I had tried to set up a tripod."[443]

As he watched the combat unfold, news arrived of the U.S. Navy's invasion of Veracruz. Americans in Monterrey, and some Mexicans, had displayed the U.S. flag, believing the Constitutionalists would not destroy property owned by Americans. After the marines' invasion, though, the stars and stripes incited violence stoked by Federal forces. The Federals and their sympathizers pulled down American flags, including one at the U.S. consulate after taking the consul captive.

Federal troops dragged the captured American flags through the streets, hoping to fuel their fellow Mexicans' outrage over the foreign invasion and turn wounded national pride into an advantage. The Federals told Monterrey citizens that forty percent of the attacking Constitutionalist forces were American mercenaries. Although that number was too high, a thread of truth ran through their rumor; the five-year-old revolution had grown beyond Mexican interests. While working with the Constitutionalists, Runyon met many Americans who had joined as soldiers of fortune.[444]

The government commander, under a flag of truce, urged González to quit the fight because of the American invasion. He asked González to unite his troops with the Federals to combat the real enemy—the United States.

González rejected the request. He replied that the United States invaded not to fight Mexico but Huerta, just as the Carrancistas were doing. González put the focus back on the capture of Monterrey. He gave the Federals two hours to surrender. When, after four hours, the Federals did not comply, González renewed the fight in the city's interior.

Runyon observed the final assault on Federal troops at the Palacio del Obispado, the see of the region's bishop, located in the hills surrounding Monterrey. Although the Federals shelled the Constitutionalists, Runyon viewed the rifle exchanges that he witnessed as much more deadly than heavy artillery. The Hague Convention of 1899 had banned dum-dum bullets in war. Mexico in 1901 ratified the declaration. Yet Runyon observed both sides ignoring that prohibition during the Revolution.

"I have made many photographs of the wounded. Both sides are using soft-nosed bullets and the Federals are using an explosive bullet and also brass and copper lined shells such as are barred by rules of war.

"Wounds inflicted by these bullets are terrible. I have seen a wound from a shot that has entered at arm with a small perforation and in going out has torn away all the

side of the arm. This was done without striking a bone and spreading as a soft nose bullet does when a bone is struck. The bullet seems to have a small hole in the end and when it enters a body it bursts. Bullets that strike the head tear it all to pieces."[445]

Despite personal danger from the shooting, Runyon followed the Constitutionalist troops as they converged on the statehouse, freed the American consul, and took over the Cinco de Mayo Plaza. Although historians generally consider the Battle for Monterrey a six-day battle between April 18 and 24, Runyon said the fighting in the city proper actually took four days.[446]

Runyon's eyes were so strikingly blue that even a newspaper reporter described him by their color after the Battle of Monterrey.[447] Anytime he traveled in Mexico, his eyes singled him out as an American. Yet he always felt comfortable traveling among the Constitutionalists and had no concerns about working alone in a country at war.

Although never a war participant himself, Runyon well understood military operations. He had served in the national guards of West Virginia and Kentucky and spent weeks observing maneuvers of U.S. Army personnel stationed at Forts Brown and Ringgold after Army protection had returned in February 1913.[448] Already, he had witnessed war's devastation in Matamoros and Ciudad Victoria. Yet, in Monterrey, his firsthand view of the conflict's brutality disturbed him. And, at this stage of the revolution, he feared what Federals would do to captives as their power continued to slip.

"I was not afraid to go with the army from Matamoras (sic), because I had been with them to Victoria, but if the tide of battle had swept the other way at Monterey (sic) I should have turned back as fast as I could."

When the Constitutionalists emerged victorious, Runyon heard soldiers boast that the winning of Monterrey showed that the power of their fighting force could defeat the U.S. military if the Navy's invasion of Veracruz turned into a full-scale war. Runyon disagreed with them. In an oblique warning to the Constitutionalist command, Runyon publicly stated that the U.S. forces at Fort Brown easily could capture Matamoros if conditions worsened between the two nations.[449]

Runyon questioned the future of the Mexican revolutionaries because of their fragmented command. Since the Battle of Matamoros a year earlier, factions in northeastern Mexico had fought internally to gain primacy even as government fortunes fell. Then, of course, there was the war's inevitable disruption of Mexico's economy. Runyon, an inveterate businessman, noted storekeepers' concerns when forced to use Constitutionalist currency despite widespread doubt about its solvency. On the other hand, the merchants had no real alternative as they feared reprisals if they contested the revolutionary notes' validity.[450]

Runyon returned to Matamoros on the first train from Monterrey to travel over a complete route of rebuilt bridges and re-laid tracks.[451] At home in Brownsville, he sent Monterrey photographs to wire services and newspapers and made many images into postcards. He probably did not regret to learn later that was his last battle assignment in Mexico.

Fortunes of war had moved all of Runyon's advocates to areas beyond his photographic reach—Blanco to the far west, Pablo González outside the northern theater, and González Villarreal eventually to Chihuahua.

After helping capture Tampico, González Villarreal had received a promotion to colonel in the Fifth Division of the Constitutionalist Army Corps of the Northeast. He was still in the border area in April 1915, when Pancho Villa's loyalists tried to take Matamoros. González Villarreal helped rebuff that attack, and he was promoted to general and assigned to command the barracks at Güemez. As Villa forces attempted to take Ciudad Victoria next, González Villarreal suffered a leg wound when the Villistas shot his horse out from under him. The Constitutionalists lost the capital, but a month later González Villarreal had recuperated and helped lead an attack on Villa's train system. That mission helped provisional Governor Caballero retake Ciudad Victoria for the Constitutionalist cause.

By autumn 1915, primer jefe Carranza appointed González Villarreal commander of the garrison at Ciudad Juárez, Chihuahua. González Villarreal was among several Carrancista officers who led the Constitutionalists in a rout of a U.S. expeditionary force at El Carrizal in June 1916. General John J. Pershing had ordered the American troops into Mexico to find Villa, but they had the ill fortune to run first into Carranza's forces. Losses were heavy, including the commanding officers for both sides.

Yet a few months after that skirmish, González Villarreal worked with U.S. soldiers to repel Villa and his men when they attacked Juárez. Villa's defeat kept the border city under Constitutionalist control and González Villarreal away from Tamaulipas.[452]

Runyon would photograph no more battles in Mexico. Still, a different kind of conflict, but conflict nonetheless, would come to him.

Chapter 17
Photos of Dead Bandits

The year 1915 began ominously for all borderlands citizens.

An anonymous group published a manifesto on January 6 urging a liberating army to retake the southern United States (Texas, New Mexico, Arizona, Colorado, and California). Soldiers of "the Latin, the Negro, or the Japanese race" would constitute the army. In paragraph seven, the plan included a genocidal component directing its adherents to kill "Every North American over sixteen years of age." Only the aged, women, and children "shall be respected."[453]

The proclamation was called the Plan de San Diego after allegedly being drawn up in that town about 150 miles northwest of Brownsville. Some historians believe the document actually was written in a Monterrey jail. Regardless of its origin, Runyon said the manifesto's message was clear to people of the borderlands: "Mexico was going to 'take' Texas." And events that occurred after January 6 did nothing to alter that interpretation.

In the Rio Grande Valley and surrounding South Texas area, after release of the manifesto, violence occurred more frequently and in ostensive coordination with the plan's goals. Borderlands insurgents initiated skirmishes and sometimes full-scale battles with ranchers, civilians, military, and law enforcement, including Texas Rangers.[454] Anyone along the border who looked deeply enough found that names linked to the Plan de San Diego often also were tied closely to a few active players in the continuing Mexican Revolution.

The intrigue boosted Newman's business, but more for information about those links than for driving. His competence as a chauffeur, his fluency in

Spanish, and his ability to mix in all strata of Mexican culture allowed him to gather intelligence in Mexico as an agent of the U.S. government on various assignments.

On the morning of March 24, Newman left Matamoros on a ninety-mile solo trip to San Fernando. At the time, Villistas reportedly were seeking an advantage over Carranza's forces in the area, but Newman reported he spotted no Villa supporters on that trip.[455]

Not long after he returned, Newman picked up the newspaper on April 8 to read a plea from Runyon's friend from the Appalachian region, William B. Cox. In his printed letter, Cox asked Newman to get him released from a Chihuahua prison.

Cox had acquired 110,000 paper pesos in Tampico after Carranza had captured the port city. Cox maintained that the funds were payment for a business transaction made in Mexico of agricultural commodities. Carranza, though, considered the paper invalid. Parties in Tampico led Cox to believe that the paper pesos could be turned into U.S. dollars in Chihuahua, a region under Villa's control.

Cox arrived in the city of Chihuahua from Tampico, after stopping briefly in Brownsville. Villa, though, charged Cox with passing counterfeit money. Cox's incarceration in prison lasted several months while his South Texas friends worked through U.S. government channels to bring him to trial as quickly as possible. They believed his innocence was evident even during turbulent times of revolution. Six individuals signed affidavits attesting that Cox had passed through Brownsville with paper pesos acquired in Tampico—not in the U.S.— before he headed west.

On April 3, Cox wrote a letter to friends in the borderlands requesting additional aid. The *Brownsville Herald* ran his letter five days later. In it, Cox pointed out "P. A. Newman and J. K. Bull [probably Jason Bull, a local farmer] know I brought this money from Tampico with me." Cox appealed to Newman to intercede on his behalf:

> "I believe that if Mr. Newman would explain to the Villa authorities that are near Matamoros now, and you and my Brownsville friends will inform them of my previous life and have them notify the authorities here I might be released—anyway, it would stay the proceedings until I have better proof."

Cox closed his letter with a warning that Villa had ordered all counterfeiters to be shot. "Get busy, brother, and help me now, and remember I am innocent of any intention of crime, or wrong intention."

Newman and Runyon were among 170 persons who signed a statement of good character for Cox after the letter ran.

Cox's wife, Ibby, traveled to Brownsville in April from Tampico and stayed with the Runyons to await her husband's fate. He was finally released in June after U.S. Secretary of State William Jennings Bryan applied added pressure.[456]

The incident showed the influence that Newman had with Villa and Carranza in the northern tier of Mexican states. It also showed why the U.S. government turned to Newman for intelligence whenever he returned from a journey.

On April 15, Newman drove a physician almost to Ciudad Victoria in record time to attend to an injury suffered by Colonel B. F. George, an American who operated a ranch deep in Tamaulipas. Newman, the physician, and George drove back to Brownsville, and Newman reported that the group experienced "little discomfort" on occasions when the group encountered either Carranza or Villa soldiers.[457]

A month later, Newman drove to Cruillas, about thirty miles from San Fernando. A rumor had reached Brownsville that Blanco had defected to the Villa forces and was near the village planning an attack on Matamoros. On the trip, Newman talked to provisional Governor Caballero. Although Caballero confirmed the Villistas held the capital at Ciudad Victoria, he told Newman the rumor about Blanco had no basis.[458]

In early December 1915, Newman traveled from Matamoros to Monterrey and then returned home via Laredo. Although Newman released no details of that trip to newspapers, his travel dates coincided with increased U.S. intelligence about the Plan de San Diego organizers. It also came as primer jefe Carranza appointed a new commander in Nuevo Laredo to allay U.S. concerns over the pro-bandit sentiment of the predecessor.[459]

Historians Charles H. Harris III and Louis R. Sadler have performed close examination of U.S. Bureau of Investigation (the forerunner of the Federal Bureau of Investigation) files as well as records of the U.S. State Department relating to internal affairs of Mexico during the years of the Plan de San Diego. In that data, they found several references to Newman's work as an intelligence agent. In at least one case report, he allowed another U.S. agent to stay at his St. Charles Street home when the agent traveled through Brownsville.

The historians cite documents showing Newman was in Tampico in May 1916 at the U.S. consulate investigating one of the Plan de San Diego's proponents. Newman claimed to have been sent into Mexico by the commanding officer, Colonel A. P. Blocksom, at Fort Brown. In June, the U.S. State Department and the bureau picked up a coded message concerning Carrancista troop movements, apparently meant for Newman. The bureau agent in Brownsville met with Newman at his garage and gained clarification on the message. In his summary, the bureau agent described Newman as "dependable" and "close mouthed and eyed and eared."[460]

In March the following year, government intelligence groups continued to mine Newman's information. The Brownsville agent in a report stated: "P.

A. Newman, who makes frequent trips into Mexico by automobile, has just returned from Victoria. He saw no Villistas or Felcistas [Felicistas] but says they were recently near San Fernando as reported."[461]

While Newman's involvement took him repeatedly below the Rio Grande, Runyon's focus on the conflicts after 1915 turned to his own region in an area stretching from about seventy miles north of Brownsville to just a dozen blocks from his home on St. Charles Street.

Runyon's photographic coverage of what would become known as the Texas bandit wars began in summer 1915 at the SLB&M's Las Norias flag station between Brownsville and Kingsville. The train stopped at a flag station only when an onboard passenger needed to disembark or a displayed flag signified someone ready to board. Yet this flag station also saw frequent comings and goings because the same location served as the King Ranch's division headquarters.

On August 8, 1915, King Ranch manager Caesar Kleberg was working in Brownsville when he received intelligence that an estimated seventy Mexican riders had been seen within the ranch's El Sauz division. At Kleberg's request, a contingent of Fort Brown troopers and Texas Rangers rode that afternoon's train north to Las Norias to investigate.

Upon arriving, the Rangers and some King Ranch cowboys rode in search of the Mexican horsemen. The bandits, concealed in the monte, reportedly watched the Rangers pass yet did not confront them. The bandits held to their faulty plan and attacked the flag station just before sunset, expecting to surprise what they believed would be a defenseless outpost. Instead, the attackers met fierce resistance from the troopers and remaining King Ranch personnel. Two hours later, the defeated bandits retreated, carrying off many wounded and leaving five dead. On the defending side, Manuela Flores, wife of a railroad employee, was the sole fatality. The bandits reportedly killed her when she refused to divulge information. The only other injuries were minor wounds to two troopers and two ranch hands.[462]

The next day, Runyon traveled to Las Norias by train and took one of his most famous and controversial photographs of the dead bandits. In the image, a Texas Ranger, who had not participated in the gun battle, a former Texas Ranger, and a local law officer roped the corpses and dragged them by horseback into a pasture. Runyon also took photographs of the unharmed Fort Brown soldiers and other images of the battle scene.[463]

On October 18, Runyon covered another bandit attack. An estimated sixty insurgents derailed a SLB&M train six miles north of Brownsville and just south of Olmito at a station near the Tandy residence. The train engine and baggage and mail cars turned over, killing the engineer. The bandits boarded

Runyon took this photograph of three armed men on horseback, including a Texas Ranger and a former Ranger, who roped and dragged four dead bandits into an open pasture. The resulting image would become one of Runyon's most widely distributed postcards and, even today, most controversial photographs. Photo by Robert Runyon, RFP, DBCAH, The University of Texas at Austin.

the remaining cars and shot at unarmed soldiers in the smoking car, killing one of them and wounding three. Before they fled, the bandits also fired into a closed toilet where two men had sought shelter. Their bullets killed one and wounded the other.[464]

In May 1916, Runyon took his camera to the Cameron County gallows to chronicle another controversial bandit narrative that started the year before. Insurgents had attacked near Sebastian, Texas, thirty-five miles north of Brownsville, on August 6, 1915, just two days before the gun battle at Las Norias. They robbed a general store and killed farmer A. L. Austin and his son, Charlie.

Authorities jailed thirteen suspects of the murders in Cameron County, but Sebastian witnesses could identify none of them. However, the witnesses did implicate two other men, José Buenrostro and Melquiades Chapa, held for unrelated offenses in the same jail.[465] The witnesses maintained that Buenrostro shot the Austins while Chapa stood guard.[466]

Buenrostro had been arrested for cattle theft earlier that year. In his arraignment, the name of Aniceto Pizaña, a Texas proponent of the Plan de San Diego, came up frequently.[467] In the trial for the Austins' killings, witnesses gave "*abrumadoras pruebas*" (overwhelming proof) of Buenrostro's and Chapa's guilt, according to a newspaper.[468] In reality, little proof existed that Buenrostro or Chapa were involved in the murders.

Buenrostro and Chapa pled innocence, but a jury in spring 1916 convicted them of murder. The two men were sentenced to death by hanging. Their Brownsville attorney, Frank C. Pierce, sought commutation of the sentence, but the state board of pardons denied the request. Pierce then traveled to Austin to request clemency, but Governor James Ferguson rejected the plea.

Authorities anticipated reprisals on May 19, the execution day. Runyon carried his camera and tripod through a hundred lawmen and thirty-five soldiers to reach the makeshift chapel at the jail where Buenrostro and Chapa awaited the hangman.

The two men had dressed in suits for their last day. No stress or concern appear on the condemned men's faces despite Runyon's photography session occurring a few hours from their hanging. In fact, before Runyon arrived, the two men had written individual notes maintaining innocence yet granting forgiveness to those who sent them to death.

The platform beneath their feet opened at 2:13 p.m. and both men died instantly, according to a report.[469] Pierce, who a year later would publish a history of the region with detailed coverage of the bandit wars, recorded the event in his book. His terse, one-paragraph account ended with a factual statement: "They were tried, convicted and duly hanged in the yard of the new Cameron County jail at Brownsville, on May 19, 1916."[470]

National news accounts referred to the double hanging as the "first legal execution" in the bandit war.[471] The hidden message was that it was not the first execution. U.S. Attorney General Thomas Watt Gregory, a Texan, in a June 16, 1916, report to President Wilson, after the president had ordered a buildup of troops along the border, cited a federal Bureau of Investigation estimate that between two hundred and three hundred Mexicans had been summarily killed in South Texas over just a few months, the majority occurring after the train derailing at Olmito.[472]

Pierce estimated the same range of deaths as "evil influences were brought to bear to clear the country of the Mexicans." Pierce's count went back to the Las Norias attack and included at least 102 persons, and more likely three hundred persons, who were killed through the Texas Rangers' self-bestowed legal process of "capture, trial, and infliction of the penalty upon those who might be suspected" of being Plan de San Diego sympathizers. Pierce's view was that political leaders believed that the public had become "indifferent" to bandit crimes that had been adjudicated through the legal process and therefore legitimized the Texas Rangers to administer "cheaper and speedier" due process.

Chapa and Buenrostro posed for Runyon on May 19, 1916, in front of a two-level altar made for them by an Oblate priest just a few hours before the two men were hanged at the new Cameron County jail. Photo by Robert Runyon, RUN00136, RRC, DBCAH, The University of Texas at Austin.

Runyon took several photos of damage caused by the bandits' derailing of the SLB&M train at Olmito, just a dozen miles north of Runyon's Brownsville residence. The Texas Rangers rounded up seven suspects in the attack the next day and summarily executed four of them. Photo by Robert Runyon, RFP, DBCAH, The University of Texas at Austin.

Pierce, through his chronicle, and Runyon, through his images, were among the individuals who helped record events as they happened. Pierce based his words on his factual observations. Runyon's photographs provided visual facts that permitted others, some thousands of miles away, to undergo a similar unraveling of thoughts about the complex series of events constituting the bandit wars.

Both sides in the borderlands conflict performed shameful acts during those troubled times. As an early photojournalist, Runyon's images had the power to subordinate the subjective words of a reporter's news story or a traveler's comments in a postcard. But giving the viewer that power, especially when it came to images like the dead bandits lassoed by law enforcement, made persons on both sides uneasy.

Late in the evening on March 31, 1916, Runyon returned from Matamoros after purchasing two developing chemicals from a Mexican merchant. At the U.S. Customs House, the agent appeared to target Runyon and frisked him. Runyon told the inspector the bottles were "something to develop pictures" and they were not subject to duty.

The agent, though, charged Runyon with a federal crime of concealment and smuggling three hundred grams of amidol and metol.

In U.S. District Court on May 12, a jury returned a not guilty verdict. Still, Runyon said the arrest had less to do with what he brought across and more because Frank Rabb, the collector of customs, sought revenge. He said Rabb did not like the criticism the public threw at law enforcement authorities after viewing Runyon's photographs. Runyon described his relationship with Rabb as "Not friendly; because I made photos of the dead bandits, etc., and he objected to it…he made objections to me personally."[473]

Nor has Rabb's narrow breadth of vision been limited to one generation or one side's viewpoint.

In 1988, when the Barker Texas History Center at The University of Texas at Austin developed *La Tierra y Su Gente*, a traveling exhibit of Runyon's photographs from the early 1900s borderlands, comments from visitors largely were positive. Yet one California activist decried its "racist photos."[474]

Runyon's work has received other critiques as well. Since 1988, when Runyon's photographs became accessible to researchers, some modern writers stated that Runyon staged his controversial shots. They noted he took multiple angles of dead bandits and he allowed the Rangers to pose. Or they suggested he moved subjects like Echazaretta to well-lighted areas or that he modified the light for Chapa and Buenrostro by covering windows.[475]

In fact, he did all that. Technological limitations of a large-format camera that often necessitated a long shutter speed to generate a viable image on the gelatin emulsion of a dry glass plate required direction and staging in most cases.

Yet many of the critics also rely on Runyon's images to tell the same story that Runyon intended them to relate when his camera captured them. On a page, his photographs counterbalance the inherent bias of the written word in newspapers, books, correspondence, or official reports. That is the true legacy of his craft.

Chapter 18
'Tenemos Perder Para Ganar'

On November 30, 1915, Runyon took a momentous photograph on Brownsville's International Bridge of scores of actors in the revolution, the American military, and the businesses and local governments of Matamoros and Brownsville. Behind the scenes, the photograph also included players in the Plan de San Diego.

The occasion marked the first time American military leaders in Brownsville had freedom to pose next to Carranza since President Wilson in September 1915 had legitimized the primer jefe's leadership in Mexico. That photograph, and the meeting it chronicled, coincided with Carranza expressing countermeasures within his army to control the border situation. Still, through the influence of Plan de San Diego proponents, including his aide, Colonel Emiliano Nafarrate, Carranza did not stop his covert support for the troubles altogether.[476]

The military already had mobilized troops of the Fourteenth Cavalry and other regular Army at Fort Brown in February 1913 when revolution tensions along the border first erupted. In 1916, in response to banditry and Villa's predations in the West, Wilson activated the National Guard and sent 110,000 soldiers to protect the border from Texas to California. That action included fifty thousand men stationed at Forts Brown and Ringgold, the latter up the river at Rio Grande City.[477] Confronted with an overwhelming and superior military force just a river away, Carranza's inner circle walked away from the Plan de San Diego. Wilson's action returned peace to South Texas. Yet memories have never faded in the borderlands over malevolent actions by both sides in those few months.[478]

For Runyon, any U.S. troops at Fort Brown meant good business. He generated healthy cash flow selling postcards and photographs of borderlands

At center is Venustiano Carranza, primer jefe of the Constitutionalists. Opposite him is Colonel Augustus P. Blocksom, commander of Fort Brown from summer 1914 to spring 1916. Just behind Carranza's right shoulder is Colonel Emiliano P. Nafarrate, responsible not only for ordering senseless executions of captured Federal soldiers after the Battle of Matamoros but also the influencer of Carranza's covert support for the Plan de San Diego and its resulting bandit war raids. Photo by Robert Runyon, RUN00001, RRC, DBCAH, The University of Texas at Austin.

conflicts to U.S. soldiers. In addition, photographs of troop maneuvers and the soldiers themselves at work and leisure gave Runyon a rich new source of photography subjects and customers. Runyon and Amelia sometimes worked all night to develop the photographs that Runyon took during the day in and around Fort Brown. Seventy years later, Amelia remembered going to the bank with bags full of gold coin payments from troopers who bought Runyon photographs in volume.[479] Nor was Fort Brown Runyon's only military market. He also received permission from the commanding officer at Fort Ringgold to sell photographs through the post exchange there. [480]

By 1917, though, the war in Europe worried Wilson more than bandits in South Texas and Villa in El Paso and New Mexico. Wilson withdrew troops from the border and shipped them to France. Those withdrawals started a business slowdown for the Runyon family at an inopportune time.

Runyon and Amelia had a second daughter, Amali, born November 9, 1915, and a third, Virginia, born September 29, 1917. In early 1920, Amelia became pregnant again. When this child, Robert Albert, was born December 16 of that year, the family of three living in the little house across from the depot had now grown to seven persons in less than a decade.[481] To make ends meet, Runyon could reinvent his photography business or move on to new ventures. He chose the former and looked to Mexico as his market expansion opportunity.

The title page of Runyon's 1911 copy of *Terry's Mexico*, a guidebook to the towns, villages, and cities of Mexico, still carries a barely visible garnet-colored, oval ink stamp with "Robert Runyon, Photographer, Brownsville, Texas" in all caps. The book's tattered and crumpled red ribbon rests at Terry's itinerary for travel from Monterrey to Saltillo to San Luis Potosí.[482]

In May 1920, Runyon followed that precise route on a two-week business development excursion to Nuevo León. Carranza, set to leave office at the end of the year, had just named his successor. In anticipation of the change, Runyon hoped that Mexico might find interest in his historical photographs.

On this trip, Runyon drove his Model T from Matamoros to Monterrey, where he arrived on May 16.[483] He again had to navigate his way through the tumult of battle as on the day he departed Carranza's loyalists holding Matamoros surrendered to forces of General Álvaro Obregón, who had designs on leading the country. Troop movements of new revolutionary factions spread throughout Mexico. And before Runyon returned, Carranza was betrayed and murdered in Tlaxcalantongo by Obregón's allies. The county rocked with unrest.[484]

In Monterrey, Runyon checked into the Hotel Iturbide, just three blocks from the Cinco de Mayo Plaza. He took photographs of the city sights and he wrote Amelia in Spanish to confirm his business plans:

"I believe that I can do good business with the photographs here in Monterrey. Perhaps tomorrow I will leave for Saltillo but I will stay much time there before arriving in San Luis (Potosí). Then I will write you again. Take care of the children and my studio.[485]

The sights Runyon witnessed on the Monterrey-Saltillo-San Luis Potosí trip were nothing like Terry had written about in his pre-revolution guide book edition. In 1920, Runyon observed how Obregón's army, operating in both urban and rural areas of Mexico, eliminated opposition by hanging them. Corpses rotted on ropes in public view since the victims' families and friends feared being considered disloyal if they removed bodies for burial.[486]

Despite his initial optimism about *"buen negocia"* from this trip, his journey was not successful. Runyon did enter into a supply agreement with the Monterrey Novelty Company, but few other vendors stepped forward.[487] Selling photographs of Mexico to Mexicans was not going to succeed.

After returning to Brownsville, Runyon began to retool his business. He focused more heavily on portrait services, a sideline he had added in 1917 to his commercial photography business.[488] By early 1920, he authorized

A family that had grown to five children by the 1920s led Robert and Amelia Runyon to purchase this home, built in 1914, at 812 E. St. Charles Street. In two adjacent lots, Runyon moved both his original photography studios. Throughout the property, he and Amelia also established and nourished several native flora gardens that became renowned around the botanical world for their diversity and uniqueness. Photo by Robert Runyon, RFP, DBCAH, The University of Texas at Austin.

construction of a new portrait studio. He designed it with a skylight for illumination and installed jute backdrops.[489] In addition, as was his custom with any new enterprise, he read and studied. His new techniques for human body photography came from sources like the *British Journal of Photography* from which he ordered manuals and guides including: *Sketch Portraiture, Human Anatomy, Portrait Studio,* and *Photography of Today*.[490]

The portrait business generated demand after Runyon promoted his services to residents in both Brownsville and Matamoros who needed a photograph for loved ones, for business, or for passports. He took photographs of blacks, Hispanics, and whites. He took adults, children, and babies.

In addition, Runyon became the official photographer for Brownsville High School, taking class portraits and action shots at baseball and football games. He consistently sought new business including extending a proposal to the border inspector to take photographs of "such Chinese or other aliens detained by the (U.S.) Immigration Service, as they might specify, to be used for identification purposes."[491]

Runyon enjoyed one prize photojournalism assignment during this portrait period. In November 1920, President-elect Warren Harding traveled to the lower Rio Grande Valley to rest up for his inauguration in March 1921 after

Runyon perfected his portrait photography skills by using his daughters as models in repeated sessions. From left, Amali, Lillian and Virginia. Photo by Robert Runyon, RFP, DBCAH, The University of Texas at Austin.

a long campaign. Runyon followed Harding and his local host, lawyer and prominent Republican R. B. Creager, from Brownsville to Point Isabel. Runyon photographed the president-elect as he played golf, fished, and made speeches at the city's November 11 Armistice Day activities.

Runyon's photographs of Harding on the Texas border brought him $9 from the *Chicago Daily News*, $15 from Underwood & Underwood, $5 each from *The New York Times* and the *Houston Chronicle*, and $3 from the *Dallas Morning News*.[492] The sum was good pay for a week's work, but few other national news opportunities came to Brownsville during those years.

In 1921, Runyon and Amelia bought a house at 812 E. St. Charles Street that was better suited for their expanded family. Although three blocks from his first Brownsville residence and his studio, the new house was larger, with two bedrooms, a parlor, two dining rooms, a kitchen, an indoor bathroom, a wrap-around porch that was screened in to provide additional beds, a garage, a gazebo-covered cistern, and living quarters meant for servants that Runyon instead used to store resources for his many individual areas of study. The house, built in 1914, also featured gardens where Runyon could grow the native plants with which he had become so fascinated. To make the house purchase, he borrowed money from González Villarreal, who had just finished a term as governor of Tamaulipas.[493]

Runyon needed his wife to access his business without disrupting her care of their children. He soon added two lots adjacent to the new house with plans for Amelia to continue providing needed photography assistance. In 1927, he would move both his studios to those locations.[494]

Existence would have been tough for the growing family without the portrait business. His once news-making revolution-era photographs had already moved into the realm of history. Despite their value, he received only occasional requests for his portfolios.

For instance, in 1921, Walter Prescott Webb had just finished his master's thesis on the Texas Rangers at The University of Texas. Webb, later a noted historian but at the time a graduate history instructor, requested prints of bandits and Texas Rangers at Las Norias, the hangings of Chapa and Buenrostro, scenes of Rurales forces in Mexico, as well as one of Texas Rangers and Customs officials pouring mescal out of confiscated contraband bottles during Prohibition.[495]

Runyon's other revenue source—the postcard business—also suffered from orders that came in spurts.[496] In 1919, J. M. Black of Kansas City, Missouri, after returning from the lower Rio Grande Valley, sent Runyon a money order for $8 to purchase two hundred postals for resale in the Midwest.[497] Locally, though, Runyon had to rely on vendors like Harry's Cigar Store and Hargrove's Book Store to promote his photography line.[498] Even his hopes for a spike in sales through the agreement with the Monterrey Novelty Company ran into difficulties when the owner could not figure out a viable price to sell them within Mexico.[499] Runyon noticed that in the 1920s the best sellers were tourist-type photographs in souvenir folders, thousands of which he sold to land development companies, and scenes of Matamoros that continued to include the popular bullfights and Plaza Hidalgo.[500]

Unauthorized use of his images complicated his quest to grow revenue from his photography assets. Runyon was astounded to find that many users, including the media, cared nothing for intellectual property rights. He decided to stem this piracy that significantly threatened his photography revenue.[501]

The Houston Chronicle used several of Runyon's postcards without authorization in its magazine supplement *Rotogravure*. Runyon sent a letter to the managing editor protesting the unlicensed use, after which the editor blamed a chaplain who provided postcards to the supplement's editor. As compensation, the editor offered to run "an item drawing special attention to your photographic work along the border." At the same time, he suggested Runyon was not harmed. "It occurs to me, however the publicity for you would be beneficial rather than otherwise," he wrote.[502]

The city of Brownsville and the Brownsville Chamber of Commerce used similar rationale in glossing over their infringement in the late 1920s. The chamber published Runyon's copyrighted photographs without permission in a brochure commissioned by the city. When Runyon confronted the chamber's manager about the issue, the man told him, "Yes, but you wont (sic) lose anything by it."[503]

This time, Runyon decided to sue the city of Brownsville for copyright infringement since the Brownsville Chamber of Commerce was an adjunct under local charter. In his suit, Runyon sought damages for nineteen photographs used without authorization times the press run of twenty thousand brochures times $1 each. The total was $380,000.

The U.S. District Court had heard both parties' evidence on the case but had not issued a judgment when the city's attorney, R. B. Creager, updated Brownsville officials. Creager predicted the loser would appeal to the U.S. Circuit Court of Appeals. He further believed the case would eventually end up before the U.S. Supreme Court. Along with that opinion, Creager billed the city his initial fee of $2,000. He noted that his final legal fees would be "fixed on the termination of the suit."

The threat of a protracted legal contest combined with mounting attorney costs moved city officials to offer Runyon an out-of-court settlement in 1929. The terms provided Runyon with a $4,750 municipal warrant. It was a small victory, and one that Creager, a staunch supporter of Republican elite businessmen, used to hound Runyon as a Cameron County Democratic Party leader in the next decade.[504]

Even as Runyon fought that infringement case, he fleshed out a new venture to create a more robust market for his postcards. By 1925, he had a business plan that utilized all his previous experience—salesman, supply chain manager, retail store official, and commercial photographer. A month after his and Amelia's last child, Delbert, was born on August 22, 1926, Runyon announced he was closing his photography business.[505] Runyon was sure he had devised a way to profit from his existing photography assets without the overhead of operating a studio.

Runyon's new enterprise was selling curios, perfume, and postcards at a store he called The Basket Place located on the main plaza in Matamoros. His partner was his brother-in-law, José C. Medrano.

Runyon's significant photography inventory, from which he could generate postcards, provided a competitive advantage over the many other curio stores in Matamoros and Brownsville that had to buy them from a supplier. Existing records, although five years of this period are missing, show he ordered 336,000 copyrighted postcards during the years he owned the curio shop. Subjects included the Catedral and plaza in Matamoros, a Mexican *jardín y patio*, the 1911 International Bridge, Brownsville buildings and residences, the Point Isabel lighthouse, and a great pictorial assortment of the region's many unique native plants.[506] Runyon promoted the postcards as a primary tourist draw to

Helen C. Kleberg of the King Ranch appreciated Runyon's customer service at The Basket Place in Matamoros. Her drawing of a blue wine glass that she requested led to a substantial order for Runyon's curio store. RRC, DBCAH, Box 2007-109/2.

The Basket Place, telling customers to "Send a Postcard from Mexico with a Mexican Stamp" in newspaper advertisements.[507]

Runyon's business plan quickly became profitable. Americans' fear of visiting Mexico had subsided with the revolution now a distant memory. Tourists and new waves of homeseekers flocked to the lower Rio Grande Valley and Matamoros throughout the 1920s. At the time of the store's opening, Americans visited Matamoros for its historic sights, its souvenirs, and its unlimited legal alcohol during Prohibition (1919 to 1935 in Texas).[508]

The Basket Place was in a high traffic location for tourists. Runyon and Medrano had set up in a building more than a century old on the northeast corner of Plaza Hidalgo. Runyon's pride was the store's patio with native plants that, he said, "alone was well worth seeing."[509]

By 1929, Runyon bought out his brother-in-law's interest.[510] After that, Runyon made all decisions. For many years, he took one or two month-long trips to Mexico's interior to buy from artists and manufacturers in Mexico City, Aguascalientes, Celaya, Puebla, and Guadalajara. From these suppliers, Runyon offered pottery, artwork, jewelry made from opals, agate, rock crystals and other semiprecious stones, the store's eponymous *canastas*, serapes and blankets, walking canes, wallets, huaraches and other items made from locally sourced fiber, leather, and horsehair. He'd also sell fragrances from Guerlain, as that company's exclusive agent in Matamoros, as well as many other French and Spanish perfume makers. He ordered Brown Betty teapot knockoffs and table crumb sweepers from Japan. He purchased Dutch meerschaum and French briar pipes. And, he'd ask his relatives in Kentucky and West Virginia to acquire all the arrowheads and tomahawk heads that the local boys could find in fields surrounding the Big Sandy River so he could attest they were authentic. He sold all these items and more, helped by Amelia, but relying on employees in Matamoros who stayed loyal to him for decades. All his children also worked there. His three daughters—Lillian, Amali, and Virginia—all of whom clerked at the store between semesters and during summers while they attended The University of Texas in the 1930s, helped attract young male shoppers to the store.[511]

Runyon built up a solid clientele not only among tourists but among repeat-buying South Texas residents. Helen C. Kleberg of Kingsville visited Matamoros from the largest ranch in the world to buy from Runyon. She was the wife of Robert Justus Kleberg Jr., ranch manager and grandson of the King Ranch founder, Richard King.[512] In 1933, Mrs. Kleberg thanked Runyon for "past favors" and ordered twelve cerveza glasses and eighteen wine glasses, sketching the shape of the latter style based on an earlier visit to the Matamoros store. She requested both in a "lighter blue" pattern. As complements, she also ordered blue plates of three different diameters in sets of eighteen each.[513]

After Prohibition ended in Texas in 1935, Runyon added another curio store on Twelfth Street in downtown Brownsville. He called it Runyon's Curio and Gift Store to cater to tourists who no longer needed to go to Matamoros for alcohol.[514]

The stores were financially successful, providing Runyon with cash flow and savings to raise his children and send each to study at The University of Texas. Yet he was not immune from all effects of the Great Depression.

Runyon had to rebuild his personal wealth after agricultural prices collapsed in the region and forced some banks to close their doors. Runyon and members of Amelia's family had deposited significant savings in Merchants Bank, the largest of the region's institutions. On March 24, 1932, the bank's board of directors closed its doors. The board turned operations over to the U.S. Comptroller of Currency with reorganization plans managed by a receiver, John M. Young, whom Runyon characterized as "a Republican Politician." Creager, the bank's attorney and Runyon nemesis, also was accused by Runyon of being in collusion with the receiver. Runyon complained to U.S. Senator Tom Connally (D-Texas) that Creager was in no hurry to reorganize the bank since he held an unpaid $74,000 loan.

Runyon's lost financial holdings were deemed substantial enough that the government eventually appointed him to the reorganization committee. Yet the bank could not be saved and that fortune was gone.[515]

Runyon, though, rebuilt rapidly. In his career, The Basket Place ranks as his most lucrative entrepreneurial pursuit.

Decades later, Amelia was asked about The Basket Place. She was sitting in a chair with her hands on the armrests. She answered in English and Spanish: "We could have been *millionarios*...but for *la politica*," referring to Runyon's involvement with the Democratic Party that would supplant his career as a merchant. Then she lifted her hands, turned her palms upward, shrugged her shoulders, and said with a wry smile: "*Tenemos perder para ganar.*"[516]

By then, Amelia did not have to explain what she meant by success gleaned from sacrifice. Everyone knew she referred to the incalculable value of what her husband did after closing The Basket Place. That was to create and leave vastly more knowledge about the borderlands' unique and often endangered flora than existed before him. And he did it, as historian and folklorist J. Frank Dobie once said, "totally apart from his business and without possible remuneration."[517]

Chapter 19
The Entrepreneur with a Scientist's Mind

In the winter of 1936-1937, unusual turbulence swept over an underwater meadow in the depths of the Mediterranean Sea between Spain and Greece. The incident—possibly caused by violent weather or a trawler—created havoc among an ancient stand of a deep-water flowering grass. In the chaos, some stems of the obscure species broke away from their roots.

Scientists in that era knew this flowering plant's botanical name, *Posidonia oceanica* (L.) Delile, and vernacular name, Neptune grass. Yet the species grew deeper on the ocean floor than researchers could descend using pre-World War II diving technology. Scientists knew nothing of this sea grass's manner of growth or particulars of its seabed meadow or even the range of its habitat. Because of that underwater turbulence, however, the science world was about to get a splash of insight.

The unattached stems hitched an ocean-current ride out of the Strait of Gibraltar into the Atlantic Ocean. They drifted west and then south toward North America. Many weeks later, they flowed into the Gulf of Mexico, swept onward by the ocean. Despite lacking roots, the truncated branches still put out pale green leaves in the warmer Gulf waters.

The amazing journey continued a while longer as the current directed the stems toward the Texas-Mexico coast. By spring, the bundle approached land. It came ashore just north of the mouth of the Rio Grande within the wrack zone for Gulf seaweed.

The improbable *Posidonia oceanica* odyssey should have ended right there. Anyone who saw the stems likely would have thought they belonged to a related species endemic to North America, *Zostera marina* or eel-grass.

More implausible was that a self-taught botanist like Runyon would scan the usual mass of sea wrack and recognize this Mediterranean vagabond as singular. Yet he did. The only explanation is that Runyon, an entrepreneur with a scientist's mind, possessed an acute sense of observation.

If a musician's ear distinguishes individual concert notes, analyzing sound waves that originate from the brass, strings, percussion, woodwinds, each in isolation, then Runyon possessed analogous talents when it came to plants, trees, cactus, or fungus. Runyon isolated the rare by searching for the unique within seemingly infinite similar elements. The difference was that Runyon did it with eyes instead of ears and with flora rather than sound waves. And, while the musician's thought process revolved around creation, Runyon's mind focused on its close relative of innovation.

It did not matter where Runyon traveled. At every location, his eyes gravitated to landscapes most persons would ignore—an ill-attended garden, an empty lot full of weeds, a brush-infested cow pasture, or a shallow pool of stagnant rainwater. Runyon critically scanned each individual item of green, gray, or brown within these habitats.

So, on May 1, 1937, Runyon followed instincts when he traveled to the mouth of the Rio Grande looking for plants. There, his eyes found those several transatlantic stems of *Posidonia oceanica*. Runyon sent samples of the "semi-succulent" branches, measured at six to ten inches long, to The New York Botanical Garden for comment. The fragments' arrival excited the scientific community. In its academic journal, a Garden scientist called Runyon's sea grass discovery "One of the most interesting botanical finds in recent years."[518]

Eighteen months later, scientists could have issued a similar pronouncement about another Runyon plant discovery. However, this plant's identification took six decades to confirm.

On October 17, 1938, Runyon's eyes focused on a shallow pond in Kenedy County south of Armstrong. He spotted a low-growing plant with a shrub-like base, yellow flowers, and a white line that ran the length of its small leaves. Runyon noted that the plant grew in moist ground in and near the pond.

Runyon originally identified this plant as *Neptunia lutea*, a Texas plant. In 1997, however, botanists at the Billie L. Turner Plant Resources Center at The University of Texas at Austin confirmed the identification of Runyon's herbarium sample as *Neptunia plena*. This plant's vernacular names are "dead-and-awake" and "water sensitive." It is native to the West Indies, parts of Mexico, and South America, but the species had not been seen in Texas until Runyon found the Kenedy County specimen. *Neptunia plena* would not be identified again in Texas for almost seven decades.[519]

When it came to borderlands' flora, Runyon sought to inspire higher awareness of little studied plants as his botanical legacy. He promoted that awareness, or what more accurately might be termed knowledge, by never hoarding information. Instead, he avidly shared both his explicit and his tacit knowledge of plants with distinguished scientists and borderlands residents.

Explicit or science knowledge is the kind that you read in books or journals. Runyon authored two books and a few articles with science data on plant life; however, most explicit knowledge of his plant discoveries resulted from collaboration with experts at the nation's leading botanical research institutions. These scientists analyzed native plant samples that Runyon sent them, and then codified facts about his discoveries in an academic periodical or in correspondence. As these science data became available, Runyon complemented that explicit knowledge with tacit knowledge in order to advance innovative and practical plans to propagate a species.

Tacit knowledge, by comparison, is the information accumulated by eye-to-eye contact with a product or service and its users. Business knowledge, sometimes called proprietary knowledge, is a form of tacit knowledge. Runyon generated tacit knowledge through physical interaction with the borderlands' ecosystem as he watched, observed, and experimented with plants in every season. In addition to viewing plants in nature, he absorbed as much information as he could from other persons and from hands-on activities while growing the plants in the gardens that surrounded his Brownsville home at 812 E. St. Charles Street.[520]

When Runyon traveled to the wet markets and yerberías in Matamoros, he gained tacit knowledge by talking to vendors as they handled the harvested produce and dried herbs. He augmented and corroborated that information by personally caring for innumerable varieties of borderlands' plants at his home, his rental properties, and at parks and resacas. From daily observation of these plants' cycles, during both droughts and wet years, he developed proprietary knowledge about their germination and growth performances, nutritional requirements, water and light needs—all data vital to their commercial or residential propagation as well as preservation in their habitat. The daily monitoring of the plants was so important to his research that he trusted only Amelia to care for his plants when he took business trips into Mexico or extended visits to family in Kentucky and West Virginia.

As Runyon accumulated tacit knowledge, always building upon the data science might generate about a species, he avidly transferred that know-how to as many persons as possible. He wrote articles on how to grow native palms for Valley newspapers.[521] He accepted all invitations to address garden clubs, service organizations, and civic groups, presenting data on the benefits of trees to the environment or how to prune shrubs properly.[522] He repeatedly conducted hands-on trainings for city park employees, showing them how to transplant, nurture, and propagate native plants to enhance the region's beauty.

His efforts' most visible benefits to the borderlands today are the native plant diversity displayed in home gardens, public parks, and resacas as well as the many nature areas that provide the vital backdrop for the lower Rio Grande Valley's ecotourism industry.

That's not to say all of the many thousands of plants Runyon collected and studied in his career qualified for this knowledge transfer process. *Posidonia oceanica* demonstrates one example of why a rare find might not advance.

Scientists in 1937 had great hopes for the seafaring branches after receiving Runyon's package. Because the pieces were found near the mouth of the Rio Grande, they anticipated that they came from unknown populations of the flowering grass in deep water meadows off the North American Atlantic coast. However, that assumption proved faulty when no subsequent specimens ever appeared. The eventual conclusion confirmed *Posidonia oceanica* is endemic to the Mediterranean Sea. Its fragments arrived on the Texas coast only because of an improbable series of events.[523] Runyon's discovery of *Posidonia oceanica* achieved nothing more than illustrate his uncanny capacity to identify unique species.

Yet, that botanical oddity aside, the door of further knowledge generation really never closes on any plant that Runyon studied. The force behind new revelations is the compounding power of explicit and tacit knowledge that Runyon initiated and transferred when applied to today's science and technology. The case of *Neptunia plena* explains how.

After Runyon's discovery, no additional evidence of *Neptunia plena* was reported in Texas. Then, on October 27, 2007, two borderlands plants experts, Dr. Alfred Richardson of The University of Texas at Brownsville (now UT Rio Grande Valley) and Ken King of Weslaco, found specimens of *Neptunia plena* growing in a Kenedy County pond in the same general area where Runyon collected the first sample. The researchers subsequently identified another population of the species in Cameron County, but no others.[524]

It was an exciting find. When he and King realized they had found *Neptunia plena,* Richardson compared the sensation to the euphoria known as the runner's high that some individuals achieve. "Finding *Neptunia* was a great thrill for us," he said, coming seventy years after Runyon's initial report.[525]

With the rediscovery, scientists now have clues about this rare plant's existence. Richardson and King theorize that *Neptunia plena* appears only during infrequent wet years in that subtropical region. During more common dry years, the researchers suggest that the species can lie dormant for extended periods. Another possibility is that its seeds stay viable in the soil for lengthy stretches of time, but only generate the leafy plant on rare occasions when climatic conditions are ideal for the species.[526]

Scientists now can test those theories by observing *Neptunia plena* in its identified locations during all weather cycles. If explicit information that flows from these observations indicates value, business knowledge may follow to utilize the species.

For instance, after scientists come to conclusions, an individual entrepreneur might investigate a series of possibilities. The first analysis is whether *Neptunia plena* solves a pain and improves life for humans, animals, or even other plants. For instance, does *Neptunia plena* generate compounds that can be used in medicine? Does its extended dormancy reveal secrets that could help vegetable or fruit species stay viable during lengthy journeys to distant universes? Can the plant's ability to emerge during wet weather aid short-term remediation or reclamation of low-lying wet areas?

Each one of those questions represents an avenue of entrepreneurship that could result when further discovery augments Runyon's research. If a path to commercialization exists, the entrepreneur can weigh the risk, then develop a business plan from the explicit and tacit knowledge to turn theoretical value into profit.[527] And that's just using one borderlands' plant as an example; Runyon researched thousands of native flora species during the last century.

Of course, a high probability exists that *Neptunia plena* has zero business value and is only important to its habitat. Nonetheless, even a dead-end process to an entrepreneur transfers valuable experience plus explicit and tacit knowledge that, taken together, will improve chances of making the next challenge work.

To understand how, one need look no further than how Runyon used the power of knowledge transfer and how it helped him persevere in his botanical studies for five decades.

Chapter 20
The Lower Rio Grande Valley Flora Authority

ow Runyon made the leap from a photographer to a merchant to a plant lover to a plant expert is an exemplary story of science entrepreneurship all its own.

Runyon wrote that plants had interested him from his childhood through his young adult years in Kentucky. In the borderlands, the diversity and beauty of subtropical and semiarid plant varieties swayed his decision to make that region home from his initial moments in Brownsville.

During Runyon's first winter living in Brownsville in 1909, he wrote Fannie Short expressing wonder at the botanical wonderland he had entered. He expressed his amazement "...to see the tropical fruits growing there in that tropical climate during our (Kentucky's and West Virginia's) winter months." [528]

Runyon later told his children that his visits to wet markets and yerberías in Matamoros intensified his interest in local plants. From Mexican vendors, he learned common Spanish names for plants—names that he came to believe were as necessary to preserve as the plants themselves.[529] In both Matamoros and Brownsville, he regularly walked through parks, groves, resaca banks, ranch pastures, and home gardens to study native plants in their habitat. These practices cultivated Runyon's persistent appreciation for the intrinsic value of all borderlands' plant species.[530]

After surprising his wife, Amelia, in 1915 by bringing home a Model T Ford, Runyon for the next decade began driving his growing family, his camera and tripod, and his plant collection materials to sites like the Rabb Palm Grove (today the Sabal Palm Sanctuary) or the old Mexican War battlefield at Palo

Alto (today the Palo Alto Battlefield National Historical Park), both in Cameron County. During these weekend family outings, he photographed trees, plants, or cactus in bloom, and he brought home specimens for further study. He often challenged his children to run ahead and bring him a blossom he had not seen.[531]

By 1918, Runyon turned to serious, self-taught study of plant taxonomy. Through research in books he bought in the U.S. and Mexico, and through correspondence with experts, Runyon taught himself botanical classification standards. He learned to identify genus and species as well as describe a plant's physical characteristics—leaves, stem, flower—in technical nomenclature.

He rapidly became a capable successor in the region to Frenchman Jean Louis Berlandier, a resident of Matamoros at the time of his accidental death in 1851. As a member of the Mexico Boundary Commission in 1827, Berlandier made many important native plant discoveries in northeastern Mexico that then included Texas.[532] A later large-scale botanical study occurred in the 1850s under naturalists with the Mexican-United States Boundary Commission that surveyed and marked the international border after the Treaty of Guadalupe Hidalgo. These scientists also identified and catalogued many additional unique and valuable borderlands species for the first time.[533]

Other naturalists studied the borderlands' flora after the Civil War, but no one until Runyon devoted a lifetime to South Texas and Tamaulipas botanical studies.[534] Runyon benefited from camera technology not available to earlier borderlands' botanists. He took close-up photographs of plants to aid his examination of a species' appearance. His photo albums feature striking shots of flowering trees and shrubs, trees, cacti and herbs growing in the borderlands' various clays, clay loam, sandy loam, and fine sandy loam.

Through dedication and effort, Runyon jumped a considerable chasm from a ninth-grade education to advanced proficiency in botany. Before long, he had picked up where Berlandier and other dedicated researchers had left off. Runyon rediscovered and collected samples of many species that these earlier botanists already had identified. Yet Runyon also identified almost two dozen other species as unique for the first time in mankind's existence (chart on page 179). The nation's botanists welcomed Runyon's energy simply because no one had committed to study the lower Rio Grande Valley and northeastern Mexico flora since the boundary commission.

Runyon's core of botanical advisors grew quickly. It included Benjamin Carroll Tharp of The University of Texas botany department and curator of The University's herbarium; John Kunkel Small, curator at The New York Botanical Garden; and Conrad Vernon Morton and Joseph Nelson Rose of the Smithsonian Institution. Rapidly, the Runyon-to-scientists collaboration sparked knowledge transfer in both directions.

Runyon just before heading out on a day spent "botanying," as he called his plant excursions, in the lower Rio Grande Valley. RFP, DBCAH, The University of Texas at Austin.

Runyon hoped scientists could corroborate his initial identification of new plants from his plant photographs. He quickly found this approach "inexact."[535] So Runyon taught himself to collect and preserve flora specimens by drying them.[536] His existing plant labels indicate that Runyon at times brought live plants to the extensive native plant gardens surrounding his Brownsville home at 812 E. St. Charles Street. Having the specimens close by allowed him to photograph and study their natural life cycles. Once a plant had flowered, Runyon would preserve voucher specimens to assist scientists in confirming the plant's identity.[537]

Runyon's first documented plant collection trip took place on April 1, 1920, when he traveled to the mouth of the Rio Grande. On that trip, he identified three plants: Virginia plantain (*Plantago virginica*), Corpus Christi fleabane (*Erigeron procumbens*) and betonyleaf thoroughwort (*Conoclinium betonicifolium*). He brought samples of each collected plant to his photography studio for further study, thus starting the Runyon Herbarium.

To preserve plants, Runyon placed specimens between numerous pages of newspaper in a homemade press under his photography studio's skylight. In that location, the sun's heat dried the plants. Often, he relied on Amelia to monitor the samples while he was working. She would rotate the presses so the specimens would follow the sunlight; on infrequent cold days, she would bring them to her kitchen, where its warmth would advance the preservation process.[538]

With each plant, Runyon entered hand-written field notes on forms, which by the late 1930s he had printed in his own *Brownsville News* print shop, telling where he had found it along with applicable descriptions including his estimation of genus and species and its characteristics. Runyon's data gathering focused on ecological or descriptive information and less on where in nature he found the plants under study.[539] As such the labels lack some valuable information, but that omission would be expected from a self-taught botanist.

In his studio, Runyon transferred his handwritten notes by typewriter to index cards and added published references from his always expanding botanical library. Runyon cross-indexed the entries so he could immediately access all available data on any mounted specimen.

In his half century of study, he followed this same procedure thousands of times. By the 1960s, Runyon considered his collection "the best and most complete private Herbarium of local plants in the State of Texas."[540] His herbarium remains listed as inactive in the Index Herbariorum, the world's database of important herbaria. At his death, the Runyon Herbarium comprised 8,750 plant specimens, the vast majority of which came from the lower Rio Grande Valley and northeastern Mexico.

Dr. Billie L. Turner, former head of The University of Texas Herbarium, found that forty percent of Runyon's Herbarium were "of such interest on account of their site and time of collection, and...complete label data."[541] These forty percent today make up the core of the 4,200-item Robert Runyon collection of The University of Texas herbaria.

After 1926, the year Runyon closed his photography studio, he dedicated as much time as possible to plant expeditions. His home gardens became a laboratory where he transplanted or grew rare specimens that he found or that other researchers sent him for observation under subtropical conditions.[542]

Runyon's daughter, Amali, remembered as a young girl listening in his studio to a discussion between a botanist and her father. The scientist came to get an update on a plant he had asked Runyon to observe in his gardens. After her father commented on how well the plant had grown, Amali slipped out to locate the plant under discussion. She did not get the reception she expected when she showed up with the specimen—roots and all. "I really got a spanking," she said.[543]

But Runyon rarely needed to employ that type of education with his family. He, his wife, and children all shared a reverence for the region's native plants. Throughout their stewardship of the properties on east St. Charles Street, the Runyon gardens were famous from Canada to Central America for their amazing varieties of unique and lush vegetation. In those years, the Runyon properties were a visually striking display of the vigor of the borderlands' subtropical native flora right in the core of central Brownsville.

In every decade, Runyon found great value in accompanying a science expert in field research. Just watching how the expert worked invariably transferred tacit knowledge to Runyon on how to approach nature studies. One of Runyon's first such excursions took place in May 1921 when he was still a commercial photographer.

J. R. Pemberton, a Stanford-educated petroleum geologist, engineer, and self-taught bird expert, asked Runyon to photograph terns unique to habitats within Cameron County resacas and on Green Island close to Point Isabel.

Runyon's close-up shots of the nests and hatchlings from that trip illustrated Pemberton's article in an ornithology journal. The printed piece advised the bird world that the lower Rio Grande Valley actually nurtured seven tern species.[544] Afterward, Runyon began to envision dissemination of a parallel "uniqueness" message about the region's equally distinct flora.

Another of Runyon's early science-based excursions was with Tharp into central Tamaulipas. In 1926, the two men spent a week studying the flora in the mountains that framed Ciudad Victoria.

The journey was under the same difficult travel conditions Runyon had encountered with Newman during the Battle of Ciudad Victoria thirteen years earlier. Yet, lack of road progress actually helped the researchers. They were able to collect en route diverse and fragile flora that road construction would have destroyed. When Runyon and Tharp readied to ascend the mountains, the research team contracted with local ranchers for horses experienced in climbing and for burros to bear their packs. In all, it was a long, arduous, yet productive trip. Despite the obstacles, the pair collected more than a hundred specimens of plants, "some of them rare, and some them thought to be new plant forms." The variety ranged from ferns to orchids. Tharp cited that excursion as the first extensive botanical survey ever made deep in Tamaulipas.[545]

Runyon also collected side by side on other excursions with the Smithsonian's Rose and Edgar Theodore Wherry, Liberty Hyde Bailey of Cornell University, and many others. His circle of influential science collaborators who came to the Valley to work with him grew every decade.

As a polymath, botany was never Runyon's sole focus. But because it was the highest on his priorities, Runyon never neglected plant studies for long. He collected specimens every decade between 1920 and 1968. He performed the majority of his work (more than sixty percent of his herbarium's existing samples) in the 1930s and 1940s, when he also was involved deeply in politics.

At the same time, Runyon did not collect every season or even every year. One reason is that he quit driving in the mid-1920s after he broke an arm cranking the engine on his Model T Ford. After that accident, he only went on plant excursions when friends, employees, sons and daughters, sons-in-law, and, later, grandchildren were available to drive him around.

Weather was another limiting factor. During the prolonged 1950s drought, Runyon collected fewer than 250 samples in the decade.[546]

When conditions were right, however, Runyon collected plant specimens wherever he traveled. When in Kentucky and West Virginia to visit family, he looked for plants. When he took periodic health checkups at Scott & White Hospital in Temple, Texas, he collected specimens in Bell and McClennan counties. When he visited his daughters, Lillian in Nueces County and Amali in Bexar County, he would seek new varieties. He even had his son, Delbert, send him plant samples from Brazos County in 1943 when he briefly attended school there.

Yet the varied, fertile soils underlying Cameron County and northeastern Tamaulipas provided Runyon with more than three-quarters of his herbarium specimens.

During his years of study, Runyon became greatly interested in external influences, including the impact of weather, especially hurricanes, on the region's plant life. Occasionally alien seeds would ride the high winds. Some might germinate and generate a specimen or two that he had never seen.

The unintentional intervention of man also interested him. Runyon kept railroad yards on his list of sites to investigate for seeds brought by cars from time to time. Prairie Mexican clover (*Richardia tricocca*) was a specimen that attracted Runyon's attention at a railyard on June 27, 1944. He believed it came in with a load of gravel.[547]

By 1937, Runyon was widely regarded as a botanical expert who provided other botanical experts with "valuable notes on (plant) distribution as well as on new species."[548]

A decade later, Runyon was considered the world authority on borderlands plants. J. Frank Dobie said, "(Runyon) knows the Lower Rio Grande flora more intimately than any other man living."[549] Tharp described Runyon this way in an academic journal: "Robert Runyon of Brownsville, Texas, a friend and for many years a student of the vegetation of the Lower Rio Grande Valley and the best living authority on it."[550] Another time, Tharp told one of his correspondents: "(Runyon) knows plants better than any other person."[551]

That reputation was well deserved. Yet Runyon's objective was more expansive than just personal recognition. He wanted his neighbors and, indeed, all citizens of the borderlands, to know and appreciate their native plants as well. To do that, he needed a business strategy.

Chapter 21
Runyon's Huaco, Topsy-Turvy, and Esenbeckia

During Runyon's first twenty-four months in serious plant study that began around 1918, he found and submitted two unique cacti specimens to Rose at the Smithsonian. At the time, Rose collaborated with Nathaniel Lord Britton of The New York Botanical Garden on what, by 1923, would become The Carnegie Institution-published, comprehensive, four-volume study of the cactus family titled *The Cactaceae*.

After Rose examined Runyon's samples and additional correspondence, he determined the submitted specimens represented new species not yet discovered. Rose in 1923 named the two discoveries *Escobaria runyonii* and *Coryphantha runyonii*, among the first of many species and one genus that the science of botany would credit to Runyon's study over the decades.[552]

Rose's encouragement inspired Runyon to expand further his research into cactus and succulents. Runyon's affinity with cactus, as with many other flora types, inspired an uncanny ability to segregate consistently unique and unknown plant life from thousands of common species already studied.

"In making the rounds" near Reynosa, Mexico, circa 1921, Runyon came upon several elegant flowering plants of the *Manfreda* genus, relatives of the agave family. Locals called the plants *huaco*, a vernacular name, Runyon said, that "was used for various species of *Manfredas*. The plant is used as a remedy for snake bite."[553]

Runyon sent living specimens of one of the more unique *Manfredas* to experts at the Smithsonian and The New York Botanical Garden. The New York-bound huaco generated surprise when it flowered the same year it

Coryphantha runyonii *was one of the first plant specimens collected by Runyon that the botanical world recognized as not yet discovered and named in his honor. He found the initial specimen about 1920 near Rio Grande City, Texas. This photograph of C.* runyonii *graced the frontispiece for Volume 4 of* The Cactaceae, *a comprehensive study of cacti authored by American botanists Nathaniel Lord Britton and Joseph Nelson Rose. Runyon contributed multiple other photographs and data to the monograph.* Photo by Robert Runyon from author's collection.

arrived. It was not because the plant was unknown. In fact, Arthur Carl Victor Schott with the Mexican-United States Boundary Commission had reported the species decades before. The John Torrey Herbarium at The New York Botanical Garden still preserved Schott's dried huaco sample. What was novel was that, after seven decades, scientists had their first opportunity to observe the species during its reproduction process because of Runyon's ability to identify uniqueness in the field.

From Runyon's living sample, scientists determined that although the roots, leaves, and growing habits resembled other species within *Manfreda*, this plant had unique differences. In Runyon's huaco, the filaments (stems of the anthers) are shorter, and the anthers themselves do not extend outside of the floral tube as other Texas *Manfreda* species do.[554] Runyon's huaco also exhibit striking "brick-red" flowers compared to the yellow-green flowers, sometimes with maroon tips, usually seen with *Manfreda*. The scientists also determined that the bulbous roots seemed closer to a tuberose or *Polianthes* (also known as *Pseudobravoa*), another agave relative.

After analysis, Runyon's plant exhibited such unique characteristics that Rose classified it between *Manfreda* and *Polianthes*. He called the new genus

Runyonia, species *longiflora* or *tubiflora*, for "Robert Runyon, a very keen collector." [555]

The name, however, never was published formally. Dr. Lloyd Herbert Shinners later renamed it *Polianthes runyonii*. Today, it is *Manfreda longiflora* or Runyon's huaco.[556]

Although Runyon never profited from it, a succulent he discovered during this period became the plant world's most marketable item among his many discoveries. Runyon identified this member of the sedum family growing in a Matamoros garden. After he submitted the specimen around 1935, Smithsonian researchers classified and named the succulent *Echeveria runyonii* Rose ex E. Walther.

Today, *Echeveria runyonii* generates significant sales for the $41 million annual cacti and succulent industry. It is a favorite offering by retail garden outlets throughout the United States.

The species stands out for its striking salmon-orangy flowers that bloom on a stem that gets as tall as four inches. The plant's light blue-gray color and distinctive rosette made up of flat, rounded leaves add to its attractive conformation. One popular cultivar is called Topsy-Turvy in recognition of its unique leaves. Combined with its reputation as an easy-to-maintain, drought-tolerant accent plant, *Echeveria runyonii* is popular for inclusion in everything from large-scale landscapes to apartment rock gardens. Gardeners have reported cold tolerance for the succulent down to seven degrees Fahrenheit as far from Matamoros as North Carolina. It performs exceedingly well within xeriscape gardens, as the species does not like excessive moisture.

One expert called it "The most tried and true (*Echeveria*) species that survives outdoors in most of Texas."[557] Yet its reach is international as well.[558]

Runyon rarely remarked on his botanical achievements. The exception was his campaign to bring the extremely rare Texas tree, known as limoncillo or Runyon's Esenbeckia or, simply, the Runyon Tree, to the world's attention.

Runyon's involvement started with his colleague, Harvey Stiles, an agricultural expert with significant knowledge about citrus varieties.[559] On April 5, 1929, Stiles catalogued a group of interesting trees with maturing fruit growing next to the Resaca de las Cuates just east of a road that led from Los Fresnos to Olmito.

Stiles' tacit knowledge about citrus cultivation compelled him to examine in detail this group of unfamiliar trees with dark green foliage that showed a similarity to orange or lemon leaves. Stiles focused on marketable citrus varieties, but he turned a herbarium sample of this strange specimen over to Runyon for further study. Stiles also sent a sample to the herbarium at The

University of Texas.[560] Although Runyon did not know it at the time, he had just a few years to examine the original trees at this location. Resaca de los Cuates underwent flood control action that coincided with expanded land clearing for agricultural production in 1933.[561] The small group of Runyon's Esenbeckia first discovered by Stiles was destroyed in the process. Fortunately, Runyon had moved quickly.

Runyon's initial observations determined that the mature tree reaches about thirty feet in height with spreading branches and a closed top. Runyon noted that the tree stays evergreen, but also puts on new leaves each year. He found out that the tree is a member of the citrus family, and in Mexico, where it grew in significantly larger numbers, it was called limoncillo.[562] Unlike orange, lime, and grapefruit trees that produce fleshy, rind-covered fruits, Runyon's Esenbeckia generates an inedible pod-like fruit.

On July 4, 1929, Runyon observed the largest of the trees in bloom. He collected a few flowers for study and dug up a three-foot seedling. He transplanted it the same day in his garden between his home and his studio.

For the rest of his life, unless he was traveling, Runyon observed this tree every day. Despite his care, Runyon's Esenbeckia operated on its schedule. From 1929 to 1940 the seedling grew only to about thirteen feet high. On May 5, 1940, it put out flowers for the first time. He described them as "small, white, paniculate and showy." He noted that his tree bloomed again in November of the same year. But it didn't bloom a third time until June 1943.

The pod-like fruit, from which Runyon detected an orange-like scent, took three to four months to mature and provide seeds. Yet he found the seeds difficult to harvest. At maturity, he noted that the pods ejected its seeds some distance from the tree. Seeds also proved resistant to germination, leading Runyon to believe they had limited viability for propagation.

To help him, Runyon asked like-minded colleagues to search for the tree whenever they visited remote locations in the Valley. That request eventually brought results. On March 20, 1940, Runyon went with W. K. (Kenneth) Clore, a U.S. Department of Agriculture plant specialist, to Barreda Station (now Russelltown). Clore, like Runyon, regularly studied native plants to observe their biological, ecological, and entomological importance to the local area. Clore identified a group of Runyon's Esenbeckia in a thicket near Resaca del Rancho Viejo. Runyon confirmed that identification. Then, on December 9, Runyon observed another group that a colleague found on a ranch eight miles east of Brownsville.

From these new observations, Runyon determined the tree's preferences. He found that Runyon's Esenbeckia in South Texas preferred thickets of the region's unique ebony (*ébano*) tree. Other compatible tree species that frequently appeared nearby were the elm (*olmos*), ash (*fresnos*), and the hackberry (*palo blanco*).

As Runyon recorded each new finding, he shared data with Morton at the Smithsonian. One finding, Runyon noted, was that three smooth and shiny leaves sprouted from each branch, a characteristic he believed made this *Esenbeckia* unique from a similar tree in Mexico. "Another specie(s) grows south of here, *Esenbeckia berlandieri*, and has a cluster of five leaves, instead of three leaves, like my tree," he wrote.[563]

By 1930, Morton determined that the three leaves per stem set Runyon's Tree apart from *E. berlandieri* and another closely related tree, *Esenbeckia pentaphylla*. Morton named Runyon's Tree *Esenbeckia runyonii*.[564] Today, some botanists believe *E. berlandieri* and *E. runyonii* are the same species and use the *runyonii* name as a synonym. Other botanists consider Runyon's Esenbeckia a distinct species.[565]

In Mexico, landowners who know both trees refer to them as different varieties. Mexican landowners call Berlandier's discovery *jopoy*, a word thought to derive from the Yucateco dialect, a Mayan language that is not used in northeastern Mexico. The vernacular name in Tamaulipas for Runyon's Esenbeckia is *limoncillo* while ranchers in the Sierra de Picachos region of Nuevo León to the west call Runyon's Tree *naranjillo*.[566] Some ranchers cut the tree's branches to use as posts for livestock pens. Esenbeckia posts will take root, branch out, and generate leaves. In time, Runyon's Esenbeckia creates a living fence for the rancher. Eco-conscious individuals appreciate the tree as a preferred host plant for larvae of beneficial pollinator insects including the giant swallowtail butterfly.

Runyon's goal in studying the tree was never its name but its preservation. He believed this beautiful species' future could be assured only by educating the public about its potential as a shade variety in the Valley. He feared, though, that the average gardener lacked skills to nurture it. He wanted data to disprove that assumption, so he conducted an inventory of Runyon's Esenbeckia in the wild.

Runyon's studies indicated that in the lower Rio Grande Valley the tree's seeds germinated most efficiently in rich alluvial clay soil near a resaca. Before widespread agricultural land clearing for crops and livestock began around 1904, more of these environments existed throughout the lower Rio Grande Valley. That knowledge led Runyon to theorize that in the last century a much larger population of Runyon's Esenbeckia grew in Texas.

Today, research by Texas State Botanist Chris Best has shown, however, that Runyon's Esenbeckia does not always need optimum conditions to thrive. In areas of Mexico, the tree does well in marginal soil on slopes of rocky debris in moist canyons. Specimens in these environments in Nuevo León have been recorded as tall as sixty feet with a three-foot trunk circumference.[567]

Runyon's theories about Esenbeckia's limitations may have been skewed by the fact that Cameron County could be the species' northernmost range. In fact, that was something Runyon always anticipated. In 1943, he told a U.S. Department of Agriculture horticulturist that Runyon's Esenbeckia "probably is a Mexican species that enters the U.S. in Cameron County, Texas."[568]

The U.S. government also contended that range limit in 1994 after experts at the Native Plant Project, a nonprofit group devoted to preserving and propagating native lower Rio Grande Valley plant life, identified Runyon's Esenbeckia as Texas' rarest tree. Under then-secretary Joe Ideker, the organization asked the federal government to list Runyon's Esenbeckia as an endangered species. Such a listing would promote management and conservation of any Runyon's Esenbeckia found on private land. The U.S. Fish & Wildlife Service rejected the petition in June 1999. One reason was that Mexico's inventory of Runyon's Esenbeckia indicated large populations in the states of Tamaulipas, Nuevo León, San Luis Potosí, Queretaro, and Hidalgo.

North of the Rio Grande, though, Runyon's fears about the endangered future of the species often have come close to reality. "The few original trees will someday in the future be destroyed and the land developed into citrus groves," Runyon predicted. At the same time, Runyon never believed that agricultural expansion and protection of resources had to be a zero sum game if developers, agriculturists, and experts collaborated to preserve rare species.

To enable that collaboration, Runyon turned to experts for assistance. He sent seeds to scientists at The New York Botanical Garden and the Smithsonian, to university experts across the nation, to the Texas Agricultural Experiment Station at Weslaco, to U.S. Department of Agriculture plant specialists in Brownsville and Beltsville, Maryland, other amateur botanists, and even to his children. Yet the results always disappointed. The tree that he transplanted on his property, which still survives ninety years later, and another that his son Delbert grew at his home in west Brownsville, were thought to be the only specimens of Runyon's Esenbeckia in Texas for most of the last half of the twentieth century.[569]

What did save Runyon's Esenbeckia for Texans in this century? It was Runyon's eagerness to transfer botanical knowledge and know-how without limits. In the 1950s, Houston botanist Robert A. Vines made repeated visits to Runyon's Brownsville home to view his gardens. He continued to meet with Amelia about plants even after Runyon's death. Vines included *Esenbeckia runyonii* in his 1960 comprehensive study, *Trees, Shrubs and Woody Vines of the Southwest*.[570]

A quarter century later, Vine's information on Runyon's Esenbeckia intrigued lower Rio Grande Valley horticulturist Mike Heep of Harlingen.

"I spent quite a few weekends walking and sometimes crawling through the woods in southern Cameron County, hoping to find *Esenbeckia* trees," he said.

His brother, Don, of San Antonio, in November 1984, finally located two specimens of Runyon's Esenbeckia in the wild. The habitat matched Runyon's description: the two trees were among a thicket of woody trees, growing in soil near Resaca del Rancho Viejo, south of San Benito. Mike discovered a third Runyon's Esenbeckia the next day. The U.S. Fish & Wildlife Service later purchased the property, and in 2018 fifteen *Esenbeckia runyonii* grow in the Ranchito tract of the Lower Rio Grande Valley National Wildlife Refuge in Cameron County.

The prized and protected population exists on just one acre of land. Although safe from development, the entire stand could be wiped out by a hurricane, tornado, flood, severe freeze, or wildfire.

Preservation of the species, in the unique ecosystem of the lower Rio Grande Valley, now falls on the current-day residents, the process Runyon long ago envisioned.

Heep, at his Valley nursery, is among those residents who contribute to a more permanent solution every day. Since 1985, he and a colleague have germinated seeds collected from that group of trees that, in turn, have resulted in more trees. "I was able to sprout about 350 (seedlings), of which most are here at our nursery," Heep said. "The Gladys Porter Zoo has purchased some from us, and they have two nice specimens."

Heep said the trees grow best if the soil is allowed to dry somewhat between waterings. That characteristic makes Runyon's Esenbeckia a good landscape choice in subtropical regions where water supplies are at risk.[571]

In 1994 and 1995, Texas State Botanist Chris Best attacked the problem of limited genetic diversity within the South Texas population of Runyon's Esenbeckia. With assistance from Santos Salgado Jacobo of Rio Bravo, Tamaulipas, a forester with Mexico's Secretaria de Medio Ambiente y Recursos Naturales, Best received permission from two ranch owners in the Sierra de Picachos near Monterrey to collect seeds from diverse populations of Runyon's Esenbeckia. Best also received permits from USDA's Animal and Plant Health Inspection Service to import the seeds into the U.S.

The seeds germinated at a nursery at the Santa Ana National Wildlife Refuge in Hidalgo County. Best's team then planted the seedlings in three separate National Wildlife Refuge tracts: Resaca de los Fresnos, about four miles southwest of La Feria; Villa Nueva, on U.S. 281 west of Brownsville; and Phillips Banco, north of the levee on U.S. 281 west of Brownsville.

Best said of the thirty-one Runyon's Esenbeckia his group planted, twenty-eight were alive in 2017 although others had survived but had not been counted. "They ranged in height from zero point three to two meters (about one foot to six and a half feet), and averaged zero point ninety-nine meters (three and a quarter feet)."

Even the well-studied Runyon's Esenbeckia at the longtime Runyon residence near downtown Brownsville continues to do its part, Best said. That original Runyon Tree provided seeds that generated two other Runyon's Esenbeckias that now grace an area near the visitor's center at the Santa Ana NWR in Hidalgo County. This Texas seedstock grows with several other *Esenbeckia runyonii* trees that Best propagated from the Sierra de Picachos seeds.

Thanks to these many champions who have continued to expand on early knowledge generated about Texas' rarest tree, the borderlands now has a powerful success story of conservation and survival to relate to the four hundred thousand ecotourists who visit each year and spend between $125 million and $150 million annually to observe and conserve the region's unique ecology.[572] Those champions' efforts demonstrate the power of entrepreneurial succession at its most complete. It brings fulfillment to Runyon's wish that this rare species remains a valued part of the lower Rio Grande Valley native flora far into the future.

Chapter 22
The Misty Figure

Newman's competitive advantage in opening automobile routes in Mexico did not last long. As automobile numbers grew along the border, Newman had no way to erect barriers to new entrants. In essence, the routes he trailblazed made possible a cottage industry for Mexican chauffeurs who displaced his abilities. So many drivers emerged that customers soon had the bargaining edge.[573] In short, by 1920 there was no profit potential for Newman in automobiles.

His value to the U.S. intelligence service faded about the same time. With cessation of the bandit battles, U.S. focus on the European theater of World War I, withdrawal of troops from the Texas border, and emergence of new Mexican leaders, interest by U.S. government agencies for intelligence shifted from Tamaulipas to the national capital at Mexico City.

Even so, Newman remained known to federal investigators. In January 1918, as World War I began its last year, Arthur, then living in San Antonio, reported to the U.S. Bureau of Investigation that he was suspicious of a German immigrant who had leased thirty-six acres of Cameron County land from Arthur's father-in-law, T. J. Lawson. The acreage was on the Rio Grande, just above a vital pumping station used for agricultural irrigation.

The German managed a creamery and dairy operation in Brownsville, but Arthur suspected he came to the lower Rio Grande Valley a year earlier for another purpose. Arthur believed the immigrant leased the land to communicate with, and to allow illegal entry to, German government agents operating out of northeastern Mexico. The Cameron County land was heavily brush-infested and Arthur said it concealed anyone crossing from Mexico.

When Lawson tried to regain possession of the land from the German, Arthur told the investigator that the lessee offered to pay more. Arthur also noted that the German had not improved the property and did not use the acreage for anything except to shelter his family in its house.

No further action exists on Arthur's complaint. However, the investigator's typed comments note Arthur's relationship to Prentice: "Informant has abrother (sic) living at Brownsville, this brother's name being P. A. Newman."[574]

In reality, Prentice stayed in contact with agents because intelligence work was hard to let go. His quest to gather information had taken him often to Matamoros' night district. Newman found there a steady and constant buzz of activity that revealed secrets. When the intrigue faded, Newman followed old habits. He continued to spend more time *en el otro lado* than he did in his garage business. His frequent absences caused his garage business to decline, and his machinist reputation suffered from unmet customer promises.

By the end of 1922, the year Newman co-developed an innovative rotary drill for oil and water wells, the creative forces had largely ceased. Aviation technology had advanced far beyond his capabilities. His aeroplane's wings were the only remaining link to his past. He stowed them in the pier-and-beam crawl space under his rented house at 107 W. St. Charles Street, a metaphor for dreams that no longer flew.[575]

Newman throughout his life had turned to Arthur for support when faced with adversity. He received a boost when Arthur moved his family back to Brownsville in 1928. By 1929, Arthur established a separate garage specializing in carburetor and ignition repairs for automobiles. He placed his shop at the rear of Bell Service Station, a company that provided service and fuel for airplanes. It was located at the Brownsville airport that opened that year as the international gateway for Pan American Airways flights to Latin America. The airport was a little over five miles from downtown Brownsville, where Prentice operated his garage.[576] The distance ensured the two garages did not compete for customers.

Arthur's reason for returning to Brownsville was so his son, Malcolm Arthur (Boy) Newman Jr., could play football for the coach at Brownsville High School. It was a good move for Valley athletics as Boy, even though slightly built, earned legendary status as the best quarterback in the history of Valley football through his high school and junior college years. Boy later played at the University of Southern California before finishing out his college career in 1932 as a walk-on for The University of Texas Longhorns.[577]

After his son's storied football career, Arthur moved to his farm at Pettus, Texas, that he had bought in 1927. There he not only worked on automobiles and machinery, but he became one of the area's leading farmers and ranchers. Like his brother, Arthur held on to a memento of those days of Texas' first aeroplanes. A large propeller blade hung for many years in his barn.

P. A. Newman, about 1930. Lorraine Owens Family Papers.

In 1941, doctors diagnosed Arthur with cancer. He moved briefly to Gonzales, then to Houston to be near his daughter's family, and finally to Aransas Pass. Arthur died in 1943 in a Corpus Christi hospital at the age of sixty-six.[578]

As Prentice's absences picked up after Arthur left, his wife physically broke. Pearl had supported her husband in moves to Fort Worth, Dallas, San Antonio, and, finally, Brownsville. She stood by him during his murder trial appearances in Hallettsville. She dissented but stayed with Newman when he dropped religion. She was there for his bold, inventive, yet ultimately inadequate efforts to equal or surpass the Wright brothers in aviation.

Yet Pearl could not tolerate his frequent absences. She turned to the message of the Jehovah Witnesses as a salve. Even with that solace, her despair at times caused her to wander barefoot through Brownsville streets, behavior that concerned family, neighbors, and friends. The conflict eventually wore Pearl down. She and Newman became estranged.[579]

Newman's aviation fame had faded by then with most borderlands citizens. About once a decade, though, reporters revisited his accomplishments in flight technology. These sporadic articles told new readers throughout Texas how Newman fell just short of making aviation history. They chronicled how Brownsville briefly became aviation's technology incubator for all the Americas south of Kitty Hawk. The readers discovered that Newman was a "quiet, kindly man" who enjoyed sitting on his porch and looking up at the sky and seeing his monoplane innovation become the industry standard.[580]

Newman, though, never totally distanced himself from aviation. He enjoyed a vicarious association with evolving technology through a son-in-law.

Newman's daughter, Lillian, on June 3, 1933, married William J. Earle, who had worked at the Brownsville airport since 1929. Earle was manager of the propeller overhaul department for Pan American Airways.[581]

In 1940, Pan Am transferred Earle and his family to Guatemala. Then around 1945, the Earles were sent to Honduras. For the next seven years, Earle worked in Tegucigalpa as maintenance supervisor for SAHSA Airlines, a Pan Am subsidiary.[582]

The chance to join his daughter's family in both countries appealed to Newman's love for Hispanic culture. His health had begun to fail him by then, and he had trouble walking. Labor in his garages had become difficult. Around 1940 Newman elected to turn his Brownsville garage over to his oldest son, P. A. Newman Jr., and join the Earles in Central America. The younger Newman, then working as a machinist in the Philadelphia Naval Shipyard, drove his wife, Elaine, from Pennsylvania all the way to the tip of Texas to take over the business. Once they arrived, however, the garage had sold. Prentice Jr. and his wife then moved to San Antonio, where he accepted a position at Kelly Air Field, later Kelly Air Force Base.[583]

During Newman's years in Central America, he would return occasionally to the Valley to visit his youngest son, Thomas Cline, in Brownsville, or Ethelyne, who had married J. L. Dahnke of Edinburg. On one such visit in 1953, Newman received a burst of recognition that renewed his aviation fame for a short time in the region. Edinburg High School student Robert Earl Good had to write a paper on Rio Grande Valley pioneer aviators. Good contacted *The Brownsville Herald* to ask if anyone remembered "a certain man who made his own plane and learned to fly it in Brownsville." William Bellinghausen in Port Isabel responded that he remembered Newman's efforts: "Mr. Newman built and flew planes. That's where Brownsville was first started on planes, and I do believe they had a company."

That was all news to the newspaper, showing how elusive both explicit and tacit knowledge can be when no one transfers it. A columnist asked: "And just what 'Mr. Newman' was that?" In the next few days, other readers who remembered Newman pointed out that he now lived in Honduras. From their comments, the columnist inferred that Newman "was a misty figure" in the history of Brownsville.[584]

Yet while the hubbub took place, Newman was in town on one of his occasional visits with his son. Newman contacted the columnist and Good and provided more information. Good wrote an essay on Newman that ran the next year in the Texas State Historical Association's *Junior Historian*.[585]

In 1954, Earle died in Honduras. Newman, his own health poor, returned to Texas for good. He lived briefly in Kingsville with his nephew, Boy Newman, and then in 1955 moved to San Antonio to live with his son, P. A. Jr., and his family. It was the last move for the misty figure.

Chapter 23
Texas Cacti and the Palm Grove

As entrepreneur, Runyon established a vision at the start of each venture. For photography, it was to become the region's pre-eminent commercial photographer through postcard sales. He achieved that goal before popular trends made postcards less fashionable. As a merchant, he wanted to own the go-to place for postcards and curios for Matamoros tourists. He made more money in this endeavor than anything else he tried.

When it came to botany, his vision was to raise scientists' and his neighbors' awareness of the Rio Grande Valley's amazing flora by identifying, classifying, recording, and describing every plant native to the region. He would recommit to this vision periodically beginning with his first collected specimens in 1920. In 1960, after more than forty years of plant study, Runyon said his "Annotated List of The Flora of The Lower Rio Grande Valley of Texas" was still being compiled.[586]

Runyon never settled upon the compilation's format. In 1942, in correspondence with Ladislaus Cutak, the principal researcher at the Missouri Botanical Garden in St. Louis, Runyon stated that he was "now engaged, in my spare time, in cataloguing the native plants of the Lower Rio Grande Valley of Texas." In 1946, he repeated this goal to a reporter, and believed his catalogue could be published, although he added he did not expect to complete the compilation soon.[587] A printed volume remained a long-term goal. He had seen the value of botanical references to both science and the common man by collaborating with other researchers on their editorial and graphics.

His first such experience was the few synopses and photographs he contributed to *The Cactaceae*. Runyon next accepted a collaboration request in the late 1920s on a study of Texas cacti species. The invitation came from Ellen Schulz Quillin, director of the Witte Museum in San Antonio. In 1931, the Texas Academy of Science published their book, *Texas Cacti*, with a run of 2,500 copies.[588]

The two authors initially intended this book as the first of a series of works on plants of the lower Rio Grande Valley. Neither Quillin nor Runyon received compensation, but even knowing that deficiency at the outset, the partnership fell short of what Runyon anticipated.

Runyon's initial charge was to write popular descriptions of all cactus species in the book except for the *Opuntias*—the prickly pear genus of cacti. Quillin also wanted to use Runyon's cacti photographs. Runyon later had to write the descriptions for the *Opuntias* when another researcher begged off.

Quillin's role was to edit the book for style and grammar. She was to use technical descriptions from *The Cactaceae*. Runyon had gained permission from The Carnegie Institution to use that copy.

Runyon and Quillin spent the last part of the 1920s working on this first comprehensive study of the state's cactus species. Runyon's daughter, Amali, remembered Quillin traveling to the Runyon home in Brownsville to draw upon Runyon's expertise during the collaboration. These visits included field trips to see the subject cacti in their native habitat.

"We rarely saw women wearing men's trousers in Brownsville," Amali said, "so she (Quillin) drew our attention from the moment she arrived. I remember she gave me a dime one time when we were all riding in Daddy's Ford to get cactus pictures."[589]

That was all the money the Runyon family made from this costly project, however. Runyon quickly became concerned over investment of expense, time, effort, and expertise in the book. In addition to his specified roles, he had to serve as the authors' business manager. He insisted that he and Quillin receive a contract from the Texas Academy. The authors signed it on March 17, 1930, just days before the manuscript went to press, but only after Runyon had ensured that he and Quillin maintained copyright privileges.

After publication, Runyon became irritated when academy members misconstrued his intellectual property advocacy as an attempt to profit from the work, a misconception he believed Quillin helped spread. Runyon insisted he was not driven by money, especially since a scholarly cactus study was too narrow to earn financial return.

"…(A)ll I want is proper credit for what I have done and not profits as Mrs. Quillin has made it appear," he told the academy president.

Runyon added that he salvaged the project after deciding Quillin did not have the expertise.

> "Mrs. Quillin started to write a book on cacti and after beginning the work in conjunction with a young man at Austin, she found out that it was not a pic-nic

(sic) *and could make no head way with the work, so she wrote to me, frankly stating that she knew nothing about cacti and ask*(ed) *me to join her in the work."*

Runyon fretted that Quillin, the scientist, projected herself as the author, and Runyon, the amateur cactus expert, merely as the book's photographer. His defense seems to have paid off as a book review published forty days after his letter to the academy president identified Quillin as a researcher and Runyon as "one of the foremost authorities of cacti in the world and (who) has nine plants named for him which he found and classified for the science of botany in the Rio Grande section." In the end, the book's printer returned all the halftone cuts to Runyon so they could not reuse his art. Although Quillin suggested a study of trees as their next collaboration, Runyon moved on to other priorities.[590]

It was 1947 before Runyon published his next work, *Vernacular Names Of Plants Indigenous To The Lower Rio Grande Valley Of Texas*. He considered this booklet his first effort in categorizing the region's flora. Its contents catalogued the core of native plants that he believed vital for lower Rio Grande Valley residents to recognize and propagate.

The booklet's organization shows Runyon's desire to preserve native plants' common names. He was concerned that vernacular names were dying away as development destroyed the natives' ancient habitat and allowed "weedy herbs" to replace them. Runyon wanted his readers to understand how to tie its common name, that he considered keys to each plants' utility, to its Latin family, genus, and species. Understanding each species' utility brought it closer to an ensured existence.

"The aborigines, through their long association with the plants, learned their uses and named each useful plant a name, which has a significant meaning in their language," Runyon said. "In many instances, these same Indian names are still in use by the native people, or at least in a modified form."

Runyon sometimes told the story of how Amelia once wanted to propagate a tree. She cut off a branch and stuck it in their garden with hopes that it would grow roots. To support the new branch, she propped it with a stick. Days later, Runyon inspected the experiment and found out that the prop was leafing out while the desired branch had withered. He teased her about her "green thumb" from that point on.

But that green thumb proved invaluable to him in finishing his booklet on local plants. He could not have performed his botanical research without her help. In this project and many others, Amelia's expertise with plants complemented her husband's explicit and tacit knowledge.

Amelia grew up using native plants for food or healing so she was more than capable to assist Runyon in matching the vernacular name to the scientific name. With her knowledge, Runyon cross-indexed more than 220 plants in a twenty-four page published compilation.[591]

With this booklet, Runyon changed his position on intellectual property in order to achieve wider awareness and transfer of knowledge. Although Runyon copyrighted the creation, he granted broad license to botanists, students, universities, and botanical gardens to reproduce the material in any form without permission.[592]

Another channel Runyon employed to extend knowledge about native plants was guest columns for *The Brownsville News*, a periodical he published for a few years. He also provided articles to other newspapers and general interest publications including *Monty's Monthly*, a periodical that focused on lower Rio Grande Valley topics. Yet, in aggregate, *Texas Cacti*, *Vernacular Names of Plants*, his columns, articles, speeches, and letters covered just a few hundred species of the thousands of plants that he studied. Although he never abandoned the idea of publishing a comprehensive catalogue of the region's plants, the two dimensions of the published page lacked the scope of his vision. He collected his plants in the real world so his true comprehensive catalogue eventually became his three-dimensional herbarium.

In time, Runyon understood that he could promote native plants more efficiently through actions and behavior than he could through published volumes. That understanding eventually drew him to seek public office. But he developed his approach as a private citizen first.

One of Runyon's far-reaching advocacies began as soon as he arrived in the region.

Sabal texana, Texas' only native palm, had enchanted Runyon since his first minutes in Brownsville in February 1909. In prehistory, this species ruled the coastal landscape of the lower Rio Grande Valley. Modern surveys indicate that the palm may have ranged as far as today's Jackson and Victoria counties two hundred miles north of the lower Rio Grande Valley.[593] The Mexican-United States Boundary Commission's naturalists estimated the *Sabal texana* habitat at about eighty miles from the Rio Grande north toward the coast. Either of those estimations were far more vast than what Runyon observed in the Valley in 1909.

Runyon's analysis of *Sabal texana* confirmed that its existence first became threatened through agricultural land clearing that began around 1904 after completion of the terminal railroad depot in Brownsville.[594] Transportation technology had a tragic effect on the palm because it generated new agricultural opportunities that required widespread removal of trees and understory vegetation. By 1920 the range of *Sabal texana* was confined to a few locations southeast of Brownsville next to the Rio Grande but miles inland from its traditional reach toward the Gulf of Mexico. The palm's population density at each location varied from just a few trees to some beautifully lush but geographically limited groves. On the other side of the river, he estimated Mexico held on to about the same range.

Runyon identified palm groves in Cameron County on both the Civil War-era Brulay Plantation as well as the nearby Piper Plantation. Other identified locations included Rancho El Salado, ten miles below Brownsville, the Burns Ranch near San Rafael, and the Grover Singer Ranch at Southmost.

Just adjacent to the Singer Ranch was the Rabb Plantation that Runyon considered the palm's last jewel. The Rabb property along the Rio Grande supported what Runyon believed was the closest representation of how the lower Rio Grande Valley appeared when Indians were sole inhabitants north of the river.

The Rabb Plantation was a rare property. Frank Rabb was a second cousin once removed to Prentice and Arthur Newman as all three descended from William and Mary Smalley Rabb. In 1887, Rabb married Lillian M. Starck, the daughter of María Vicenta Kenedy Starck who had inherited the twenty thousand-acre Rancho San Tomás from her mother, the former Petra Vela, the wife of rancher Mifflin Kenedy.

Rabb, the son-in-law, received one-half undivided interest in Rancho San Tomás. As owner, Rabb oversaw construction of a stately Queen Anne-style mansion on the property. He also supervised the plantation's cotton, sugarcane, and bean operations. Runyon's photographs of Rabb's farmland in the early 1900s show he also grew cabbage and corn on his property. Interestingly, Runyon's farming photographs reveal that Rabb's practice was rarely to clear-cut his land for crops. He often left individual palms growing undisturbed between crop rows. For Runyon, though, Rabb's most impactful land management practice was preserving a significant portion of the property's native palm grove from any disturbance.[595]

Runyon visited this grove frequently throughout his six decades in the lower Rio Grande Valley. Even before 1920, he and Amelia took Willie, Lillie, Amali, and Virginia to Rabb's property for weekend outings. There, Runyon utilized the varied tropical backgrounds and lighting to test new photography techniques with his children as subjects.[596]

For his botanical pursuits, the palm grove offered Runyon a pristine habitat from which to study, classify, and identify *Sabal texana* and other diverse native plants that thrived under the palms' subtropical influence. One time, in mid-December 1939, he recorded *Sabal texana* in mature fruit, *Iresine palmeri* (Palmer's bloodleaf) in flower, and a legume (*Bradburya virginiana*) in fruit all at the same time. Runyon once estimated that he had collected and identified at least sixty rare specimens just at the Rabb Palm Grove. He considered the property the lower Rio Grande Valley's most valuable plot of land because of the "many tropical plants growing in the grove, that have never been found any other place in this region of South Texas."[597]

Runyon and Rabb had a complex relationship. In 1919, Runyon blamed Rabb, at the time holding office as the powerful collector of customs, for orchestrating his arrest for smuggling. Yet the two men always seemed in harmony about the need to preserve the palms. When plant scientists visited Runyon, he asked for, and always received, Rabb's permission to bring the experts to the grove.[598]

In 1925, Runyon hosted three such prestigious botanists on a milestone visit. Runyon explained the grove's value to experts Liberty Hyde Bailey of Cornell University, Edgar Theodore Wherry of the Smithsonian, and John Kunkel Small of The New York Botanical Garden. In 1927, Small published a paper based on that visit. His article described the native palm's shrinking range by using significant data documented through Runyon's studies. Small's article also used Runyon's photographs, included his biography, and listed his botanical accomplishments to date. That scientific article both furthered Runyon's botanical credentials and brought needed attention to Texas' native palm within the environmental world.[599]

A year later, Runyon hosted Bailey, who this time came as president of the American Association for the Advancement of Science, on another inspection of the grove. Bailey asked Runyon to accompany him again on a visit to the grove on April 22, 1940.[600]

Each authority that Runyon hosted at the grove expanded international understanding of the native palm's true last preserve and its value to mankind. The experts' interest, in turn, inspired Runyon to amplify his own palm studies that built on knowledge generated by two palm researchers of the previous century. W. C. Gorgas, a yellow fever scientist and U.S. Army surgeon general, conducted pioneer studies into *Sabal texana* when stationed at Fort Brown from 1882-1884. He collaborated with famed botanist C. S. Sargent of Massachusetts. Sargent's analysis of the Sabal palm's commercial utility influenced much of Runyon's later conclusions about the palm's high value potential to the local economy.[601]

Runyon's personal expanded study examined the palm holistically from its propagation to its economic utility. He understood that his neighbors had given the species the nickname of Rio Grande palmetto, but he agreed with Bailey that the vernacular name that evoked the comprehensive benefits of *Sabal texana* was palma de micharos. Runyon said the term combined the Spanish word for palm with the Indian name for its "delicious" and "date-like" fruit. Consumer demand for the micharos in the wet markets of Matamoros and Brownsville always impressed him.

As to propagation, Runyon believed seed-grown palms were usually successful, but that transplants done without removal of a large ball of earth around its roots often failed. He found that early winter, when the palm was dormant, was the best season for transplants.[602]

For decades, Runyon personally planted the palm in every possible location, including "a few thousand *Sabal texana* seedlings along the Resaca in the City Limits."[603] He wanted residents to do the same in their yards. In a discussion with the Weslaco director of the Texas Agricultural Experiment Station, Runyon lamented that the imported *Washingtonia robusta* had become the variety of choice for many Valley landscape gardeners.

"The Washington is of quick growth and easy to transplant, which makes it an ideal palm for commercial use, but in the long run the *Sabal texana* is undoubtedly the best," Runyon argued. "My opinion is that the *W. robusta* grows too tall to stand strong winds and the tall trees are ugly in appearance."[604]

In a presentation to the Kiwanis Club, Runyon again explained plant utility as the key to the Sabal palm's assured existence. He urged local entrepreneurs to create multiple products from the native palm.

> "The Rio Grande Palmetto also has an economic value that should not be overlooked. The trunks make excellent fence posts and last for many years when in contact with the earth. The fruit is edible and finds a ready sale in our own market. The leaves produce the best material for hat braid, and the braid produces a high grade hat. It is a pity that the poor people of this region are not taught the process of making hat braid. This would lessen the relief problem in our city. The leaves are also used extensively to cover the small 'Jacals' and for ornamental thatch roofs."[605]

Runyon long advocated for the grove to go under public ownership to maintain its integrity as nexus of the native palm's viability. Rabb actually had offered the grove to the federal government as a national park as early as 1917, but received no action. Dr. Tharp helped Runyon advocate establishment of a national park at the grove in 1922 but that also led nowhere. Runyon continued the cause and worked on it in every decade. The national awareness Runyon stirred up in the botanical science community made it difficult for Rabb ever to waver on preserving the grove. Yet Rabb, an inveterate businessman, did change his approach even if he did not change his mind.

Botanist David Fairchild of Coconut Grove, Florida, visited the grove with sculptor Gutzon Borglum in the early 1930s, years before the artist started on Mount Rushmore. Later, Fairchild told Runyon that he and Borglum asked Rabb about securing the grove's future.

"Rabb said he would give the grove for a National Monument if he would be permitted to build and run a hotel in it and we said good bye to him and left," Fairchild told Runyon.

After Rabb divorced his wife, he married Margaret McCormick in 1932. Rabb died that same year and the estate passed to the second Mrs. Rabb. Runyon impressed upon her stewardship the continued need to preserve the grove. She assured Runyon "that the trees will not be disturbed so long as she owns the land." In the mid-1940s, it looked as if the transfer to a government park would occur. Fairchild wrote Runyon congratulating him that the grove "has come into hands that will preserve the beautiful *Sabals* for perhaps centuries to come."[606]

Yet the transfer plans fell through again.

Runyon, by the late 1950s, became deeply concerned about the grove's future when he noticed that plant diversity had diminished. He had not made a major botanical discovery for years and worried that many rare birds and wildlife once drawn to the grove for food and shelter also had disappeared.[607] The grove's preservation had to wait until 1972 when the National Audubon Society purchased the palm grove as a wildlife sanctuary for an undisclosed amount. The grove's stewardship changed again in 2010 when The Gorgas Science Foundation, a nonprofit conservation group, leased the sanctuary. The foundation preserves the native palm's habitat on the Rio Grande and has restored the old plantation house. Fittingly, the foundation's participation returned Gorgas' name to the Sabal Palm Sanctuary more than 125 years after his research aided some of Runyon's own studies.[608]

Runyon died four years before the grove management first fell to nonprofit groups. Yet he would have seen the change of stewardship favorably. He believed high awareness of the grove's uniqueness within the Valley's ecosystem—whether through profit or nonprofit—was the path to assuring its future.

The following tables provide an incomplete look at the scope of plant species that Robert Runyon collected, which either generated a new published study by the science community or added information to existing science knowledge. The authors of the studies and journals in which they appeared are included in the tables using the recognized botanical abbreviations. Other data includes each specific published article's bibliographic data, graphics (if any), and date of publication. The source for this information is Tropicos® (www.tropicos.org) and The International Plant Names Index (www.ipni.org).

Runyon Epithets — Vascular Plants								
Family	Genus	Epithet(s)	Author	Publication	Volume	Page	Illustration	Publication Year
Acanthaceae	*Justicia*	*runyonii*	Small	*Addisonia*	15	29	Pl 495	1930
Acanthaceae	*Ruellia*	*runyonii*	Tharp & F.A.Barkley	*Amer. Midl. Naturalist*	42	52	fig. 23	1949
Agavaceae	*Runyonia*		Rose	*Addisonia*	7	39		1922
Agavaceae	*Polianthes*	*runyonii*	Shinners	*Sida*	2	335		1966
Alliaceae	*Allium*	*runyonii*	Ownbey	*Res. Stud. State Coll. Wash.*	18	198		1951
Asteraceae	*Helianthus*	*debilis* Nutt. subsp. *runyonii*	Heiser	*Madroño*	13	161		1956
Cactaceae	*Coryphantha*	*runyonii*	Britton & Rose	*Cactaceae* (Britton & Rose)	4	26	(t. 1, fig. 1).	1923
Cactaceae	*Echinocereus*	*runyonii*	Orcutt	*Cactography*	5			1926
Cactaceae	*Escobaria*	*runyonii*	Britton & Rose	*Cactaceae* (Britton & Rose)	4	55	fig. 53	1923
Cactaceae	*Neomammillaria*	*runyonii*	Britton & Rose	*Cactaceae* (Britton & Rose)	4	81	Plate 10, 2	1923
Convolvulaceae	*Cuscuta*	*runyonii*	Yunck.	*Bull. Torrey Bot. Club*	69	541	fig. 1	1942
Crassulaceae	*Echeveria*	*runyonii*	Rose ex E.Walther	*Cact. Succ. J. (Los Angeles)*	7	69		1935
Cyperaceae	*Cyperus*	*aristatus* var. *runyonii*	O'Neill	*Rhodora*	44	56		1942
Fabaceae	*Casparia*	*runyonii*	Britton & Rose	*N. Amer. Fl.*	23 (4)	210		1930
Lamiaceae	*Scutellaria*	*drummondii* var. *runyonii*	B.L.Turner	*Phytologia*	76	365	fig. 1	1994
Poaceae	*Digitaria*	*runyonii*	Hitchc.	*J. Wash. Acad. Sci.*	23	455		1933
Rutaceae	*Esenbeckia*	*runyonii*	C.V.Morton	*J. Wash. Acad. Sci.*	20	136		1930
Urticaceae	*Urtica*	*chamaedryoides* var. *runyonii*	Correll	*Wrightia*	3	129		1965
Verbenaceae	*Verbena*	*runyonii*	Moldenke	*Phytologia*	2	25		1941
Verbenaceae	*Verbena*	*runyonii* Moldenke f. *rosiflora*	L.I.Davis	*Nature Leafl. Lower Rio Grande Valley Nat. Club*	No. 2 (4)			1945
Non-Vascular Plant (Moss)								
Pottiaceae	*Acaulon*	*runyonii*	Grout	*Bryologist*	48	25		1925
Other Plants In Which Published Study Names Robert Runyon as "Collector"								
Amaryllidaceae	*Cooperia*	*smallii*	Alexander	*Addisonia*	21 (1)	7	Pl. 676	1939
Asteraceae	*Grindelia*	*oolepis*	S. F. Blake	*Proc. Biol. Soc. Washington*	41	139		1928
Brassicaceae	*Selenia*	*grandis*	R.F. Martin	*Rhodora*	40 (472)	183		1938
Euphorbiaceae	*Euphorbia*	*innocua*	Wheeler	*Contr. Gray Herb.*	127	62	Pl. 3	1939
Rosaceae	*Rubus*	*riograndis*	L.H. Bailey	*Gentes Herbarum*	5 (4)	209	f. 87	1941

Chapter 24
Brownsville's Stormy Petrel

The untapped value network that native plant opportunities offered to Rio Grande Valley residents began to jell in Runyon's entrepreneurial mind by the mid-1930s. It was the era when he received letters bragging on Florida's beauty from aunts, uncles, and cousins who had left Kentucky and West Virginia for the Sunshine State to avoid cold winter weather.[609]

Runyon never traveled to either Florida or California. But when he discussed those regions with botanists who had lived and studied there, including Fairchild, they convinced him that the lower Rio Grande Valley, the Gulf Coast, and Brownsville had weather and beautiful subtropical native plants that rivaled any other region.

"The Valley flora is not as showy as that in Florida," Runyon admitted, "but from a botanical standpoint it is extremely interesting because of the number of plants that have commercial value. A host have medicinal properties; and, in almost all plant groups, this area has something new."[610]

That "something new" meant visitors to Brownsville could see and touch semitropical treasures from the jungles and forests of northeastern Mexico without ever leaving the United States. As the lower Rio Grande Valley is the northernmost range of many unique subtropical plants and wildlife native to Mexico, it offers natural diversity other states cannot match. In Runyon's view, if the lower Rio Grande Valley promoted its unique native trees and flowers—and the wildlife and insect life they support—all of which are not found elsewhere in the United States—the region could give the other coasts a run for their tourist dollars.

In essence, Runyon had conceived an ideal circular economy business model—one that was renewable, brought value to the public, and provided businesses in the lower Rio Grande Valley with competitive advantages against their California and Florida counterparts.

As one Valley editor once wrote about Runyon's concept:

"That isn't the sentimental stuff of Ferdinand the Bull's love of flowers or love of the beauties of nature but is a belief that beautification pays cash dividends which are paid through for rental of houses, purchases in stores, patronizing of hotels and restaurants, theatres and contributions, through friendship to public or semi-public funds."[611]

Runyon, though, could only do so much as a private citizen. He needed support from local government to further his plan. And to secure that support he needed to follow his lifelong dream to become a politician.

Runyon had worked within the election process his whole life. Within a year of marrying Amelia, he jumped right into Texas politics in February 1914 as an election judge. For each of the next fifty-two years, Runyon continuously served his Democratic Party as county chairman, election judge, presiding judge, supervisor, or clerk.[612]

So, Runyon seemed well positioned to enter politics as a candidate for public office. Even his political philosophy was a plus. Runyon was an old-school Democrat who believed in an ethical, well-managed government that espoused lower taxes and demanded bureaucratic efficiency.

Yet the Brownsville political flow, under its boss-run rule legacy, was a difficult current in which to leap and survive. Runyon found out early that local successful politicians did not come from independent entrepreneurs like him. They came from what locals called the elite business class.

After the April 1912 election, the first Texas campaign in which Runyon actively supported candidates, all of whom lost, Runyon was among five hundred persons who attended his group's election post-mortem. The newspaper coverage said Runyon told the group that he was from old Kentucky "where they say politics are the d_____." It was a line he paraphrased from "In Kentucky," a famous poem by James Mulligan that, unlike the Brownsville newspaper censor, always used the full word. Nonetheless, to readers of the article, Runyon's meaning was clear. He said it was the "'crookedest election' he had ever seen."[613]

Over the next decade Runyon monitored how local factions mobilized their voters. By the mid-1930s, Runyon had formulated his own political philosophy for Brownsville that revolved around the concept of "civic betterment." The philosophy advocated a more beautiful city to generate revenue from more tourists and to draw new residents to Brownsville. Runyon theorized that increased tourist spending, combined with new residents paying property taxes, would result in less frequent tax increases and improved property appraisal management. The philosophy also held that the city had to pare its budget and watch unnecessary spending.

In 1935, Runyon ran for a city commission seat on a slate of local Democratic merchants headed by mayoral candidate Fausto Yturria. Runyon's political emergence worried the elite businessmen. Their leader, R. B. Creager, a seasoned political boss on the national scene, publicly belittled Runyon's business accomplishments.

"Robert Runyon," Creager said, "is a pain in the neck." Creager then changed body parts and said Runyon's name would be more descriptive if a "'B' were substituted for the 'R.'"

In his speech, Creager said Runyon's sole accomplishment was keeping his Model T Ford in working condition in order to have someone drive him daily to The Basket Place over the international bridge. Creager added: "He makes his living in Matamoros by selling picture cards and watered perfume to suckered tourists."

Creager also alleged that Runyon financed his business by "mulcting Brownsville citizens of $4,700" received in the 1929 copyright infringement settlement with the city. Creager did not mention that the city paid him several thousand dollars as its attorney in the case.[614]

Runyon lost the election for his seat. Yturria forced a runoff for the mayor's position, but incumbent R. B. Rentfro won.[615]

Runyon began laying the foundation for another campaign in summer 1936. He networked with Democrats from throughout the Valley who shared his philosophy. In communications to voters, Runyon told citizens to take control of their city. "Break the chain" in order to "break the Machine," he said. "...(R)e-establish free representative, progressive county and city governments. It means the abolition of discord and hatred and the establishment of co-operation and good will between the square dealing citizens of Brownsville and Cameron County as a whole."[616]

Runyon filed for mayor in the 1937 election under a fresh umbrella called the Greater Brownsville Party. The party's platform stood for lower property and business taxes, a smaller bureaucracy, more efficient city utilities, reduced city indebtedness, and enhanced commercial opportunities for the Port of Brownsville. Runyon's platform included elements of civic betterment as it committed the mayor's office to beautifying parks. In addition, Runyon advocated a lower tax assessment for any homes and businesses with attractive lawns and gardens since they contributed to Brownsville's goal to be a beautiful city.[617]

Runyon lost the mayoral election to incumbent Rentfro by a razor-thin margin on December 14, 1937, yet voters elected the remainder of his slate to the city commission.[618] The outcome convinced Runyon that the system was rigged. As he wrote a cousin:

> *"I was defeated by thirty-three votes for mayor, but my entire ticket for commissioners was elected; and I consider it a great victory even though I, myself, lost. At the last when they* [the elite businessmen cabal] *saw the tide was against them, they concentrated against me and the thirty-three majority that Mayor Rentfro received are all illegal votes. However, it will turn out all right in the long-run. My Commissioners will take office on the 24th of December. They have offered me the position of City Manager. It is more important than the Mayor's job and carries a larger salary."*[619]

Runyon proved a pragmatic city official. One of his first actions was to cut his city salary in half, and he urged the commissioners and mayor to do the same.[620] Yet Runyon also angered easily. Brownsville historians William L. Adams and Anthony K. Knopp called him "Principled but temperamental."[621] His contemporary, B. C. Tharp at The University of Texas, termed him Brownsville's "stormy petrel in politics."[622] Runyon, though, believed he was merely fighting "all kinds of malicious propaganda" foisted upon him by his opponents and their mouthpieces that included *The Brownsville Herald*.[623]

As city manager Runyon doggedly battled *The Brownsville Herald* editorial staff. *The Brownsville News*, Runyon's periodical, became his vehicle to slice up the establishment editors.

A *News* editorial writer, Wm. Brown, coined Runyonism to describe the city manager's style of government. The editor tied Runyonism to positive benefits for Brownsville by "application of (Runyon's) time-tested business methods to the business of the city" for taxpayer benefit.

The *News*' circulation was small so its editorial impact was minimal. Yet it helped Runyon promote his agenda in the face of constant controversy. And he did achieve a lot. As city manager, he upgraded the electric, water, and gas infrastructures and improved the city's sewer system. He paid all the city's interest-bearing debts and made sure city employees received salaries on time. He reimbursed employees for any paychecks in arrears.[624] He also rewrote the city charter that established the governing system for Brownsville's elected officials.

True to his principal goal, Runyon made Brownsville a more beautiful city by promoting native plants in public and private gardens. He sought local buy-in by explaining his beautification campaign's benefits to civic groups. "The botanical beauty of Brownsville can be made equal to any city in the United States probably at less cost," he promised.[625]

He espoused action by residents to nurture native plants, including palma de micharos and ébano, so these species would endure despite continued land clearing. His view was not to halt progress, but to use nature's cure—the plants themselves—to undo any damage caused by bulldozers. Simply replanting trees works wonders for the soil, the ecology, the environment, and the beauty of the area, he said.

"Man cannot stop the work of Nature," he explained in an address as city manager. "Man can destroy the great work that Nature has done. He can denude the Earth and finally perish himself. But he cannot stop Nature from working."

To complement palms, he envisioned planting ornamental plants and shade trees in parks and resacas as picnic locations for both residents and tourists. Runyon, relying on experience as a curio store manager and owner, argued that a vigorous tourist trade was vital to the local economy.

"From the business standpoint, the tourist trade is well worth bidding for," Runyon said. "When the tourist visits our city, he is interested in seeing things new to him, things that are strange and attractive. It behooves us to plant trees of subtropical appearance, or at least trees that are attractive to the tourist."

Runyon's important resources within Brownsville were its park system and resacas. He believed the city would need little investment to develop the most beautiful park system in Texas. Even though inexpensive, he also knew efficient park management for robust plant life required top-down commitment.

> "Building beautiful parks is not an overnight piece of work to be taken lightly. It is long and serious work, the result of careful planning and management. But I believe with this hard work and management and with the natural resources available, trees, climate and natural water courses, that in ten years our parks will be developed into lovely show places, attractive alike to the tourist and the resident."

Runyon promoted the beautification concept for his entire city manager term. He estimated that by 1938 he had personally planted two thousand plants and shrubs, including many native palms. In the same time, he directed and supervised the planting of ten thousand seeds of palms and other native trees that he expected to germinate by the following spring. [626]

Runyon targeted many of the city parks then existing—Lincoln (just underway because of his efforts), Washington, Resaca, Belvedere, Filmore, and Ringgold[627]—as well as streets including the aptly named Palm Boulevard with sponsorship from Mrs. R. A. Porter. Runyon held to his promise to reduce costs by utilizing New Deal financial aid and employment opportunities of the Works Progress Administration (WPA) and the National Youth Administration (NYA).

His approach produced several temporary and many full-time jobs for local citizens. He put fifty youngsters to work at Ringgold, just in time for the next election. The youths cleared the land's encroaching brush and invasive species, planted desirable trees and shrubs both from pots and seeds, and built a shade-providing jacal to showcase the utility of the palma de micharos.[628]

In 1939, city voters re-elected all city officials with the exception of Rentfro, who declined to run. Commissioner Royce Russell filled the mayoral position. Runyon was appointed to another term to implement the city beautification program.

By the beginning of the 1939 growing season, visitors to the Valley noticed the results of Runyon's planting agenda over almost twenty-four months. Parks had put on new color, and an impressive assortment of new shade trees made resacas more hospitable.

In mid-March, W. H. Feagin of Tulsa, Oklahoma, wrote a letter complimenting the city for its beauty he enjoyed on a recent visit. Runyon replied that more was to come. "The resacas as we have in Brownsville and the vicinity are very valuable assets to this community and the development of the resacas into beautiful lakes is a small and inexpensive project," he told Feagin. "With the resacas properly developed, and planted to shade trees and palms, they will become extremely attractive and valuable additions to our flat landscape."[629]

By summer of that year, Runyon had convinced WPA to hire twenty-one men to expand the initiative, although this time he had to accept non-native plants provided by government and private industry. Runyon reluctantly agreed, as he had committed to carrying out the beautification project at the least cost possible. Yet he emphasized that his plan must focus on natives.

"I have planted a number of exotic plants in the park and many of them seem to be quite at home in their new surroundings," Runyon told the WPA engineer in charge. "But on the other hand I am not going to overlook the planting of a number of our local trees and shrubs which I know to be acclimated to the severe changes in our climatic conditions, which occur periodically in this region."[630]

Despite his agenda's impressive progress, Runyon's city manager tenure started to show rough edges. The relationship between Runyon and Mayor Russell became frosty. Runyon also felt attacked by editorials in *The Brownsville Herald* that criticized the city commission for rubber-stamping Runyon's agenda. In time, that journalistic harping created a rift between his office and those same commissioners who appointed him.

The situation became untenable for all sides when Runyon unilaterally fired the chief of police. In response, city commissioners adopted a resolution to relieve Runyon of his duties. Yet Runyon, who knew the city charter better than any city attorney, proved he could stay in office for another thirty days. Runyon was at his desk on the last day he was legally allowed to serve, leading some observers to wonder if he was inciting a coup of city government. Yet he showed up that last day just to effect transition of responsibilities.[631] His calendar states:

"I was removed from office at 8 a.m. and Ben Freudenstein was made city manager. I went over the work with him and came home at noon. The people are astonished."[632]

Before Brownsville citizens could forget the value of his city service, Runyon launched a bid for mayor. As he wrote: "My record as city manager in a short period of two and one-half years probably will never be equaled in Brownsville."[633]

During the mayoral campaign, Runyon explained how he improved voters' daily lives. He pointed to the city's enhanced sewer system and upgraded utilities as concrete examples. He reminded residents that he repaired the city's financial standing so it could once again receive credit.

And, he continued to show the long-term value of drawing more tourists to a more beautiful Brownsville. By then, even *The Brownsville Herald* could no longer dispute the benefits his beautification program had already shown. One editorial noted: "Robert Runyon, who was city manager of Brownsville from January 1, 1938, until June 24, 1940, probably was more interested in park development in Brownsville than any other man has been." [634]

Runyon built his 1941 election alliance under the Better Brownsville Party aegis. The party's platform again included park improvements along with fiscal responsibility in city administration. Although Russell's opposing party had *The Brownsville Herald* editors on his side, Runyon responded in kind. He had *The Brownsville News* regularly lambast Russell even though Runyon pledged "no mud-slinging." Still, by Brownsville standards, it was a gentlemanly campaign. Even *The Brownsville Herald* said, "Both tickets have been conducting active, but quiet campaigns, relying largely on person-to-person contacts in soliciting support."[635]

Runyon and his ticket won the election on November 4, 1941. He was sworn into office thirteen days later.[636] Less than three weeks after taking office, Japan bombed Pearl Harbor, and the United States entered World War II.

Chapter 25
Given the Chance to Serve

Running city hall in wartime January 1942 imposed new demands on the Brownsville mayor. Besides heading city government's ceremonial, administrative, legislative, and operational duties, Runyon also led the region's Civil Defense wartime efforts.

Beginning with his first months as mayor, his official focus changed from pruning branches at parks to paring the omnibus city budget to meet the challenge of defense-related demands.

One early action eliminated the city's $500 monthly stipend of taxpayer dollars to the Brownsville Chamber of Commerce. Runyon long had resented the cozy relationship between the city and the elite business members who ran the chamber. He explained the cut was needed because: "The city can very well use that money for other and more important purposes as we expect extra financial burdens because of war conditions."

A week later, Runyon irritated Elizabeth Pettit Davenport, chairman of the Public Health Nursing Association and wife of powerful attorney Harbert Davenport. Runyon directed the city commission to cut the city health department budget by almost $13,500. In addition, Runyon refused Mrs. Davenport's request to add a registered nurse to the city's health clinic.

As mayor, Runyon wanted small businessmen to see that his administration would not spend their tax dollars frivolously. Historians Adams and Knopp wrote: "Runyon's challenge to the elite establishment was not a proletarian revolution but an attempt by bourgeois entrepreneurs and businessmen to wrest power from an entrenched establishment."[637] Yet Runyon never received strong backing for his maverick approach. He heard appeals for him to resign as mayor within the first ninety days of his term.

Runyon eroded support further when he fell under suspicion of voter fraud. He was cleared of the charges a year later, but his defense, combined with ubiquitous criticisms, impacted his health. Although he remained firm in holding onto office, he took a sabbatical.

"I do so on the urgent direction of my doctor who has told me several times recently that it is either rest or death," Runyon said in a statement. "My political opponents seem unwilling to give me a rest."

Before he could depart, Runyon's friend, investor, and brother-in-law, General Francisco González Villarreal, died of heart problems on June 17, leaving a significant void in Runyon's circle of personal counselors.

By month's end, Runyon headed to Quapaw Baths at Hot Springs, Arkansas, where he had traveled regularly since 1928 for mineral water bath treatments. His original plan called for him then to spend time in West Texas where "I can be free of political bickering and where I can continue my studies and researches in botany," he said.[638]

However, he returned to Brownsville from Hot Springs by the end of July. By August 1, he approved the city commission's recommendation to sell the rails of the old Brownsville streetcar system to the War Production Board. The abandoned rail system comprised forty-five tons of steel—a quantity estimated to render American fighting forces three tanks, 1,800 fifty-caliber machine guns, and 150 three-inch anti-aircraft guns. [639]

The final year of Runyon's mayoral term offered few opportunities for further implementation of his city park beautification plan. One option did arise when the U.S. government offered to plant two hundred eucalyptus trees in Brownsville. Before deciding, Runyon first studied how Brazil had used eucalyptus imported from Australia to reforest land. He also examined a eucalyptus tree planted in Ringgold Park in 1929. He liked both results, so he accepted the offer. Runyon again would have preferred to stay with native trees yet the government gift provided wartime expediency to park improvement.[640]

His official actions, in fact, show that defense matters dictated most decisions during that year. Runyon stressed publicly that wartime protection of the city's population ranked above any other goal. As Runyon watched young men and women leave the lower Rio Grande Valley to serve in Europe or the Pacific, he committed to keeping the border, port, and city of Brownsville safe for their families until their return.

His son, Bob, had been among the Valley young adults who had been drawn into the conflict. Bob, recently married, had enlisted at Fort Sam Houston just as Runyon became mayor.

Texas Governor Coke Stevenson appointed Mayor Runyon municipal defense coordinator for Brownsville. He received a civilian Federal Bureau of Investigation diploma from Director J. Edgar Hoover on January 16, 1942. On

October 20, 1942, he completed the bomb reconnaissance agent's course of the U.S. Army. Although suffering from pernicious anemia, he attended all Civilian Defense trainings, gained certification in critical areas, and disseminated defense instructions to city dwellers. He considered his wartime leadership a highlight of his mayoral career. [641]

"I did not shirk my duty as coordinator of the Civilian Defense," he later said. "The best Civilian Defense organization for a town the size of Brownsville, in the state of Texas, was our record."[642]

That record, though, was not enough to get him re-elected in a November 1943 three-way race that included the elite merchants' party headed by H. L. Stokely as well as a new faction called the People's Ticket headed by produce salesman Dean Porter. Stokely's slate came in second. Runyon garnered just six percent of the vote to come in third and his commissioners performed even more poorly. Yet Runyon was magnanimous to the victor.

"I wanted that city bunch out of office," he said. "I know Mr. Porter and his commissioners will give Brownsville a good administration. I'm glad to be relieved of a job but happy that I was given the chance to serve."[643]

Runyon, though, was far from finished with public service. He proposed to Porter's administration that he oversee the parks' beautification effort at no salary. To the regret of several commissioners, the city attorney accepted Runyon's offer.

Runyon used the volunteer position to make up for two wartime years he had to set aside beautification efforts as mayor. He worked with a passion, directing neglected pruning of the plants to give the parks a more manicured appearance. He solicited and received additional plants donated to Brownsville by Southern Pacific Railroad, the federal government, and various botanical gardens.

One unforeseen consequence in appointing Runyon, despite costing the city nothing for his expertise, was his administrative authority over city park workers. And many workers found Runyon a tough taskmaster.

Before long, the employees said they wanted their own foreman to replace Runyon. When some workers quit because Runyon did not allow half days off on Saturdays, a charge he denied, change had to happen.[644]

Runyon convinced the city to replace the dissidents, yet some commissioners feared the replacements were loyalists to Runyon's political faction. As criticism grew, Runyon withdrew from park supervision. He was tired of controversy, and the impact of the war still weighed on his thoughts. Bob had finished officers' training school as a lieutenant and had been ordered to England with the Eighth Tank Battalion of the U.S. Army's Fourth Armored Division. With D-Day on everyone's mind, Runyon's focus again turned to all the Valley's young soldiers now overseas.

The action he took was unanticipated. Runyon neither liked nor trusted reporters in that era. But he also knew how to leverage them when needed. As national attention focused on the Allied Forces' invasion of the Continent, Runyon decided it was time to use the press.

Runyon invoked prayer for solace and turned to newspaper editors for assistance. He worked with a *Brownsville Herald* columnist to petition Mayor Porter to proclaim the anticipated invasion day "as a day of sincere prayers to the Almighty God to spare the lives of our brave soldiers, who fight for our liberty, and for Him to have mercy on those who fall in battle."

In response, Porter did proclaim the anticipated D-Day as a "day of sincere prayer." He urged all citizens of Brownsville to avoid actions of "hilarity and celebration" when they heard city sirens signal that the invasion of the Continent had begun.[645]

As it turned out, Runyon had good reason to be concerned. Lieutenant Runyon arrived in France just after D-Day on June 6, 1944. By August 13, after twenty-seven straight days on the front line, Lieutenant Runyon took time from a location he could not disclose to write a sister and her husband.

> *"This outfit is called 'the traveling circus' and believe me it is well named. Our mission is to speed down main highways, take big guns, towns, big rail centers, etc. and cut the enemy off. Usually they are encircled. Then the infantry comes up, slowly mopping up. The air corps has been great in this team of tanks and air power and infantry. The doughboys who fought for days after D-day actually kiss our tanks. They really love them."*[646]

He was promoted to first lieutenant on October 6 and made leader of the first platoon. On November 10, 1944, Lieutenant Runyon's tank was in the advance unit leading trains through the village of Viviers as part of the Lorraine campaign pushing the German Army. As the force moved forward, a nest of German soldiers attacked with forty-millimeter anti-tank guns. Lieutenant Runyon's tank was hit by fire and exploded in flames. Three of the men under his command were killed. Runyon put his life at risk to help his gunner leave the burning tank before further gunfire wounded him in the shoulder and he was taken prisoner.

Lieutenant Runyon used the overnight hours to advise his ten captors that they would experience the same Allied Forces' military strategy that he had outlined in his earlier letter to his sister. The Germans surrendered to Lieutenant Runyon before the U.S. Infantry arrived. Runyon turned the prisoners over to the Allied Forces and returned to duty four days later after receiving field medical treatment for his wound. He held off surgery on his shoulder until he could be transported to England in late February 1945. For his battle wound and his meritorious service, Lieutenant Runyon was awarded the Purple Heart, the European Campaign Ribbon with five

Bronze Stars, a presidential citation, a Bronze Star medal, and an American Campaign Ribbon.[647]

After serving as mayor and learning about so many of his neighbors' losses in the war, Runyon often remarked to friends and relatives how fortunate he felt that his son was able to serve and live. He knew other families in the Valley, and several members of his family back in Kentucky and West Virginia were not as fortunate. As one aunt wrote him after the war ended: "I know you are glad this war is over and your son has survived to get home again. So many are very sad now over their loved ones who will never return."[648]

Runyon never again held public office, although he ran in some races and had a voice in who ran in others. He considered a draft by his party for another run for mayor in November 1945, but decided against it. As he told a relative, "my health will not permit me to get into a position where there is lots of work."[649] From 1946 to 1949, he served as a member of the Brownsville Park Board.[650] In 1947, observers speculated Runyon would run for mayor as part of an anti-administration ticket. However, he chose not to file for election after failing to get a ticket formed.[651]

He returned in 1949 with a platform promoting lower taxes and higher wages through a stronger economy.[652] Runyon lost that election, polling half as many votes as incumbent Stokely. Runyon did get a consolation prize that same year when his home state honored him with its highest tribute. Kentucky Governor Earle C. Clements commissioned Runyon as an aide-de-camp and Kentucky colonel. Runyon told Clements: "There is nothing I know of that would have pleased me more than a Commission with the rank of Colonel from the State of Kentucky."[653]

In 1952, Runyon ran for a newly created House of Representatives seat in the Texas Legislature, but lost. Runyon, who had become angered by the city's sale of parkland and failure to keep existing parks maintained, again ran for a Brownsville city commission post in 1955 with political protégé Margal L. Vicars leading the ticket. Runyon lost his seat by less than a hundred votes, but Vicars beat Stokely in a close election. The Texas Supreme Court overturned that victory seventeen months later when it upheld lower court rulings that gave Stokely the office after a recount.[654]

Stokely, though, did not run for re-election six months later. Vicars regained the mayor's post, but Runyon did not run with him.[655] Nonetheless, one observer quoted Runyon as saying after the election: "Boy, I feel good. After twenty years, Brownsville is free (of politics favoring big business)."[656] Vicars did appoint Runyon to Brownsville's Planning and Zoning Board. He served from 1959 to 1961 as a member and chairman.[657]

Although elected office eluded him, Runyon stayed active in Democratic Party affairs for decades. He made news in 1948 as chairman of the Cameron County

Democratic Party in support of President Harry Truman for re-election. Runyon vocally opposed the Dixiecrats—the faction within the Democratic Party that opposed civil rights and backed Strom Thurmond of South Carolina for president. Runyon directed the Cameron County delegation to oppose the Dixiecrats' agenda. Runyon said he would not tolerate defections from that directive when the delegation attended the state Democratic Convention that year.

"I am, and have always been, a moderate Democrat, neither to the right nor to the left, nor do I hold with party bolters," he said.[658]

In 1954, though, Runyon's support for party policies of Democrat Ralph Yarborough, a U.S. senator from Texas, over Texas Governor Alan Shivers, leader of conservative Democrats in the 1940s and 1950s, placed him in the liberal category of his party. Runyon gave his faction a policy advantage by taking the Cameron County Democratic Party chairmanship on a technicality over the conservative candidate, A. M. Kent of Harlingen. The battle over the legality of that technicality went back and forth in the courts for years.[659]

Ultimately, the courts affirmed Kent as chairman. Runyon blamed his opponents' successful challenge on meddling by Republicans who wanted one of their own to run Cameron County's Democratic Party.[660]

Despite occasional and sometimes bitter internal party squabbling, local, state, and national leaders always thought highly of Runyon's unwavering commitment to the American political system under the then-prevalent single party rule in Texas. Longtime Runyon ally and Cameron County Judge Oscar Dancy once described Runyon to U.S. Speaker of the House Sam Rayburn (D-Texas) in these words: "There is no stronger Democrat in the State of Texas. He is a Democrat through good and evil. He was former Mayor and City Manager and also former County Chairman of this County. No question about his Democracy or loyalty to the Ticket. He will go down the line."[661]

Chapter 26
The Entrepreneurs' Twilight Years

In 1955, when Newman returned to the Alamo City to live with his son and his family, he was eighty-four years old with diminished mobility. He had been diagnosed with Charcot-Marie-Tooth disease, a neurological condition that is not fatal but severely weakens lower extremity muscles.[662] Newman could walk with a cane, but he found it easier to stay close to his bed.

Newman also suffered from psoriasis, and he sometimes sent his grandson, Robert, to the drugstore to get hydrogen peroxide to treat the scaly patches. Robert looked forward to those trips because Newman gave him a dollar for a bottle that cost a dime and let him keep the change.

Robert had heard tales about his grandfather all his life, but it was just during those last years of Newman's life that Robert came to know him. At times, Newman would move from his bed to a nearby rocking chair, and tell life stories to his grandson. Robert thought little about it at the time, but the conversations focused on Newman's experiences in Mexico rather than contributions to aviation history.

"The way he told me—I was about seven or eight years old when he used to tell me these stories—he said he was a war correspondent and he'd send stories back to The Brownsville Herald. He had pictures standing next to piles of Mexican bodies from those battles. There were so many killed they had to burn them because there were too many to bury. In those days in Mexico it was a pretty wild time and if he was involved as a secret agent then I can believe it. He frequented Mexico quite often. He was always a very kind person to me. He treated me well. He was always talking about history. He loved Mexico and loved the Mexican people and their food. He'd get me to try cabrito telling me it was just like chicken, but I wouldn't believe him. I wouldn't eat it."

As Robert grew older and discovered his grandfather's aviation feats, he came to view P. A. Newman as a self-made man who started with nothing yet succeeded as an innovator. Most striking to Robert was that his grandfather never feared failure. Robert wonders today what might have happened if, with all Newman's mechanical talent, he had received more funding and recruited a larger team to help him and Arthur in their Brownsville flight experiments.

> "His innovations made aviation history. If he wouldn't have suffered his setbacks due to fate, luck or whatever, he might have made even more lasting impressions on today's aircraft scene. With a little bit of luck—and he had little luck, it seems, through the years—he could have possibly beaten the Wright brothers. But luck or fate was just not there."

Newman became severely ill in his ninety-fourth year. On his deathbed, he took care of one last piece of business by listening to prayers of a friend of Robert's mother. Then he re-embraced Christianity after years of professing to be an atheist.[663] Newman died of a stroke on June 28, 1964.[664]

His obituary ran in newspapers from Texas to New York, a fitting flurry of publicity for a man who once received international attention simply for manning a glider for a quarter mile over the Texas coastal prairie. *The New York Times* ran the only account that gave his full name as Prentice A. Newman; all the rest used his initials. Yet all obituaries, including the *Times*, identified Newman as the U.S. inventor of the monoplane.[665] Newman's family buried him at Buena Vista Cemetery in Brownsville.

The 1960s was a busy decade for Runyon. In the first half, he continued his, often single-handed, agitation of the "entrenched establishment" within city government that he had started three decades earlier.[666] He continued to attend Brownsville city commission meetings as a citizen to ensure that commissioners followed the city charter that he had helped amend in 1939 and to fight any alternative amendments.[667] As he once advised at a public meeting, "The citizens should make it their responsibility to see that the public officials are never permitted to abuse the City Charter."[668] In 1961, he also ramped up his longtime advocacy for preservation of Padre Island as a national park. Runyon called it "the last frontier of the virgin flora and natural resting and breeding place for the fast diminishing waterfowl and wild life." Congress established the South Padre National Seashore the following year.[669]

Runyon and Amelia celebrated their fiftieth wedding anniversary on July 4, 1963, with hundreds of family members, friends, political allies, and some opponents attending.[670] Then, on October 4, 1966, after fifty-two years of serving the Cameron County Democratic Party in politics, two terms as Brownsville city manager and one as mayor, and several decades as watchdog of city government, Runyon dropped all political affiliations. He sent a letter

Robert Runyon in a 1962 author's photograph for his genealogy on the Runyon family. RFP, DBCAH, The University of Texas at Austin.

to his old friend, County Judge Oscar Dancy, and the city commissioners, and withdrew from all activities.

"I am doing research in local botany and plan to finish the botanical work during the next six months; also I have much other work and business matters that require my daily attention," Runyon explained.[671]

Her husband's departure from politics did not come soon enough for Amelia. As she later told journalist Juan Montoya:

"That was the one bad thing I didn't agree with, politics. He [Runyon] was such a sincere man and so honest in trying to do something for the city, but people still said terrible things about him. That was the one thing I didn't agree with him, getting into politics."[672]

Runyon's focus after that point went solely to botany and to genealogical research. In most years of his life, beginning about 1937, he had spent a month to six weeks during hot summers traveling. He went first to his mineral bath treatments in Hot Springs, Arkansas, then on to Kentucky, West Virginia, Virginia, the Carolinas, or Tennessee to research his family through interviews with relatives and record searches in county court houses. Between 1952 and 1962, he authored three books on the Lawson and Runyon families, always with plans to expand them with new information. He maintained genealogical files comprising thousands of documents and correspondence with other family researchers.

Runyon's non-family visitors to 812 E. St. Charles Street in the 1960s included many botanists who made special trips to the Valley to mine his knowledge. In December 1967, Runyon and Donovan S. Correll, head of the botanical laboratory at the Texas Research Foundation in Renner, jointly conducted a plant survey along a levee of the Rio Grande. Correll shared Runyon's view that Texans needed a comprehensive guide to their state's flora. In fact, that visit with Runyon was research for Correll's book, *Manual of the Vascular Plants of Texas*, published in 1970.

That was Runyon's last recorded plant-finding excursion. He died suddenly on March 9, 1968, in Brownsville at the age of eighty-six. He was buried close to the grave of an infant grandson in an ébano-shaded plot at Buena Vista Cemetery in Brownsville.

Although Runyon never saw Correll's finished work, the book would have pleased him. Its transfer of knowledge fit Runyon's objective to reach the public with information on the region's flora. Correll's preface listed Runyon first among the "number of highly skilled amateurs (who) have either directed us to new elements in the flora or have provided assistance in one way or another."[673]

Runyon had written his will eleven years before his death. In it, he stipulated that his heirs sell or donate his herbarium. The University of Texas in 1968 accepted Runyon's 8,750 specimens and accompanying field notes. The Runyon collection remains a component of the million-specimen herbaria at The University of Texas Billie L. Turner Plant Resources Center in Austin.[674]

Runyon also asked his heirs to dispose of his multiple libraries— botanical, genealogical, historical, and miscellaneous—as they saw fit. In 1970, Amelia and her six children donated the entire botanical collection to the James C. Jernigan Library at Texas A&I University (now Texas A&M University at Kingsville). The more than 950 books, pamphlets, and other research materials make up the Robert Runyon Collection within the library's South Texas Archives.[675]

Today, evolving explicit knowledge within the science of botany has determined that some unique species Runyon collected in the lower Rio Grande Valley were plants that had been discovered and named previously. Runyon's huaco (named *Runyonia tubiflora* but never formally published as such) and Runyon's water willow (*Justicia runyonii*) are among his discoveries that scientists consider synonyms of, or conspecific with, previously identified plants.

That evolution is valuable as science always advances through accumulation of new knowledge. At the local level, though, such knowledge evolution can be regressive. If tacit ecological knowledge tied to Runyon becomes lost— including his belief that preservation and utilization of native plants can make the lower Rio Grande Valley more beautiful and more economically solid— someone has to rediscover it all over again.

In 1995, former Mayor Margal Vicars returned to Brownsville city hall to raise awareness of the borderlands' ecological knowledge advanced by Runyon in the twentieth century. Vicars supported a motion by City Commissioner John Wood to name a new park after Runyon as the city's first official recognition that Runyon's explicit and tacit ecological knowledge has brought value to the borderlands. The site would replace the Lincoln Park acreage, with its many trees and palms personally planted by Runyon, that was scheduled to be destroyed during construction of the Veterans International Bridge at Los Tomates. The bridge opened in 1999.

Vicars might have unnerved commission members when he reminded them that Runyon "is the only city manager in history to cut his salary in half." The news account indicated the commissioners eventually gave less weight to Runyon's lifelong accomplishments that benefited their city than to the historical footnote that "Lincoln helped Mexico win their independence from the French."[676] The commissioners kept the Lincoln Park name for the new location.

However, many individuals in the borderlands every day do contribute greatly to extending that same knowledge Runyon created. Although in most cases it takes some travel from where Runyon lived and worked for six decades, twenty-first century ecotourists can still experience a small part of his botanical legacy to the region thanks to these unsung individuals. The closest site that grows a few Runyon's Esenbeckia is the Gladys Porter Zoo in Brownsville. The zoo is within a mile of the old Runyon homestead where his original Esenbeckia also still lives.

Beyond that, visitors must make the drive to the national wildlife refuges where several Runyon's Esenbeckia grow in Cameron and Hidalgo Counties, both locations accessible to the public. In addition, thirty miles north of Brownsville, a good sampling of native flora is at The Robert Runyon Garden, located along one of the trails within Harlingen's Hugh Ramsey Nature Park. At this unique and free garden, volunteers with the Rio Grande Chapter of the Texas Master Naturalist honor Runyon by nurturing many of his plant discoveries, including Runyon's Esenbeckia and Runyon's Violet Wild Petunia. And, of course, Runyon's decades-long persistence in raising awareness of the native Sabal palm helped preserve the Rabb Palm Grove. Today that site is maintained under the name of the Sabal Palm Sanctuary, located along the Rio Grande east of Brownsville. A walk along its trails allow visitors to view the same pristine habitat for native plants that enthralled Runyon throughout his botanical career.

Runyon's actions and words while he was alive show he would not have spent much time worrying about the sparse recognition he has received. He was never driven by having a plant receiving a Latinized form of his surname or seeing a park named after him. He never sought recognition beyond what his discovery and his work merited. As Runyon once told a fellow plants researcher, "During my many years of collecting I have never asked for the rights for publication, nor joint authorship, however it might be a splendid idea."[677] Still, he never acted on that idea. He just wanted to transfer knowledge so experts and the public became aware of the bounty, variety, utility, and beauty of borderlands' flora.

Most borderlands residents today think of Runyon's expansive photography record when they hear his name. But that wasn't always the case. Decades before he died, Runyon had stored away his fourteen thousand glass-plate and celluloid negatives in scores of labeled wooden cigar boxes in his smaller studio. Runyon once told a reporter he planned to sort the negatives and catalogue them.[678] But he never started that project. In his last years, he kept focus on his botanical research, his gardens, and genealogy. The images remained remarkably stable despite the subtropical temperature and humidity changes they experienced over half a century of storage with no climate control.

Runyon's will, which specified disposition of all his botany resources, did not mention his photography materials. That omission shows the personal and historical value he placed upon his botanical studies in the borderlands compared to his photography assets. Amelia, though, always understood the photography collection's importance. After all, many unique images in the collection exist because of her family's influence and her assistance in the studio.

Amelia kept watch over the photography assets for almost twenty years after her husband died. Then, in 1986, Amelia and her children donated Runyon's vast inventory of more than fourteen thousand glass-plate and nitrate negatives, prints, postcards, and lantern slides, and some of his business papers to the Barker Texas History Center (now the Dolph Briscoe Center for American History) at The University of Texas at Austin. Amelia did not live to see historians use the Runyon photographs to open a long-closed window into borderlands' daily life during tumultuous years of the early twentieth century. She died in Brownsville in 1987 and was buried beside her husband. But her goals had been met.

With those donations of Runyon's botanical, photography, and business resources, Amelia and her children permit other entrepreneurs to find inspiration in understanding that Runyon was never merely just a professional photographer or a learned botanist. Despite having no more than a ninth-grade education, Runyon dedicated himself through self-learning to run a railroad service business; to become a commercial photographer and war photojournalist; to conduct international commerce; to identify and preserve more than two dozen obscure native plants; to become a leader of a political party, a city manager, and mayor of Brownsville; to author five books; and much more. Runyon is the borderlands' Renaissance Man.

Folklorist and historian J. Frank Dobie was among the vast network of persons whom Runyon influenced in various disciplines. Through Dobie's command of the English language, he once summarized in twenty-six words the perfect elevator pitch for Runyon's entrepreneurial being: "One has to admire a man who cuts off a little hunk of the world and dedicates a lifetime to its study like Robert Runyon has."[679]

Epilogue

This story unites P. A. Newman and Robert Runyon as dynamic entrepreneurs and innovators who lived and worked contemporaneously in Texas' intellectually fertile borderlands. Their trip into the Mexican battle zone in November 1913 is the only event that personally linked the two innovators, and even that collaboration was for a brief week. Importantly, though, the trip demarcated their entrepreneurship—Newman decelerating his technology career as an engineer and Runyon, the polymath, just beginning to accelerate many avenues of study.

On that danger-filled journey, the engrossing *los compañeros de viaje* photograph presents today's viewers with a metaphor of twentieth century borderlands science and technology entrepreneurship. It embodies the teamwork required between a generalist and a specialist, a polymath and an engineer, to accomplish a project, to complete a task, to create an innovation.

The most important consideration for this photograph is that it exists only because other convoy participants—Constitutionalist officers with vastly higher obligations to reach their destination—had fled to avoid looming danger.

Newman and Runyon persisted because they called on important entrepreneurial attitudes of commitment and determination. As products of those attitudes, only Newman and Runyon shunned safety to forge into the unknown and complete the mission.

Runyon had become a technically accomplished photographer by 1913. On occasion he experimented with creativity. Yet vastly more of his exposures showed his practical nature. His practical category included photographs that always were well composed for a commercial purpose—to illustrate a news article, a promotional brochure, or one of his postcards.[680]

The singular photograph Runyon took of Newman and two Carrancistas near the war-torn capital of Tamaulipas on that blustery November day in 1913 is as interpretive of human entrepreneurial spirit as any Old Master genre painting from the 1700s might have portrayed. The powerful automobile represents technology, the Winchester and Mauser rifles signify the need to manage risk and uncertainty, Newman's centered position symbolizes leadership, the Carrancistas represent the entrepreneur's management of any situation by assembling proper teams, and the dust and dirt covering the automobile's fenders and wheels translate into finishing a goal. Even the half-empty bottle of tequila can suggest the sense of humor any entrepreneur needs to cope with the certainty of repeated failures before success is approached. The image simply is the perfect study of these early twentieth century South Texas entrepreneurs. Photo by Robert Runyon, RUN00062, RRC, DBCAH, The University of Texas at Austin.

Yet this image is completely different from either the creative or the commercial categories. It is a singular instance of a third category of Runyon's photography—a candid side that Runyon's other exposures rarely showed.

What we know is when and approximately where the group stopped to take the photograph, the responsibilities of the main subjects (even if we do not know all the names), and the valued functions of their accoutrements. And that knowledge colors this black-and-white image with the symbolism of entrepreneurship.

Runyon took the photograph on November 25, 1913, somewhere between Padilla/Santander Jiménez and Ciudad Victoria. As photographer, Runyon does not appear in the scene. Yet his hand is strong in symmetry of composition as revealed by the tequila bottle at left foreground and the long stick at opposite right to delineate the outer limits where his subjects could stand and still be in the image frame. Deep in Tamaulipas on that cloudy morning, Runyon set up this shot just as he lived his entire innovative life—by standing back, viewing, assessing, contemplating, and then building around the big picture. That same approach over decades compelled him to tackle other large-scale projects including preservation of a grove of Texas' only native palm and propagation of the state's rarest tree. He again employed those characteristics to seek political office to beautify Brownsville, then boldly and unilaterally improved every city park and resaca as a public servant and later as a private citizen. Still, his generalist nature drove him to do more in his lifetime. Runyon also dedicated decades to locate, research, study, and catalog all native plants of the Texas-Tamaulipas borderlands. His life's effort became a world-class herbarium that comprised 8,750 individual specimens.

Runyon over decades of borderlands study received no grants and had no patrons. He did all conservation, preservation, and knowledge transfer at his own expense with the exception of the years he served as city manager and mayor. Yet even then he never promoted his agenda over the welfare of the city. When he took office in 1938, city finances showed a significant deficit. Yet at the time he left as city manager, all debts had been paid and he had placed the city on a cash basis.

Even when he applied for federal New Deal dollars for park beautification, he put the city first. He committed the bulk of WPA funding to updating the city's aging sewer system over thirty months. For park construction, he received $40,058 from WPA compared to a city investment of only $12,518. And he leveraged those dollars skillfully. When his term ended, he considered beautification "one of the most valuable pieces of construction and improvement work done through WPA labor."[681]

The broad-shouldered, square-jawed Newman occupies the image's center. The position befits his penchant for leadership in his ventures. His singular stance symbolizes his specialist engineering approach that had its origins years before the invention of the automobile or the airplane. Then, during a heady twelve months of successes and failures, efforts that helped make 1909 the most exciting year of early aviation, Newman gambled everything on his aeroplane concept. A bit more success with a larger team of associates to quicken the development pace, and the Newman brothers aeroplane might have been the one that the military tested at Fort Myer, that won all the competitions, and that advanced the commercial aviation model. No one can say how his hand in killing Shell Mason in 1905 impacted his innovative mind in 1909. His record shows, however, that despite the anxiety of possibly being sentenced to death, he still was focused, creative, and aware of his technology goals for the entire twelve months.

His last creation, the monoplane, was the earliest machine to incorporate multiple innovations ultimately adopted by modern airlines. The list includes single, fixed, dihedral wings, an engine in front of the pilot and between the wings, a tractor propeller configuration to pull the airship through the air rather than push it, and a clear view for the pilot with all controls in the rear. To his credit, by year's end and just after acquittal, he realized he had come up short against aviation's leaders, and he shut down his engineering efforts. This photograph, though, is proof that his entrepreneurial spirit had rebounded thirty-five months later as a trailblazer of roads through northeastern Mexico.

For entrepreneurs, the photograph also demonstrates the value of building a team. Newman and Runyon chose two Carrancistas as bodyguards after investing "some effort" to persuade them. But they chose well. The revolutionaries came prepared to face any eventuality through their obvious ease in handling the required tools—bandoliers, pistols, and rifles. The slightly bow-legged man to the right, certainly the youngest traveler in the group, shows neither anxiety nor fear even though he carries both a holstered pistol and a rifle. Not so with the older revolutionary. He, like Newman, holds his rifle at ready. He is positioned to move forward quickly. It is uncertain whether a movement would be for defense or to reach for the half-full tequila bottle just in front of him. But it does not matter. The traditional clear liquor simply provides that bit of whimsy entrepreneurs must possess to maintain perspective during arduous times.[682]

After they took the photograph and folded back into the vehicle to continue their journey, it is easy to imagine Newman behind the wheel, the Carrancistas sitting two abreast beside him, watching the road and the brush as they passed. And Runyon, alone in the rear seat to Newman's left, guarding his strapped-in camera cases and tripods as the Cole "30" bounced on Firestone Non Skid Tires over wagon ruts that served as a road.

Once this trip had ended, neither man abandoned his dreams. Newman forever marveled at mankind traveling through the heavens, and Runyon spent his life studying his corner of the earth. Failure never dissuaded them from tackling new challenges because solutions always seemed worth pursuing. And at the end of their decades of wanderings and adventures, they showed that a satisfying entrepreneurship is nothing more and nothing less than good management of risk and reward punctuated by innovation and transfer of new knowledge.

Their lifelong efforts did not result in fabled wealth, corporate empires, or vast lands for themselves and their families. But glitter was never their primary objective anyway. Newman wanted to make aviation as accessible to the common man as an automobile, and Runyon wanted to preserve all borderlands' native flora. Had either man achieved legendary success, the fortune gained likely would have been less valuable than the journey taken.

Acknowledgments

In late March 1952, theaters in the lower Rio Grande Valley prepared for the movie premiere of *Viva Zapata!* starring Marlon Brando and Jean Peters with screenplay by John Steinbeck.

Emiliano Zapata never fought close to the borderlands during the 1910-1920 Mexican Revolution. But director Elia Kazan did film a good part of the quasi-biographical movie at Roma in the lower Rio Grande Valley as well as further up the Texas side of the river at San Ygnacio. A few weeks before the release date, local interest started building, so a *Valley Morning Star* reporter interviewed my grandfather, Robert Runyon. The reporter wanted Runyon, as one of America's earliest war photojournalists, to tell readers what really happened in the borderlands during the conflict.

In 2008, I found that March 7, 1952, article in a cache of Runyon's papers that my mother, Amali Runyon Perkins, had preserved after her father's death. The article held interest because it is the only document that captured my grandfather's thoughts about several critical incidents—including the Battle of Ciudad Victoria—that he experienced during that violent era. I also sent the article to my uncle, Delbert Runyon, to see if he could add anything. Delbert, who at the time was the last living child of Robert and Amelia Runyon, said he had never seen the article. Yet he thought it was interesting, but incomplete. He said: "It doesn't say why my father left his Model T Ford in [Ciudad] Victoria and it doesn't say that he had a companion, a blacksmith, (I think his name was Newman) who was along in case he was needed to fix the Model T."

My uncle's comment was intriguing. Besides being an accomplished photographer, my grandfather also was a lifelong serial entrepreneur. I wondered if Newman had played a significant role in any of the Runyon endeavors. As it turned out, minimal research showed that in their careers Prentice Alexander Newman and Runyon collaborated only for a mere week. Yet scant research also showed that Mr. Newman was, like my grandfather, an entrepreneur of the highest caliber. Both Newman's and Runyon's stories invited much more examination.

Journey's Reward developed from that deeper scrutiny into the lives of both men, but only after gaining the assistance of many outside experts. These individuals helped gather information, transfer knowledge, edit, and correct multiple areas of the manuscript. Their contributions were so complete that errors in the final treatment are solely the author's shortcomings.

Thanks to Patty Newman Turner of Odessa, Texas, author of the Newman family genealogy, for introducing me to Robert L. Newman of San Antonio, the grandson of Prentice A. Newman, and Lorraine Owens of Lake Lotawana, Missouri, granddaughter of Malcolm Arthur Newman. Their valuable contributions of Newman family stories helped put logical order to the events surrounding the Newman brothers' success at making aviation history. Mrs. Owens' genealogical records also held amazing clues into the Newman brothers' past. In addition, Mike Owens, Mrs. Owens' grandson, graciously scanned Newman family photographs for inclusion in the book. And Regena Williamson of the Lavaca County TXGenWeb project provided great help in accessing legal records for Prentice and Arthur Newman's murder indictments and district court trials.

I am also indebted to the many experts who steered me away from multiple manuscript mishaps to make this treatment as accurate as possible in covering multiple technology and science areas.

For the sections on photography, thanks go to Amy Bowman, photographs archivist at the Briscoe Center for American History at The University of Texas at Austin. She helped verify and point out vital facts concerning Runyon's decade-and-a-half career as a commercial photographer and photojournalist.

Dr. Joe Lee Janssens of Houston, this century's leading military historian of the Mexican Revolution, explained attack strategies, troop movements, and specific terms underlying the 1913-1914 Battles of Matamoros, Ciudad Victoria, and Monterrey. Much additional detail for that era became possible through Dr. Janssens' personal comments and edits as well as his landmark two-volume studies of 1913-1914 entitled *Maneuver and Battle in the Mexican Revolution*.

George W. Cox of Santa Fe, New Mexico added personal perspective on the Revolution years. Mr. Cox, who had initially contacted my Uncle Delbert, related the saga of his grandfather, adventurer William B. Cox, whose freedom from Pancho Villa's prison in Mexico required intervention with Revolution leaders from both Runyon and Newman.

My brother, Richard D. Perkins of Houston, put his decades of engineering experience and aviation knowledge to work to interpret century-old news reports on mechanical and structural changes that the Newmans made to their aeroplanes. The Newman engineering architecture had to be reconstructed from newspaper reports as no diaries or sketches still exist. My brother also provided many high-resolution scans of photographs out of the Runyon Family Papers.

Although several authors have documented Runyon's photography career, this book is the first account to delve deeply into Runyon's botanical achievements. Its scope became possible only through advice and additions to text of Dr. George Yatskievych, botanist and curator of the Billie L. Turner Plant Resources Center at The University of Texas at Austin. The center maintains the Runyon Herbarium as a component within the University's massive Herbaria collection. Dr. Yatskievych also was gracious to give me a crash course on botanical citation protocols.

The section on Runyon's Esenbeckia (*Esenbeckia runyonii*) became a story of contemporary ecological conservation importance through information provided by Chris Best, Texas state botanist, U.S. Fish and Wildlife Service. Mr. Best shared data on his remarkable efforts to preserve and diversify populations of Runyon's Esenbeckia in Texas through seed sourced in Mexico. Mr. Best has built exceptional relationships among Mexican researchers and ranchers where Runyon's Esenbeckia grows in larger numbers than north of the Rio Grande.

Also thanks to horticulturist Mike Heep of Harlingen for explaining how he and his brother, Don, rediscovered Runyon's Esenbeckia in Cameron County late last century, more than fifty-five years after Runyon began studying the tree. Mike too is propagating Runyon's Esenbeckia seedlings that grow in many new locations.

Dr. Alfred Richardson, professor emeritus of biological sciences at The University of Texas-Rio Grande Valley, reviewed and enhanced the section on Runyon's unique capacity to identify rare plants. Dr. Richardson's exceptional field guides to borderlands flora, including *Plants of Deep South Texas*, co-authored with Ken King, have become vital resources for any plant-lovers' library. Dr. Richardson also validated assumptions regarding Runyon's knowledge transfer.

The power of knowledge transfer in innovation proved a persistent theme in the careers of Runyon and Newman. I am in debt to Meg Wilson of Austin, a fellow with the IC^2 Institute at The University of Texas at Austin, for confirming the two entrepreneurs' knowledge generation and transfer practices. She and many other professors who have taught in the masters of science in technology commercialization program, formerly at IC^2 and now under the auspices of the McCombs School of Business at UT-Austin, emphasize knowledge transfer flow as essential to innovation commercialization.

Thanks also to staffs at UT's Briscoe Center and the Benson Latin American Library, for helping locate Runyon, Newman and borderlands research materials; Jolene Clark, librarian and archivist of the George Banker Owens Collection, Midwest Genealogy Center, Mid-Continent Public Library, Independence, Missouri, for scans of Newman family photographs; Lori K. Atkins, archivist at the James C. Jernigan Library at Texas A&M University-Kingsville, for facts on the Robert Runyon Collection in its South Texas Archives; and Omar Corona, library assistant at the Harlingen Public Library, for newspaper research.

In reality, this book exists only because Runyon's wife, sons and daughters, all of whom have passed on, were far-sighted in preserving his historical documents. I thank Lillian Runyon Mahoney and Robert Albert Runyon, executors of the Runyon estate, for spearheading the placement of both the Runyon Herbarium at UT-Austin and the Runyon Botanical Library at Texas A&I University (now Texas A&M-Kingsville). Also to Amelia Runyon, Virginia Runyon Gilbert and Delbert Runyon for preserving the Runyon photographic assets now secured at the Briscoe Center for American History at UT-Austin.

Amelia Runyon also protected a massive volume of her husband's business papers for two decades after his death. In turn, her daughter Amali Runyon Perkins preserved them for another two decades. Amali also used these papers to write several short accounts of her father that provided priceless clues to different elements of Runyon's life. These papers are now at the Briscoe Center.

Also vital were the thousands of Runyon genealogical records, including diaries, biographies and books, that Amali and her oldest brother, William T. Runyon, maintained and expanded until their deaths. Other Runyon family papers used in this book have been shared with me over time by my cousins, Ginger Gilbert Liening, Madeleine Gilbert Spangler, and Mike Burney. Access to all these data helped define unknown facts about Runyon's earliest years.

Finally, thanks and love to my wife, Susan, for her support for more than forty years. She spent a sizable portion of that time listening to tales of Robert Runyon from my grandmother, Amelia, my mother, Amali, my aunts and uncles, and my brothers, sisters, and cousins. Those tales inspired her to encourage me repeatedly to make this book happen.

Endnotes

LOFP: Lorraine Owens Family Papers
RRC, DBCAH: Robert Runyon Collection at the Dolph Briscoe Center for American History, The University of Texas at Austin
RRML: Robert Runyon Mexico Library (Runyon's personal collection of volumes on Mexico, one of many libraries he maintained, consisted of more than 125 volumes. See "Runyon Library: A List of Books on Mexico, 1947," RFP.)
RFP: Runyon Family Papers

Prologue

1. "Flying Machine, Invention of a San Antonian, Is Nearing Test," *The San Antonio Light*, December 31, 1908, 3; "Airship Test Brings Victory to Inventor," *The San Antonio Light*, January 3, 1909, 1, 4.
2. As science fiction writer and historian H. G. Wells said, "By 1909 the aeroplane was available for human locomotion." H. G. Wells, *The Outline of History* (Garden City, New York: Garden City Books, 1956), II, 763.
3. "New Schedule Is Announced," *Brownsville Daily Herald*, January 28, 1909, 9.
4. Robert Runyon, Kodak Exposure Record, December 12, 1907, to January 13, 1911, RRC, DBCAH Box 2007-223/4.
5. For a comprehensive analysis of classical entrepreneurs in the Rio Grande Valley, see Alicia M. Dewey, *Pesos and Dollars: Entrepreneurs in the Texas-Mexico Borderlands 1880-1940* (College Station, Texas: Texas A&M University Press, 2014).

Chapter 1

6. P. A. Newman, *Selected Passports*, National Archives, Washington, D.C., Ancestry.com, *U.S. Passport Applications, 1795-1925*, [database online], Provo, Utah, http://interactive.ancestry.com/1174/USM1490_1113-0329, accessed August 1, 2015.
7. "Airship Test Brings Victory to Inventor;" "Make Faulty Aeroplane Drop Like Parachute," *The Daily Express*, San Antonio, Texas, January 11, 1909, 12.
8. "Brothers Held After Shooting," *Fort Worth Telegram*, May 16, 1905, 8.
9. Patty Newman Turner, George Newman, and Betty Newman Nauer, *Joseph and Rachel Rabb Newman An Old Three Hundred Family of Texas and Their Descendants* (Wyandotte, Oklahoma: The Gregath Publishing Company, July 1998), 19-23; Victor C. Wegenhoft, "Rabb, William," *Handbook of Texas Online*, http://www.tshaonline.org/handbook/online/articles/fra07, accessed April 5, 2017; Barbara L. Young, "Newman, Joseph," *Handbook of Texas Online*, http://www.tshaonline.org/handbook/online/articles/fne23, accessed April 5, 2017.
10. "William P. Newman," *Veteran Biographies*, The Herzstein Library, San Jacinto Museum of History, http://www.sanjacinto-museum.org/Library/Veteran_Bios/Bio_page/?id=629&army=Texian, accessed October 28, 2015.
11. Turner, Newman, and Nauer, *Joseph and Rachel Rabb Newman*, 20; "Joseph Austin Newman," LOFP.
12. U.S. Census Bureau: 1870, Smith County Texas, Ninth Census of the United States; LOFP; Robert H. Thonhoff, "Gillett, TX," *Handbook of Texas Online*, http://www.tshaonline.org/handbook/online/articles/hlg16, accessed April 5, 2017; Joseph Austin Newman's tombstone at the Runge Cemetery is the source for his Confederate service affiliation.
13. Turner, Newman, and Nauer, *Joseph and Rachel Rabb Newman*, 20-23; LOFP.
14. LOFP.
15. "The Prize Composition," Laredo, Texas, circa 1888, LOFP.
16. "Laredo Local News," *Galveston Daily News*, April 5, 1889, 3; Patricia L. Duncan, "Texas Spring Palace," *Handbook of Texas Online* http://www.tshaonline.org/handbook/online/articles/lkt06, accessed December 13, 2015; Sandra L. Myres, "Fort Worth, 1870-1900," *The Southwestern Historical Quarterly*, 72, No. 2, October 1968, 204.
17. LOFP.
18. "Personals," *Laredo Daily Times*, December 5, 1915, 5.
19. Harry Foehner, "America's First Monoplane Was Constructed by Brownsville Man," *El Heraldo de Brownsville*, November 8, 1936, 5.
20. "Aeronautics," *The Source Book* (Chicago, Illinois: Perpetual Encyclopedia Corporation, 1926), I, 24.
21. Lorraine Owens, telephone interview, September 23, 2016.
22. P. A. Newman, "Boiler Feeder and Indicator," US Patent 485976, filed April 26, 1892, and issued November 8, 1892.
23. "Joseph Austin Newman," "Malcolm Arthur Newman," LOFP.
24. David McCullough, *The Wright Brothers* (New York, New York: Simon & Schuster, 2015), 25.
25. "Karnes County," *San Antonio Sunday Light*, July 31, 1898, 8.
26. Lorraine Owens, telephone interview, September 23, 2016.
27. LOFP; Turner, Newman, and Nauer, *Joseph and Rachel Rabb Newman*, 20.
28. U.S. Census Bureau: 1900, Runge Village, Karnes County, Texas, Twelfth Census of the United States.
29. McCullough, *The Wright Brothers*, 31.
30. Stephen Meyer, "Automobile in American Life and Society: The Degradation of Work Revisited: Workers and Technology in the American Auto Industry, 1900-2000"[database online], the University of Michigan, http://autolife.umd.umich.edu/Labor/L_Overview/L_Overview.htm, accessed April 5, 2017.
31. No Title, *The Cuero Daily Record*, July 16, 1902, 3; "Prentice A. Newman, Dallas, 1903-04," Ancestry.com, *U.S. City Directories 1882-1995*, [database online], Provo, Utah, accessed August 28, 2015.
32. Turner, Newman, and Nauer, *Joseph and Rachel Rabb Newman*, 21.
33. "Prentice A. Newman, Dallas, 1904-05," Ancestry.com, *U.S. City Directories 1882-1995*, [database online], Provo, Utah, accessed August 28, 1905; "Prentice A. Newman, Dallas, 1905-06," Ancestry.com, *U.S. City Directories 1882-1995*, [database online], Provo, Utah, accessed August 28, 2015.
34. "Brothers Held After Shooting."

35 State of Texas Drivers License Certificates, Robert Runyon, 1941, 1943, 1949.
36 Robert Runyon and Amos Runyon, *Runyon Genealogy* (Brownsville, Texas: Privately Printed, 1955), 1-7; Robert Runyon, *Supplement to Runyon Genealogy* (Brownsville, Texas: United Printers and Publishers, 1962), 195-202; "Runion, Isaac, Petition," December 8, 1818, Record No. 000300353 (database online), Legislative Petitions Digital Collection, Library of Virginia, Richmond, Virginia, http://digitool1.lva.lib.va.us:8881/R/D2U23RPD6S6BNRCBQFF7M3LPHIJNJJGCTH76S6RIG4IDEV2LY1-00888?func=search-advanced-go&LOCAL_BASE=1505&ADJACENT=N&find_code1=WPA&request1=legpet&find_operator=AND&find_code2=WRD&request2=Runion&find_operator2=AND&find_code3=WCV&request3=Tazewell+County&pds_handle=GUEST, accessed April 5, 2017.
37 Robert Runyon, "Runyon Families Migrate to Eastern Kentucky and Southern West Virginia," unpublished paper, circa 1962, RFP.
38 Amos Runyon to Robert Runyon, April 28, 1958, Amos Runyon Folder, RFP.
39 Robert Runyon, "Notes of the Data of the Runyon Family," no date, RFP. (Runyon's notes state that Mitchell Runyon bought a 213-acre farm from D. W. and Isabelle Eba); Runyon and Runyon, *Runyon Genealogy*, 7-84; Runyon, *Supplement to Runyon Genealogy*, xxii-xxiv, 199-205; Alfred H. (Bud) Peterson, Jr., to Robert Runyon, April 8, 1961, RFP.
40 Runyon, "Notes of the Data of the Runyon Family."
41 "Anthony Lawson family, Brig Active," Ancestry.com, *Philadelphia Passenger Lists, 1800-1945* [database online], Provo, Utah.
42 Anthony Lawson's customers traveled so frequently to Lawson's general store that they called the new community Lawsonville and then corrupted it to Lawnville before giving it the official name Logan in honor of an Indian chief in the Mingo tribe. Lawnville also was known as Logan Court House or Logan CH. See Robert Y. Spence, the *West Virginia Encyclopedia*, "Logan," http://www.wvencyclopedia.org/articles/1440, accessed July 19, 2018.
43 Robert Runyon, *Genealogy of the Descendants of Anthony Lawson of Northumberland, England* (Brownsville, Texas: The Brownsville News Publishing Company, 1952), 2-13; G. T. Swain, "Execution of Slave for Murder First Public Execution in Logan," *The Charleston Gazette*, May 20, 1928, 2.
44 Runyon. *Genealogy of the Descendants of Anthony Lawson of Northumberland England*, 9-12; John Britton Wells III, James M.Prichard, *10th Kentucky Cavalry, C.S.A.* (Baltimore: Gateway Press, Inc., 1996), 179. In correspondence to Amali Runyon Perkins, James M. Prichard of the Kentucky Department for Libraries and Archives, public records division, archival services branch, and co-author of the *The 10th Kentucky Cavalry, C.S.A.*, wrote: "In regard to your recent request, there are no service files of pension records available for George Lawson in Kentucky. As co-author of the book you cited I recall that (co-author) Mr. (John Britton) Wells and I reconstructed the roster of Melvin Lawson's company from county level civil and criminal case files after the war, hence the PWR (Post War Record)."
45 F. Keith Davis, "CHRISTMAS-TIME 1879: Christmas Eve Frolic and Gun Battle," *The Logan Banner*, Logan, West Virginia, December 24, 2013, http://www.loganbanner.com/news/news/2888510/CHRISTMAS-TIME-1879:-Christmas-Eve-Frolic-and-Gun-Battle, accessed July 22, 2014.
46 Runyon, *Genealogy of the Descendants of Anthony Lawson of Northumberland, England*, 11.
47 Amali Runyon Perkins to the National Genealogical Society (NGS), Arlington, Virginia, June 17, 1997, June 21, 1999, RFP; G. W. Lawson, *Directory of Deceased American Physicians, 1804-1929* [database online], Ancestry.com, Provo, Utah: MyFamily.com, Inc., 2004. Original data: Arthur Wayne Hafner, editor, *Directory of Deceased American Physicians, 1804-1929*, American Medical Association's Deceased Physician Masterfile (Chicago, Illinois: American Medical Association, 1993), accessed April 23, 2011.
48 Runyon and Runyon, *Runyon Genealogy*, 29-30; U.S. Census Bureau: 1940, Brownsville, Cameron County, Texas, Sixteenth Census of the United States
49 Robert Runyon scrapbook, "Ideal Mounting Book Domestic Art," RRC, DBCAH; Tom Sanford, "Robert Runyon, New Cameron County Democratic Chairman, Opposes Bolters," Brownsville Herald, July 29, 1948, 15.

Chapter 2
50 "Annual Report of the Surgeon-General of the Public Health and Marine-Hospital Service of the United States for the Fiscal Year 1904," 58th Congress, (Washington, D.C.: U.S. House of Representatives, 1904), 303-325.
51 Based on the 1900 census, San Antonio was the largest population center in Texas with 53,321 residents. Houston was second with 44,633. *Texas Almanac*, "City Population History from 1850–2000," Texas State Historical Association, https://texasalmanac.com/sites/default/files/images/CityPopHist%20web.pdf, accessed February 7, 2017.
52 T. J. Heard, M.D., "Report on Medical Topography, Meteorology, and Epidemic Diseases of Texas," *The Galveston Medical Journal*, Vol. 3, No. 3 (Galveston, Texas: Greensville Dowell, May 1868), 475-478.
53 U.S. Census Bureau: 1880, Cuero, DeWitt County, Texas, Tenth Census of the United States.
54 U.S. Census Bureau: 1900, Cuero, DeWitt County, Texas, Twelfth Census of the United States.
55 J. M. Reuss, M.D., "An Outbreak of Yellow Fever in De Witt County," *Transactions of the State Medical Association of Texas*, paper presented at the 36th Annual Session (Texas Medical Association: Austin, Texas, April 25-29, 1904), 135-139.
56 J. H. Reuss, M.D., *United States deceased physician file (AMA), 1864-1968* [database online], American Medical Association: Chicago, Illinois, Reh, Wm. S. - Reynolds, George E., Image 2548, accessed March 21, 2017.
57 Reuss, "An Outbreak of Yellow Fever," 136-137.
58 Reuss, "An Outbreak of Yellow Fever," 137.
59 "Another Fever Case in DeWitt County," *The Daily Express*, San Antonio, Texas, November 4, 1903, 3.
60 "Cuero," *The Galveston Daily News*, April 26, 1903, 20.
61 The 1902 Goliad F4 tornado today is considered the second deadliest tornado to hit Texas in recorded history. It killed 114 persons and caused 250 injuries. See "Top Ten Deadliest Tornadoes in Texas (since 1900)," National Oceanic and Atmospheric Administration (NOAA) National Weather Service Weather

Forecast Service, https://www.weather.gov/ama/top10_tornadoes, accessed April 10, 2017. For Dr. Reuss' and Lily Newman's response to the tornado see "Local and Personal," *The Victoria Weekly Advocate*, May 24, 1902, 8.
62 LOFP.
63 "Society News Over the State: Runge." *The Galveston Daily News*, November 1, 1903, 20.
64 "Recovering," *The Victoria Weekly Advocate*, November 14, 1903, 8.
65 Reuss, 137.
66 John P. Carrier, PhD., "Medicine in Texas: The struggle with yellow fever, 1839-1903," *Texas Medicine*, November 1986, 62-65.
67 "Newmans Gave Bond," *The Galveston Daily News*, May 18, 1905, 4.
68 LOFP.
69 Runyon, "Runyon Families Migrate;" William Ely, *The Big Sandy Valley: A History of the People and Country From the Earliest Settlement to the Present Time*, Facsimile Reprint Edition (Bowie, Maryland: Heritage Books, Inc., 1987), 99-100.
70 U.S. Census Bureau: 1860, Wayne Township, Adams County, Ohio, Eighth Census of the United States; U.S. Census Bureau: 1880, Wayne Township, Adams County, Ohio, Tenth Census of the United States.
71 Julia C. Ford to William T. Runyon, April 19, 1958, Julia C. Ford File, RFP.
72 William T. Runyon to Robert Runyon, January 3, 1956, RFP.
73 U.S. Census Bureau: 1900, Catlettsburg, Boyd County, Kentucky, Twelfth Census of the United States.
74 Runyon and Runyon, *Runyon Genealogy*, 35; also Julia C. Ford to William T. Runyon, June 16, 1963, Julia Ford File, RFP. The Runyons actually were shirt-tail relatives to Nora Young Runyon's Mims relatives. Robert Runyon's aunt, Jennie Runyon, had married Tandy Lewis Ford, a first cousin to Nora's mother, Mary Louise Mims Young.
75 U.S. Census Bureau: 1880, Catlettsburg, Boyd County, Kentucky, Tenth Census of the United States. Young and Runyon lived close to each other on the same census record.
76 Both Ashland and Catlettsburg, Kentucky, had offered ferry service to Ohio ports including Ironton since 1857. Ashland Centennial Committee, *A History of Ashland, Kentucky 1786-1954* (Ashland, Kentucky: Graber Printing Company, 1954), 50; Catlettsburg Centennial Committee, *History and Program Commemorating the Founding of the City of Catlettsburg, Kentucky* (Catlettsburg, Kentucky: Catlettsburg Centennial Committee, 1949), 28-29.
77 Runyon and Runyon, *Runyon Genealogy*, 31; Marriage License Application, Probate Court, Lawrence County, Ohio, Robert Runyon and Nora Young, No. 1412, September 16, 1901; "Ohio Marriages, 1800-1958," database, FamilySearch (https://familysearch.org/ark:/61903/1:1:XD8F-1VC : 10 February 2018), Robert Runyon and Nora Young, 15 Sep 1901; citing Lawrence Co., Ohio, reference 2:3KR0LK8; FHL microfilm 317,723.
78 Robert Runyon, "These Records Is the Property (sic) of Robert Runyon," Catlettsburg, Boyd County, Kentucky, May 12, 1908, RFP.
79 Tom Sanford, "Robert Runyon, New Cameron County Democratic Chairman, Opposes Bolters;" Robert Runyon to James N. Kehoe, Maysville, Kentucky, April 17, 1933, RRC, DBCAH Box 2007-109/1.
80 Marriage License Application; Amali Runyon Perkins Notes on Robert Runyon, RFP.
81 Robert Runyon, "Property of Robert Runyon—Family Records," RFP.

Chapter 3
82 U.S. Census Bureau: 1900, Yoakum, Lavaca County, Texas, Twelfth Census of the United States.
83 Nancy Beck Young, "San Antonio and Aransas Pass Railway," *Handbook of Texas Online*, http://www.tshaonline.org/handbook/online/articles/eqs06, accessed November 5, 2015; Mary M. Orozco-Vallejo, "Yoakum, TX," *Handbook of Texas Online*, http://www.tshaonline.org/handbook/online/articles/hfy01, accessed November 5, 2015.
84 No title, *The Yoakum Daily Herald*, December 21, 1898.
85 No title, *The Moulton Eagle*, Moulton, Texas, January 27, 1905; "Bought Yoakum Property," *The Houston Chronicle*, July 28, 1907, 16.
86 "Advertisement: The Lane Hotel," *San Antonio Express*, January 7, 1900, 17.
87 U.S. Census Bureau: 1910, Yoakum, Lavaca County, Texas, Thirteenth Census of the United States.
88 U.S. Census Bureau: 1910, Yoakum, Lavaca County; The State of Texas v Prentiss (sic) Newman, Lavaca County District Court, 1905-1909.
89 Newmans Gave Bond.
90 "Shell Mason Killed At Yoakum," *The Hallettsville New Era*, May 19, 1905, 1.
91 "Runge," *The Galveston Daily News*, July 3, 1904, 17; "Killing at Yoakum," *The Victoria Weekly Advocate*, May 17, 1905, 1.
92 "Shell Mason Killed by Newman Boys," *The Houston Chronicle*, May 16, 1905, 1.
93 Newmans Gave Bond.
94 "Shell Mason Killed At Yoakum."
95 Court documents referred to the location as "a house of ill repute," before a clerk crossed out the last two words and replaced them with "questionable reputation." The State of Texas v Prentiss Newman.
96 The State of Texas v Prentiss Newman.
97 "History of Williamson," City of Williamson, The Official Website of Williamson, West Virginia, http://www.cityofwilliamson.org/history-of-city-hall.html, accessed March 29, 2016; "Industrial and Commercial Williamson, West Virginia's Youngest and Most Prosperous City," business promotional pamphlet, circa 1910, RFP.
98 Robert Runyon, "Robert Runyon," circa 1952, RFP.
99 "State of West Virginia," RFP.
100 "Registers to Vote." Runyon Perkins Notes, RFP; William T. Runyon to Lillian Runyon Burney, June 20, 1963, Perkins-Runyon Correspondence, RFP.
101 "State of West Virginia."
102 "Notes on Robert Runyon;" Kalamazoo Nurseries to Robert Runyon, May 16, 1910, RRC, DBCAH Box 2007-223/3.

103 "These Records Is the Property (sic) of Robert Runyon."
104 Robert Runyon, *The Mirror Plater's Guide* (Catlettsburg, Kentucky: Privately Printed, 1906), RRC, DBCAH Box 2007-223/2.
105 "These Records Is the Property (sic) of Robert Runyon."
106 *History and Program Commemorating the Founding of the City of Catlettsburg, Kentucky,* 15; Robert Runyon, Kodak Exposure Record.
107 "These Records Is the Property (sic) of Robert Runyon."
108 "Kentucky State Guard," RFP.
109 Photostat of Southern Fire Insurance Company appointment of Robert Runyon as agent, September 5,1908; Runyon Perkins Notes, RFP; Tom Sanford, "New Cameron County Democratic Chairman, Opposes Bolters."
110 Author interview with Amelia Leonor Medrano Longoria de Runyon, Brownsville, Texas, April 1987.
111 "Big Sandy News," *Big Sandy News,* Louisa, Kentucky, December 11, 1908.
112 Robert Runyon, "Property of Robert Runyon: Family Records," circa 1908, RFP.

Chapter 4
113 The State of Texas v Prentiss Newman.
114 "Death Record," *The Daily Express,* San Antonio, Texas, April 30, 1905, 2.
115 "Shell Mason Killed by Newman Boys."
116 U.S. Census Bureau: 1900, Runge Village, Karnes County, Texas, Twelfth Census of the United States; U. S. Passport Applications, 1795-1925; Ethelyne Dahnke to Lorraine Owens, Joseph Austin Newman Genealogy, LOFP.
117 Turner, Newman, and Nauer, *Joseph and Rachel Rabb Newman,* 21.
118 "Shot By Girl's Brother," *The Washington Post,* Washington, D.C., May 17, 1905, 1.
119 The State of Texas v Prentiss Newman.
120 Robert L. Newman telephone interview with author, October 27, 2015.
121 "Shell Mason Killed At Yoakum."
122 "Shell Mason Killed," *The Dallas Morning News,* May 17, 1905, 4.
123 "Shot By Girl's Brother."
124 "Shell Mason Killed."
125 "Killing At Yoakum," *The Victoria Weekly Advocate,* Victoria, Texas, May 20, 1905, 1.
126 "Crime Scene Map," The State of Texas v Prentiss Newman; Investigative Reports of the Bureau of Investigation 1908-1922, NARA M1085, boi_mexican_851-874_0007, https://www.fold3.com/image/225788609, accessed July 23, 2018.
127 "Crime Scene Map."
128 "Shell Mason Killed by Newman Boys." The Yoakum correspondent for *The Houston Chronicle* claimed in his account to be at the location of the shooting between the Lane Hotel and Mason residence that morning and saw Shell Mason leave his home. The correspondent's report also contradicted the investigation report that the first two rifle shots were simultaneous before a third shot occurred. The correspondent said he heard one shot followed by the sound of an empty cartridge being ejected. Then he heard a second and final shot.
129 "Shell Mason Killed From Window of Lane Hotel in Yoakum," *The Daily Express,* San Antonio, Texas, May 17, 1905, 1.
130 "Shell Mason Killed At Yoakum;" "Shell Mason Killed From Window of Lane Hotel in Yoakum."
131 "Shot By Girl's Brother;" "Slain at Entrance," *Bryan Morning Eagle,* May 17, 1905.

Chapter 5
132 "Shell Mason Killed From Window of Lane Hotel in Yoakum."
133 LOFP.
134 "Shell Mason Killed." Of the 20 men from Karnes County supporting Prentice and Arthur Newman, at least two were relatives: their uncle, William Leckie, and Prentice's father-in-law, T. S. Williams of Cuero.
135 "Newmans Gave Bond."
136 The State of Texas v Prentiss Newman.
137 *The Hallettsville New Era,* October 27, 1905, 2.
138 Evan Anders, *Boss Rule in South Texas: The Progressive Era* (Austin, Texas: University of Texas Press, 1982), 175.
139 Robert M. Ireland, "The Libertine Must Die: Sexual Dishonor and the Unwritten Law in the Nineteenth-Century United States," *Journal of Social History,* 23, No. 1 (Oxford University Press, Autumn 1989), 27-44; http://www.jstor.org/stable/3787563, accessed August 27, 2015.
140 The State of Texas v Arthur Newman, Lavaca County District Court; The State of Texas v Prentiss Newman.
141 Dale Lasater, *Falfurrias: Ed C. Lasater and the Development of South Texas* (College Station: Texas A&M University Press, 1998), 91.
142 "Arthur Newman Makes Invention," *The Hallettsville New Era,* April 19,1907, 1.
143 Thomas E. Clark, assignee, "Device for perforating well-casings," US Patent 702128A, June 10, 1902.
144 "Social World Throughout Southwest Texas," *The Daily Express,* San Antonio, Texas, May 28, 1905, 22.
145 *Directory of the City of Fort Worth 1905-06* (Galveston, Texas: Morrison & Fourmy Directory Company, 1905), texashistory.unt.edu/ark:/67531/metapth46812/m1/374/?q=Newman, accessed February 22, 2017, University of North Texas Libraries, The Portal to Texas History, texashistory.unt.edu; crediting University of Texas at Arlington Library.
146 Notes from Ethelyne Dahnke, LOFP
147 Prentice Newman, 1906-1907, *U.S. City Directories, 1822-1995* [database online].
148 "District Court," *The Shiner Gazette,* Shiner, Texas, March 28, 1906, 4.
149 "District Court," *The Shiner Gazette,* November 7, 1906, 1.
150 The Thirtieth Texas Legislature in the 1907 session broadened the statute to punish physicians prescribing drugs for abortions by adding the words "or knowingly procure to be administered." See "The Evidence Sufficient to Sustain a Conviction for Abortion," *Texas State Journal of Medicine,* III, No. 11, March 1908, 275.

151 *United States Deceased Physician File (AMA), 1864-1968,* images, FamilySearch, https://familysearch.org/pal:/MM9.3.1/TH-1951-31279-35284-27?cc=2061540, accessed April 14, 2016, Botts, Edwin H-Boyle, Arthur R > image 2461 of 3007; American Medical Association, Chicago.
152 "District Court Doings," *The Hallettsville Herald,* November 5, 1909, 3; "Newman Acquitted," *Brownsville Daily Herald,* November 9, 1909.
153 "Unwritten Law Case," *The Austin Statesman,* April 17, 1907, 1.
154 "Arthur Neuman Not Guilty," *The Hallettsville New Era,* April 19, 1907, 3.
155 "Acquit Arthur Neumann," *Fort Worth Star-Telegram,* April 21, 1907, 12.
156 The State of Texas v Arthur Newman.
157 "Arthur Neuman Not Guilty."
158 "Lavaca County Court," *The Austin Statesman,* October 29, 1908, 7.
159 Anders, *Boss Rule,* 52-53.

Chapter 6
160 Robert Earl Good, "Texas' First Airplane Flight," *The Junior Historian,* 14, No. 6, May 1954, 9.
161 Advertisement, "Alamo Automobile Co.," *San Antonio Gazette,* May 23, 1908, 2.
162 LOFP.
163 No Title, *The Cuero Daily Record,* August 21, 1908, 1.
164 Henry Woodhouse, "The Conquest of the Air," *The World's Great Events* (New York: P. F. Collier & Son Corporation, 1945), VIII, 370-371.
165 McCullough, *The Wright Brothers,* 156-159.
166 "Have Solved Problem of Navigating Air," *The San Antonio Light,* May 15, 1908, 12.
167 McCullough, *The Wright Brothers,* 184; J. R. Hildebrand, "Man's Amazing Progress in Conquering the Air," *National Geographic,* XLVI, No. 1, July 1924, 93.
168 "Aeronautics," *The Source Book.*
169 "Wilbur Wright Makes Successful Airship Flight," *The Daily Express,* San Antonio, Texas, August 9, 1908, 7.
170 Foehner, "America's First Monoplane."
171 McCullough, *The Wright Brothers,* 92; Woodhouse, *"The Conquest of the Air,"* 365-366.
172 "Flying Machine, Invention of a San Antonian, Is Nearing Test," *The San Antonio Light,* December 31, 1908, 3; "First Flight of Airship in San Antonio," *San Antonio Gazette,* December 31, 1908, 1. Newman's first flight was the only aeroplane on which Massey contributed. He remained a San Antonio automobile mechanic until his death at age twenty-five on December 11, 1911, at his parents' home in San Antonio ("Massey," *The San Antonio Light,* December 11, 1911, 3).
173 Texas had recorded many other previous attempts at flight prior to 1903. See the aviation entry in *The Handbook of Texas* for a list.
174 Margaret Guroff, *The Mechanical Horse: How the Bicycle Reshaped American Life"* (Austin, Texas: The University of Texas Press, 2016), 85-86; McCullough, *The Wright Brothers,* 38-39; "Inventing a Flying Machine: The Breakthrough Concept," The Wright Brothers, Smithsonian National Air and Space Museum, https://airandspace.si.edu/exhibitions/wright-brothers/online/fly/1899/breakthrough.cfm, accessed November 14, 2018.
175 Although no engineering diaries or notes exist for Newman, newspaper accounts show that he meticulously went over every critical control point on every aeroplane he built before each flight test. His San Antonio reports also indicate he created an engineering quality measuring system that monitored each detail of the craft's basement construction for components of his first iteration.
176 H. L. Eustace, "Brownsville Aviation Pioneer Encountered Many Obstacles," *The Brownsville Herald,* July 7, 1929, 17.
177 "Airship Test Brings Victory to Inventor."
178 "First Flight of Airship in San Antonio."
179 McCullough, *The Wright Brothers,* 49.
180 Foehner, "America's First Monoplane;" "Newman Aeroplane Trial," *Brownsville Daily Herald,* October 29, 1909, 5; "Aeroplane Flies 100 Yards, Then Swoops to Earth," *The Daily Express,* San Antonio, Texas, January 3, 1909, 20.
181 Robert Esnault-Pelterie, "Expériences D'Aviation," *L'Aérophile,* June 1905, 132-138; McCullough, *The Wright Brothers,* 240.
182 "Gyroscope," Britannica School, Encyclopædia Britannica, Inc., 2015, http://www.austinlibrary.com:2241/levels/referencecenter/article/38664#2950.toc, accessed November 16, 2015.
183 "Elmer Ambrose Sperry," Britannica School, Encyclopædia Britannica, Inc., 2015, http://www.austinlibrary.com:2241/levels/referencecenter/article/69088, accessed November 16, 2015.
184 Foehner, "America's First Monoplane."
185 "Expect to Fly in Test at Fort Sam Houston," *The San Antonio Light,* December 30, 1908, 1.
186 "Flying Machine, Invention of a San Antonian, Is Nearing Test."
187 "First Flight of Airship in San Antonio."
188 McCullough, *The Wright Brothers,* 92.
189 "Expect to Fly in Test at Fort Sam Houston."
190 "Flying Machine, Invention of a San Antonian, is Nearing Test."
191 "Delay in Aeroplane Test," *The Daily Express,* San Antonio, Texas, January 2, 1909, 12.
192 "Airship Test Brings Victory to Inventor."
193 Ethelyne Dahnke to Lorraine Owens, February 18, 1973, LOFP.
194 "Expect to Fly in Test at Fort Sam Houston."
195 "Airship Test Brings Victory to Inventor." Competing San Antonio newspapers gave different accounts of the results of Newman's first flight. While the *San Antonio Light* article, referenced in the text, focused on positive achievements of Newman's first flight, San Antonio's *Daily Express* focused on the problems Newman experienced in the air and on his rough landing. Even so, even the *Daily Express* reporter concluded "the demonstration was successful." See "Aeroplane Flies 100 Yards, Then Swoops to Earth" *Daily Express,* San Antonio, Texas, January 3, 1909, 20.

[196] Ethelyne Dahnke to Lorraine Owens; "Airship Test Brings Victory to Inventor."
[197] "Airship Test Brings Victory to Inventor."

Chapter 7
[198] "Newman Aeroplane," *Aeronautics*, IV, No. 4, March 1909, 120.
[199] Good, "Texas' First Airplane Flight," 9.
[200] "Newman Will Build Improved Aeroplane," *The Daily Express*, San Antonio, Texas, January 4,1909, 1.
[201] "Make Faulty Aeroplane Drop Like Parachute."
[202] Harry Foehner, "Unsung Early Aviator Now Leads Quiet Life," *Dallas Morning News*, August 24, 1930, 3. Foehner lists the following San Antonio residents as potential investors: Dr. Frederick J. Fielding, J. M. Vance, J. M. Nix, George B. Taliaferro, G. A. C. Halff, H. G. Stack, and Nat M. Washer. The article also suggested this same group had contributed funds to Newman's original aeroplane built in the basement of Alamo Automobile Company, but, if so, not one of them invested in Newman's second iteration.
[203] "Eyes of World on San Antonio Balloon Race," *The Daily Express*, San Antonio, Texas, November 1, 1908, 18.
[204] Christian Brannstrom and Matthew Neuman, "Inventing the 'Magic Valley' of South Texas, 1905-1941," *Geographical Review*, American Geographical Society, 99, No. 2, April 2009, 126, http://www.jstor.org/stable/40377377, accessed November 23 2015.
[205] James C. Nagle, *Irrigation in Texas* (Washington, D.C.: Government Printing Office, 1910), Google Books, https://archive.org/details/irrigationintex00naglgoog, accessed November 23, 2015.
[206] Brannstrom and Neuman, "Inventing the 'Magic Valley' of South Texas," 123, 126-127.
[207] "In Our Valley," *The Brownsville Herald*, July 9, 1929, 1.
[208] "Flying Machine for Brownsville," *Brownsville Daily Herald*, January 15, 1909.
[209] Original Brownsville investors included: Geo. J. Head, Thos. R. Tumlinson, R. B. Creager, Noah Allen, D. L. Spero, E. F. Rowson, Jno. McClintock, W. O. Coleman, J. S. Rowe, T. Crixell, L. E. Brunnaugh, J. G. Fernandez, Burt E. Hinkley, Jas. A. Browne, E. A. McGary, R. B. Rentfro, A. C. Brokaw, W. M. Lastinger, P. Champion, J. H. Cross, M. Besteiro, James B. Wells, Jno. Bartlett, E. L. Hicks, J. C. Wreford, J. B. Scott, Alba Heywood, A. W. Wood, Louis Crixell, A. C. Weyman, José Celaya Jr., B. G. Stegman, Jno. B. Rutledge, and R. N. Magill.
[210] "Brownsville Aeroplane Co.," *Brownsville Daily Herald*, January 20, 1909.
[211] "Work Is Begun On Aeroplane," *Brownsville Daily Herald*, February 4, 1909; "Brownsville Aeroplane Co."
[212] "To Buy Aeroplane Material," *Brownsville Daily Herald*, January 22 1909.
[213] "To Fly Aeroplane at Uniform Elevation," *The Daily Express*, San Antonio, Texas, February 1, 1909.
[214] No title, *Brownsville Daily Herald*, February 9, 1909, 2.
[215] "Aeroplane is About Finished," *Brownsville Daily Herald*, February 19, 1909; "To Fly Aeroplane at Uniform Elevation."

Chapter 8
[216] George W. Cox to Delbert Runyon, September 12, 2008, RFP.
[217] Robert Runyon, "Contents of trunk left at W. T. Youngs;" Robert Runyon, "Records, Property of Robert Runyon," December 3, 1908-January 29, 1909, RFP.
[218] Advertisement: "Hotel Richelieu," *New Orleans Times-Picayune*, January 28, 1900, 1.
[219] Runyon, "Records, Property of Robert Runyon."
[220] Runyon, "Records, Property of Robert Runyon;" Kodak Exposure Records.
[221] Classified advertisement, *The Houston Post*, January 25, 1909, 8; Classified advertisement, *The Houston Post*, December 29, 1909, 10; "New Schedule Is Announced." George C. Werner, "St. Louis, Brownsville and Mexico Railway," *Handbook of Texas Online*, http://www.tshaonline.org/handbook/online/articles/eqs30, accessed November 17, 2015.
[222] Kodak Exposure Records.
[223] George W. Cox.
[224] Fannie Short to Robert Runyon, March 4, 1909, RRC, DBCAH Box 2008-106/1.
[225] Fannie Short, April 6, 1909, RRC, DBCAH Box 2008-106/1.
[226] Ada Spears to Robert Runyon, June 18, 1909, RRC, DBCAH Box 2008-106/1.
[227] Evelyn French to Robert Runyon, June 9, 1909, RFP.
[228] Evelyn French to Robert Runyon, December 4, 1909, RRC, DBCAH Box 2008-106/1.
[229] Evelyn French, October 11, 1909.
[230] "Delightful House Party," *Brownsville Daily Herald*, June 18, 1909, 1.
[231] Evelyn French, June, 20 1909; Evelyn French, July 1, 1909.
[232] Evelyn French; letter is dated June 9, 1909, but postmark was July 9, 1909.
[233] "Delightful House Party."
[234] Evelyn French, June 2, 1909, to August 2, 1910.
[235] Kentucky State Guard, RFP.
[236] Evelyn French, July 1, 1909.
[237] Evelyn French; letter is dated June 9, 1909, but postmark was July 9, 1909.
[238] Evelyn French, July 12, 1909.
[239] Evelyn French, July 27, 1909.
[240] Evelyn French, January 11, 1910.
[241] "Lunch Room Changes Hands," *Brownsville Daily Herald*, September 1, 1909.
[242] "Late Personals," *Brownsville Daily Herald*, September 28, 1909.
[243] "Arrested on Charge of Opening Letters, *Brownsville Daily Herald*, October 7, 1909.
[244] "Case Dismissed," *Brownsville Daily Herald*, October 16, 1909.
[245] Evelyn French, October 11, 1909.
[246] Edyth Christie to Robert Runyon, November 9, 1909, RRC, DBCAH Box 2008-106/1.
[247] Gulf Coast News and Hotel Company, circa 1909, RRC, DBCAH Box 2.325/v46.
[248] Linda Peterson, "From Commerce to History: Robert Runyon's Postcards of the Lower Rio Grande Valley and Brownsville, 1910-1926," *The Southwestern Historical Quarterly*, Texas State Historical Association, 102, No.

2, October 1998, 213.
[249] Evelyn French, January 24, 1910; Evelyn French, November 20, 1909.
[250] "Companies B, C, and D, Twenty-Fifth United States Infantry," *Congressional Serial Set,* IV (Washington, D.C.: Government Printing Office, 1911), 1396.
[251] Garna L. Christian, "Brownsville Raid of 1906," *Handbook of Texas Online,* http://www.tshaonline.org/handbook/online/articles/pkb06, accessed November 18, 2015.
[252] "Companies B, C, and D, Twenty-Fifth United States Infantry," 2172.
[253] Evelyn French August, 23, 1909; November 5,1909; January 24, 1910; April 9, 1910; April 9, 1910.
[254] Fannie Short, July 24, 1909.
[255] Robert Runyon to International Correspondence Schools, April 13, 1910, RRC, DBCAH Box 3B110.
[256] Kodak Exposure Records.

Chapter 9
[257] "Brownsville's Air Navigator," *Brownsville Daily Herald,* March 6, 1909, 8. Despite Tumlinson's remark, there is no mention of anyone actually accompanying Newman on any of his attempts.
[258] "Airship Did Not Fly Saturday," *Brownsville Daily Herald,* March 8, 1909, 1.
[259] "Airship Still Refuses to Soar," *Brownsville Daily Herald,* March 9, 1909, 1.
[260] "Will Fly to Corpus, Of Course, But—," *Brownsville Daily Herald,* March 9, 1909, 2.
[261] "Texan Flies Twelve Miles," *The Sun,* New York, March 24, 1909, 1; "Flying in Texas," *Flight International,* I, No. 16, April 17, 1909, 227.
[262] "Texan Flies Half an Hour," *Baltimore Sun,* March 24, 1909, 1; "Texas Aeroplane Flies," *The Evening Star,* Washington, D.C., March 24, 1909, 9.
[263] The State of Texas v Prentiss Newman.
[264] Foehner, "America's First Monoplane;" Good, "Texas' First Airplane Flight," 9.
[265] "E.H.R. Green Purchases Large Wright Aeroplane," *Dallas Morning News,* February 18, 1909, 5. Green later changed his purchase to a Glenn Curtiss aeroplane, but failed to receive delivery in time for the 1909 State Fair. See "Curtiss Aeroplane Purchased by E. H. R. Green of Dallas For Use Here During the State Fair of Texas," *Dallas Morning News,* September 12, 1909, 24.
[266] "San Antonio Man Invents Aeroplane," *San Antonio Light and Gazette,* May 30, 1909, 23.
[267] "Local Man Invents New Aeroplane," *San Antonio Light and Gazette,* September 22, 1909, 1-2.
[268] Martin Donell Kohout, "Brodbeck, Jacob Friedrich," *Handbook of Texas Online,* http://www.tshaonline.org/handbook/online/articles/fbr63, accessed November 30, 2015.
[269] "Aeroplane Co. Holds Meeting," *Brownsville Daily Herald,* May 25, 1909, 1.
[270] "12-Day Fair is Decided Upon," *The San Antonio Light,* March 25, 1909, 2.
[271] "Aeroplane Co. Holds Meeting."
[272] Vijay K. Jolly, *Commercializing New Technologies: Getting from Mind to Market* (Boston: Harvard Business School Press, 1997), 256.
[273] "Aeroplane Co. Holds Meeting."
[274] McCullough, *The Wright Brothers,* 239-240.
[275] "Motor for Aeroplane," *Brownsville Daily Herald,* June 18, 1909, 1.
[276] "Aeroplane Exhibition," *Brownsville Daily Herald,* May 26, 1909, 3.
[277] "Accident Marred Flight of Airship," *Brownsville Daily Herald,* May 31, 1909, 1.

Chapter 10
[278] "Aeroplane Announcement," *Brownsville Daily Herald,* May 31, 1909, 2.
[279] "Brownsville Airship Flight," *Brownsville Daily Herald,* June 2, 1909, 1; "Brownsville Is Proud," *Brownsville Daily Herald,* June 2, 1909, 2.
[280] "From Brownsville, Texas," *The Automobile,* XX, No. 24, June 17, 1909, 976, https://books.google.com/books?id=xGUxAQAAMAAJ&lpg=PA1000&ots=cBqh7XeCLP&dq=The%20Automobile%20magazine%20June%2017%2C%201909&pg=PA976#v=onepage&q=The%20Automobile%20magazine%20June%2017,%201909&f=false, accessed April 13, 2017.
[281] "Aeroplane Meeting," *Brownsville Daily Herald,* June 2, 1909, 3.
[282] "Airship Makes Another Flight," *Brownsville Daily Herald,* June 4, 1909, 1.
[283] "Mission Statement," Metropolitan Museum of Art, https://www.metmuseum.org/about-the-met, accessed January 22, 2018.
[284] Robert Runyon portrait by Gilhousen Studio, Brownsville, Texas, circa 1909, RFP.
[285] "Photos of Flying Machine," *Brownsville Daily Herald,* June 4, 1909, 3. Gilhousen left Brownsville the next year, leaving a void for portrait photography that Runyon eventually filled.

Chapter 11
[286] "Motor for Aeroplane."
[287] Today's city of Port Isabel, Texas, was known as Point Isabel from the community's founding in the 1830s until it was incorporated in 1928. We use the prevailing name for the site in the years discussed in the text.
[288] "Aeroplane May Not Fly," *Brownsville Daily Herald,* July 1, 1909, 3.
[289] "Isabel and Tarpon Swept By The Storm," *Brownsville Daily Herald,* July 1, 1909, 1.
[290] "Aeroplane May Not Fly."
[291] "Brownsville's Air Navigator."
[292] Robert Earl Good, "Conquering The Last Frontier—Aviation," *The Junior Historian,* March 1956, 27; McCullough, *The Wright Brothers,* 92; "Santos Dumont's Cross-Country Flight," *Flight International,* I, No. 16, April 17, 1909, 227; Robert Runyon, "Letters to the Editor: Hurricane List," *The Brownsville Herald,* June 30, 1963, 6.
[293] "Aeroplane Will Try To Fly Friday," *Brownsville Daily Herald,* August 4, 1909, 1.
[294] "Airship Trial Flight Tomorrow," *Brownsville Daily Herald,* August 5, 1909, 3.
[295] "Big Bird May Soar Monday," *Brownsville Daily Herald,* August 7, 1909, 3.
[296] "Shower Prevented Flight," *Brownsville Daily Herald,* August 9, 1909, 5.
[297] "Electric Theater Tonight," *Brownsville Daily Herald,* August 9, 1909, 5.
[298] "Great Day in Aviation Contests," *Brownsville Daily Herald,* August 28, 1909, 1.

[299] "In Our Valley," *The Brownsville Herald*, March 20, 1953, 4. In this column, Newman stated he made a successful hop with his aeroplane under its own power after being initially pulled by an automobile. In the article, he identified A. Cueto as the driver.
[300] "Airship Flight Almost a Success," *Brownsville Daily Herald*, August 20, 1909, 5; "America's First Monoplane Was Constructed by Brownsville Man."
[301] Eustace, "Brownsville Aviation Pioneer Encountered Many Obstacles;" Foehner. "Unsung Early Aviator Now Leads Quiet Life."
[302] "Airship Injured," *Brownsville Daily Herald*, August 28, 1909, 3; "To Rebuild Airship," *Brownsville Daily Herald*, August 31, 1909, 3.
[303] "Santos Dumont's Cross-Country Flight."
[304] "May Make Trial Flight Todal (sic)," *Brownsville Daily Herald*, October 28, 1909, 2.
[305] Foehner, "Unsung Early Aviator Now Leads Quiet Life."
[306] "Repairing the Brownsville Airship," *Brownsville Daily Herald*, September 17, 1909, 2.
[307] "Newman Aeroplane Trial."
[308] Good, "Conquering The Last Frontier—Aviation," 27.
[309] "Prentice A. Newman, Built 1-Wing Plane," *The New York Times*, June 30, 1964, 33.
[310] Turner, Newman, and Nauer, *Joseph and Rachel Rabb Newman*.
[311] "Newman Aeroplane Trial;" "Local Items: Another Attempt was made," *Brownsville Daily Herald*, October 30, 1909, 5.
[312] The State of Texas v Prentiss Newman.
[313] "Hallettsville New Era," *Weimar Mercury*, Weimar, Texas, November 18, 1909.
[314] "Newman Acquitted."
[315] "Attempt Flight Next Week," *Brownsville Daily Herald*, November 19, 1909, 6; McCullough, *The Wright Brothers*, 55.
[316] "To Try Its Wings Again," *Brownsville Daily Herald*, December 3, 1909, 8.
[317] "Wouldn't Go Up," *Brownsville Daily Herald*, December 4, 1909, 2.
[318] "Tired of Living," *Yoakum Weekly Times*, December 11, 1909, 6.
[319] H. L. Eustace, "Local Man Made and Flew Planes in 1909 Here for Publicity," *The Brownsville Herald*, September 22, 1929, 12.
[320] Roger Bilstein, "Aviation," *Handbook of Texas Online*, http://www.tshaonline.org/handbook/online/articles/epa02, accessed March 2, 2014.
[321] Eustace, "Brownsville Aviation Pioneer Encountered Many Obstacles."

Chapter 12
[322] Evelyn French, September 4, 1909.
[323] Fannie Short, August 13, 1910.
[324] Ella Lawson to Robert Runyon, January 29, 1911, RFP.
[325] "Brownsville Borrows Some Boom Timber From Catlettsburg," *The Catlettsburg Tribune*, November 30, 1910, 1, DBCAH Newspaper Collection.
[326] E. T. Pierce to Robert Runyon, July 26, 1910, RFP.
[327] Evelyn French, January 2, 1910.
[328] Edyth Christie, January 6, 1910.
[329] Evelyn French, March 12 and March 29, 1910.
[330] Evelyn French, April 18, 1910; Julia C. Ford (Mrs. J. C. Lallance) to Robert Runyon, April 8, 1910, RRC, DBCAH Box 2008-106/1.
[331] Fannie Short, June 9, 1910.
[332] Kodak Exposure Records.
[333] "Personals," *Brownsville Daily Herald*, July 9, 1910, 5.
[334] William Runyon, St. Joseph College School Roll of Honor certificates, October 1910 to April 1911, RFP.
[335] Eastman Kodak to Robert Runyon, June 1, 1910, RRC, DBCAH Box 3B110. Runyon continued to enter contests through 1918, once drawing a commendation from *American Photography* magazine for his landscape shot entitled "The Rio Grande." See *American Photography*, 12, No. 4, April 1918, 234.
[336] Robert Runyon to C. U. Williams Co., September 30, 1910, RRC, DBCAH Box 3B107.
[337] Runyon Perkins Notes, RFP.
[338] Peterson, "From Commerce to History," 214.
[339] Robert Runyon, photography inventory on Gulf Coast News and Hotel Company letterhead, circa 1910, RRC, DBCAH Box 3B107.
[340] Peterson, "From Commerce to History," 214.
[341] Runyon Perkins Notes, RFP.
[342] Ella Lawson to Robert Runyon, January 29, 1911, RFP.
[343] William Runyon to Lillian Runyon Burney, June 20, 1963.
[344] Robert Runyon to H. G. Zimmerman & Company, June 12, 1911, RRC, DBCAH Box 3B107.
[345] "The Rio Grande Railroad Company 1870-1911," *Journal of Texas Shortline Railroads*, Lester Haines, editor, 1, No. 2, August-October 1996, 36.
[346] Robert Runyon to George E. Knauff, May 15, 1911; Bee Candy Manufacturing Company to Robert Runyon, July 12, 1911; Rueckheim Bros. & Eckstein to Robert Runyon, July 18, 1911, RRC, DBCAH Box 3B107.
[347] Runyon Perkins Notes, RFP.
[348] Robert Runyon to George E. Knauff, general manager, Gulf Coast News and Hotel Company, October 7, 1911, RRC, DBCAH Box 3B107.
[349] "Good Pictures," *Brownsville Daily Herald*, January 17, 1912, 9.
[350] Robert Runyon to José T. Medrano, October 12, 1912, RFP.
[350] Charles Gilhousen portrait of Robert Runyon, RFP; "Popular Couple Wed," *Brownsville Daily Herald*, November 25, 1912, 3. The folio on this issue gives the year as 1913 rather than the accurate year of 1912.

Chapter 13
[351] Frank Cushman Pierce, *A Brief History of the Lower Rio Grande Valley* (Menasha, Wisconsin: George Banta

Publishing Company, 1917), 20; Craig H. Roell, *Matamoros And The Texas Revolution* (Denton, Texas: Texas State Historical Association, 2013), 33.
[353] Daniel D. Arreola, "Plaza Towns of South Texas," *Geographical Review*, American Geographical Society, 82, No. 1, January 1992, 56-73, http://www.jstor.org/stable/215405, accessed November 17, 2012.
[354] Robert Runyon, "The Old Board Walk," December 25, 1964, RFP; Joseph J. Macek to Robert Runyon, September 25, 1965, RRC, DBCAH Box 2007-223/4.
[355] H. Hamilton Fyfe, *The Real Mexico: A Study on the Spot* (New York: McBride, Nast & Company, 1914), 33, RRML.
[356] Runyon Perkins, *Just Another Family Cookbook* (San Antonio, Texas: Privately Printed, 2006), 144.
[357] William Runyon to Lillian Runyon Burney, June 20, 1963.
[358] Omar S. Valerio-Jiménez, *River of Hope: Forging Identity and Nation in the Rio Grande Borderlands* (Durham, North Carolina: Duke University Press, 2013), Kindle Edition.
[359] Florence Johnson Scott, *Historical Heritage of the Lower Rio Grande* (San Antonio, Texas: The Naylor Company, 1937), 92; Garry Mauro, *Guide to Spanish and Mexican Land Grants in South Texas* (Austin, Texas: Texas General Land Office, 1988), 199.
[360] Eliseo Paredes Manzano, *Homenaje a los Fundadores de la Heroica, Leal e Invicta Matamoros en la Sesquicentenario de su Nuevo Nombre* (H. Matamoros, Tamaulipas: El H. Ayuntamiento de Matamoros, Tamaulipas, 1976), 94, 96.
[361] "México, Tamaulipas, registros parroquiales, 1703-1964," images, FamilySearch (https://familysearch.org/pal:/MM9.3.1/TH-1-11056-36039-34?cc = 1790934&wc = MCQ8-D66:144322701,144319702,144322702 : accessed 8 May 2015), Matamoros > Nuestra Señora del Refugio > Bautismos 1800-1854 > image 137 of 2202; paróquias Católicas, Tamaulipas (Catholic Church parishes, Tamaulipas).
[362] Paredes Manzano. *Homenaje a los Fundadores de la Heroica, Leal e Invicta Matamoros*, 8.
[363] "Ruth Clark Scrapbook," untitled, unbylined news article, McAllen Public Library, McAllen, Texas.
[364] Jeffrey William Hunt, "Palmito Ranch, Battle Of," *Handbook of Texas Online*, http://www.tshaonline.org/handbook/online/articles/qfp01, accessed May 8, 2017; Kathleen S. Dodds, Seton Hall University, to Celeste Perkins McEntire, January 26, 2005, RFP.
[365] César González Gómez, "El Juego Liberal: Beisbol Mexicano En La Época Del Fin Del Segundo Imperio, 1866-1870," September 8, 2008, http://ciudadanosenred.com.mx/el-juego-liberal-beisbol-mexicano-en-la-epoca-del-fin-del-segundo-imperio-1866-1870/, accessed November 26, 2018; González Gómez email to author, July 17, 2017; "The Base Ball Match" and "The Base Ballers," *The Brownsville Ranchero*, December 27, 1868, 1.
[366] "Ruth Clark Scrapbook."
[367] Amelia Leonor Medrano Longoria to Robert Runyon, September 3, 1912, RFP.
[368] Robert Runyon to Amelia Leonor Medrano Longoria, October 3,1912, RFP.
[369] Joseph T. Medrano to Robert Runyon, October 10, 1912, Celeste Perkins McEntire Family Papers.
[370] Robert Runyon to Joseph T. Medrano, October 12, 1912, RFP.
[371] Delbert Runyon to author, June 25, 2009, RFP.

Chapter 14
[372] Advertisement, "P.A. Newman with Hinkley & Batz," *Brownsville Daily Herald*, July 12, 1911.
[373] "Irrigation Machinery for Mexican Plant," *Brownsville Daily Herald*, June 6, 1911.
[374] "Model of Drill and Stabilizer Ready in 30 Days," *The Brownsville Herald*, December 31, 1922, 2; "A. P. Newman Invents New Rotary Drill," *The Brownsville Herald*, September 30, 1923, 4.
[375] "Chauffeur," *The Oxford Dictionary of Word Origins*, Julia Cresswell (Oxford University Press, Online 2010), http://www.austinlibrary.com:2057/view/10.1093/acref/9780199547920.001.0001/acref-9780199547920-e-946?rsk, accessed February 23, 2017.
[376] Carl S. Chilton, *From Steamboats & Stagecoaches To Jet Aircraft* (Brownsville, Texas: Brownsville Historical Association, 2011), 42; Francisco J. Alvarez de la F., "Ciudad Victoria, Capital de Tamaulipas," *La Verdad de Tamaulipas*, April 26, 2014, http://www.laverdad.com.mx/desplegar_noticia.php?nota = 166240, accessed February 19, 2016.
[377] Fyfe, *The Real Mexico*, 38, RRML.
[378] J. Lee Stambaugh and Lillian J. Stambaugh, *The Lower Rio Grande Valley of Texas* (Austin, Texas: Jenkins Publishing Co./San Felipe Press, 1974), 254.
[379] Herman Schnitzler, compiler and editor, *The Republic of Mexico: Its Agriculture, Commerce & Industries*, Library of Latin-American Information (New York: Nicholas L. Brown, 1924), 494-544, RRML.
[380] Walter Clore, "Roots of the Valley: Depression childhood adventures recalled," *Valley Morning Star*, January 8, 1995, C-1; José Raúl Canseco Botello, *Historia de Matamoros* (Matamoros, Tamaulipas: Talleres Tipograficos de Litografica Jardin, S. A. de C. V., June 20, 1981), 249; "Matamoros-Victoria Highway to be Finished June 1," *The Brownsville Herald*, April 14, 1948, 7.
[381] Philip Terry, *Terry's Mexico* (Boston and New York: Houghton Mifflin Company, 1911), 11-12, RRML.
[382] Toribio de la Torre, et al, *Historia General de Tamaulipas* (Ciudad Victoria, Tamaulipas: Instituto de Investigaciones Históricas de la Universidad Autónoma de Tamaulipas, 1986), 44.
[383] "Hunting in Mexico," *Brownsville Daily Herald*, November 18, 1912, 11; "Will Return Home from Monterrey," *Brownsville Daily Herald*, November 26, 1912, 1.
[384] Joe Lee Janssens, *Maneuver and Battle in in the Mexican Revolution: A Revolution in Military Affairs, 1913* (Houston, Texas: Revolution Publishing, 2016), xxxviii, 54.
[385] Janssens to author, June 24, 2018. Janssens' review of the Mexican secretary of war's registry, entitled *Escalafón general del Ejército*, shows that in September 1911 de la Peña was a first captain assigned to the Ninth Infantry Battalion. Also see "Captain Penn (sic) Not Killed at Torreon," *The Brownsville Herald*, November 25, 1910, 1.
[386] Richard F. Weingroff, "On The Right Side of the Road," *Highway History*, U.S. Department of Transportation, Federal Highway Administration, https://www.fhwa.dot.gov/infrastructure/right.cfm, accessed January 28, 2016.
[387] "Pistol and Gun in Deadly Duel," *Brownsville Herald*, February 22, 1913, 1; Mexicans Fight Duel, *Dallas*

Morning News, February 23, 1913, 2.
[388] "Is Killed in Chihuahua," *Brownsville Herald*, December 5, 1913, 1. Although the headline stated de la Peña was killed in Chihuahua, the article states he died in Coahuila where General Pablo González had implemented an end-of-year strategy following the capture of Ciudad Victoria.
[389] Janssens, *Maneuver and Battle in in the Mexican Revolution, 1913*, 54-61; Ciro R. de la Garza, *La Revolución mexicana en el Estado de Tamaulipas* (Mexico, D. F., Mexico: Librería de M. Porrúa, 1973-1975),162.
[390] de la Garza, *La Revolución mexicana*,164; José Carlos Mora Garcia, *La Revolución Mexicana en Tamaulipas: Raíces, Origen y Desarrollo del Movimiento Constitucionalista, 1913-1914* (Ciudad Victoria, Tamaulipas, Mexico: Comisión Organizadora para la Conmemoración en Tamaulipas del Bicentenario y de la Independencia y Centenario de la Revolución Mexicana, D. R Gobierno del Estado de Tamaulipas, July 15, 2009), 140.
[391] William Runyon to Lillian Runyon Burney, June 20, 1963.
[392] Oscar Rivera Saldaña, *Diccionario Biografico De La Heroica Matamoros*, Edición Especial (H. Matamoros, Tamaulipas, Mexico: Librería Española, 2001), 273.
[393] Janssens to author.
[394] Frank N. Samponaro and Paul J. Vanderwood, *War Scare on the Rio Grande: Robert Runyon's Photographs of the Border Conflict, 1913-1916* (Austin, Texas: Texas State Historical Association, 1992), 57.
[395] Joe Lee Janssens, *Maneuver and Battle in the Mexican Revolution, 1913*, 146-150; de la Garza, *La Revolución Mexicana*, 165.
[396] "Lower Valley Had Grandstand Seat at Battle of Mexican Revolution," *Valley Morning Star*, March 7, 1952, 12.
[397] Janssens, *Maneuver and Battle in the Mexican Revolution, 1913*, 149.
[398] Kodak Exposure Records; Janssens to author.
[399] "Bandits are Terrorizing Ranchers Near Matamoros," *Houston Chronicle*, February 21, 1913, 12.
[400] "Echazaretta Is Reported Killed," *Brownsville Herald*, December 19, 1913, 1.
[401] Runyon Perkins Notes, RFP.

Chapter 15
[402] "México, Tamaulipas, Registro Civil, 1800-2002," images, Archivo General del Registro del Estado de Tamaulipas, Matamoros > image 70 of 475, FamilySearch, https://familysearch.org/ark:/61903/3:1:33SQ-GT98-D1S?cc=1916237&wc=MD55-G36%3A203415001%2C204272901 : May 21, 2014, accessed April 19, 2017.
[403] Delbert Runyon to author.
[404] Jules Gouffé, *El Libro de Cocina*, Rodriguez y Co., editor (Mexico, D. F., Mexico: Dublan y Comp., 1893).
[405] Runyon Perkins, *Just Another Family Cookbook*.
[406] Janssens, *Maneuver and Battle in in the Mexican Revolution, 1913*, 280; de la Garza, *La Revolución Mexicana*, 190; Samponaro, Vanderwood, *War Scare on the Rio Grande*, 49-52.
[407] For an analysis on Carranza's action to transfer Blanco for failure to follow commands, see Joe Lee Janssens, *Maneuver and Battle in the Mexican Revolution, 1913*, 278-280. Also, Janssen's *Strategy and Tactics of the Mexican Revolution 1910-1915* (Houston: Revolution Publishing, 2019), 94.
[408] Amali Runyon Perkins, notebook inventory of Runyon photography glass plate negatives, "Matamoros, Tamps," Note 17, 1986. The cited note quotes Amelia Runyon explaining to her daughter, Amali, her family's involvement in the November 1913 Battle of Ciudad Victoria. The note states: "Mother said Tió Pancho (Francisco González Villarreall) and Tió José (José Cecilio Medrano Longoria) were with the Carrancistas, and Daddy (Robert Runyon) and others followed troops to Victoria."
[409] "Bombarding C. Victoria," *Brownsville Herald*, November 14, 1913, 1. (The printer did not remove the slug for the previous date when he composed this edition's page, although the day in the folio is correct.)
[410] Janssens, *Maneuver and Battle in in the Mexican Revolution, 1913*, 308.
[411] "State Capital Is Destroyed," *Brownsville Herald*, November 29, 1913, 5.
[412] Janssens, *Maneuver and Battle in the Mexican Revolution, 1913*; 318-319; de la Garza, *La Revolución mexicana*, 221-222.
[413] Rivera, *Diccionario Biografico*, 272; "Victoria Captured After 49 Hours of Continuous Fighting," *Brownsville Herald*, November 19, 1913, 1. The article states José Telésforo Medrano received the telegram from his son and General Pablo González, but the editor confused the general with Medrano's son-in-law, Francisco (Pancho) González Villarreal.
[414] Ancestry.com. Puebla, Mexico, Civil Registration Marriages, 1861-1930 [database online], Lehi, Utah: Ancestry.com Operations, Inc., 2014; "D'Cuir's Sad Death," *Brownsville Herald*, November 26, 1913, 1.
[415] Janssens, *Maneuver and Battle in the Mexican Revolution: A Revolution in Military Affairs, 1914* (Houston, Texas: Revolution Publishing, 2016), 211.
[416] The National Archives and Records Administration; Washington D.C.; Nonstatistical Manifests and Statistical Index Cards of Aliens Arriving at Eagle Pass, Texas, June 1905-November 1929; NAI: 2843448; Record Group Title: Records of the Immigration and Naturalization Service, 1787-2004.; Record Group Number: 85; Microfilm Roll Number: 05.
[417] Newspaper reports may have had wrong information about Major Raúl Gárate being among the aides who accompanied Decuir. Janssens lists Gárate among the Constitutionalist officers who attacked the Federals' positions at Las Virgenes on November 17 (see Janssens, *Maneuver and Battle in the Mexican Revolution, 1913*, 316). It seems unlikely that Gárate would make the multi-day trip back to Matamoros after the battle was won just to turn around and head to Ciudad Victoria again. It may have been a different Gárate with the convoy that departed Matamoros on November 21. The death certificate for the convoy's commanding officer, Colonel Luciano Decuir, dated November 23 in Santander Jiménez, was witnessed by Fernando Gárate of Matamoros.
[418] "Leave for Victoria," *Brownsville Herald*, November 21, 1913, 1; "Colonel Accidentally Shot," *The San Antonio Light*, November 24, 1913, 2.
[419] Photocopy, RRC, BCAH, RUN00090.
[420] José Carlos Mora Garcia, *La Revolución Mexicana en Tamaulipas*; "Looking to Sept. 15," *Brownsville Herald*,

September 12, 1913.
[421] "D'Cuir's Sad Death."
[422] It is possible that both Newman and Runyon had traveled by automobile with General Jesús Carranza to the military meeting at Santander Jiménez on November 11. Runyon's negatives show a photograph of a jacal taken at nearby Padilla that is dated November 11, 1913. Newspaper reports too state that Carranza traveled to this meeting by automobile (See "Bombarding C. Victoria," *Brownsville Herald*, November 14, 1913, 1). Newman's driving experience, and the fact he was chosen again in a few days to drive in the military convoy, makes it possible he was one of the chauffeurs who returned Carranza and his subordinates to Matamoros early on November 14 with Runyon among the passengers.
[423] "State Capital Is Destroyed;" "Lower Valley Had Grandstand at Battle of Mexican Revolution."
[424] de la Garza, *La Revolución mexicana*, 224-225; Revolutionary Sentinel Kills Leader, Mistaking Him for Federal General," *The Washington Herald*, November 25, 1913, 10.
[425] "D'Cuir's Sad Death;" Ancestry.com. Tamaulipas, Mexico, Civil Registration Deaths, 1860-1987 [database online], Lehi, Utah: Ancestry.com Operations, Inc., 2015; Janssens, in communication with author, states that Constitutionalists sometimes used *capitalista* as a derogatory term and may have employed it on the death certificate to cover up their error in killing one of their own.
[426] "State Capital is Destroyed;" "Lower Valley Had Grandstand at Battle of Mexican Revolution."
[427] Delbert Runyon to author.
[428] "Lower Valley Had Grandstand at Battle of Mexican Revolution."
[429] "Runyon Returns from Victoria Last Night," *The Brownsville Sentinel*, November 28, 1913, transcribed copy, RFP.
[430] "Labor and Material Bill," Hill Sign Company, December 2, 1913, RRC, DBCAH Box 3B110.
[431] "Dreamland Theatre," *Brownsville Herald*, December 1, 1913, 4.
[432] Robert Runyon, "Postcard Album," RFP.

Chapter 16
[433] Janssens, *Maneuver and Battle in the Mexican Revolution: 1914*, 211.
[434] "Troops to Tampico," *Brownsville Herald*, December 16, 1913, 6.
[435] Advertisement, *Brownsville Herald*, August 15, 1914, 1.
[436] Classified Advertisement: "Automobiles," *Popular Mechanics*, February 1915, 19.
[437] Turner, Newman, and Nauer, "*Joseph and Rachel Rabb Newman*," 21.
[438] Advertisement, *Popular Mechanics*, April 1914, 22; August 1914, 17; September 1914, 21; advertisement, *Modern Electrics and Mechanics*, 28, No. 5, May 1914, 699.
[439] Advertisement, *Popular Mechanics*, March 1914, 21;
[440] Photocopy, C. Eleuterio Reyna, "Pase del Ferrocarril Constitucionalista por Roberto Runyón," March 19, 1914, RRC, DBCAH RUN0022.
[441] Runyon and Runyon, *Runyon Genealogy*, 32.
[442] "Lower Valley Had Grandstand Seat at Battle of Mexican Revolution."
[443] Gordon Shearer, "Brownsville Boy Travels With Revolutionary Army Picturing Battles," *Fort Worth Star-Telegram*, May 14, 1914, 5.
[444] "Lower Valley Had Grandstand Seat at Battle of Mexican Revolution."
[445] Shearer, "Brownsville Boy Travels With Revolutionary Army Picturing Battles."
[446] Janssens corroborates Runyon's timeframe in his *Maneuver and Battle in the Mexican Revolution, 1914*, 151-157.
[447] Shearer, "Brownsville Boy Travels With Revolutionary Army Picturing Battles."
[448] Frank Cushman Pierce, *A Brief History of the Lower Rio Grande Valley*, 155.
[449] Shearer, "Brownsville Boy Travels With Revolutionary Army Picturing Battles."
[450] "Lower Valley Had Grandstand Seat at Battle of Mexican Revolution;" ironically, Brownsville merchants had a higher acceptance of Constitutionalist currency with more favorable exchange rates than their counterparts in Matamoros (see Janssens, *Maneuver and Battle in the Mexican Revolution: 1914*, 25.)
[451] "Brownsville Boy Travels with Revolutionary Army Picturing Battles."
[452] Rivera, *Diccionario Biografico*, 272-273; Mariano B. Marin, *Recuerdos de la Revolucion Constitucionalista* (Ciudad Victoria, Tamaulipas, Mexico: Universidad Autónoma de Tamaulipas, Instituto de Investigaciones Historicas, 1977), 9, 10, 30, 34, 40-41.

Chapter 17
[453] Don M. Coerver, "Plan of San Diego," *Handbook of Texas Online*, http://www.tshaonline.org/handbook/online/articles/ngp04, accessed April 19, 2017; Charles R. Harris III, Louis R. Sadler, *The Plan de San Diego* (Lincoln, Nebraska: University of Nebraska Press, 2013), 1-5.
[454] "Lower Valley Had Grandstand Seat at Battle of Mexican Revolution."
[455] "Brownsville Autoist Has No Fear of War," *The Brownsville Herald*, March 24, 1915, 4.
[456] George W. Cox to Delbert Runyon, September 12, 2008; "Friends of Cox Sign Petitions In His Behalf," *The Brownsville Herald*, April 8, 1915, 4; "Mrs. Cox Says Was Misquoted In Interview," *The Brownsville Herald*, April 29, 1915, 4; "William B. Cox Released," *Dallas Morning News*, June 22, 1915, 2.
[457] "Injured Man Here From Point in Mexico," *The Brownsville Herald*, April 9 1915, 10.
[458] "Says He Heard Nothing of Lucio Blanco Rumor," *The Brownsville Herald*, May 14, 1915, 4.
[459] "Personals." *Laredo Weekly Times*.
[460] Charles R. Harris III, Louis R. Sadler, *The Plan de San Diego*, 161-162.
[461] Investigative Case Files of the Bureau of Investigation 1908-1922, National Archives NARA M1085, roll 857, 198, J. B. Rogers report, March 4, 1917.
[462] Pierce, *A Brief History of the Lower Rio Grande Valley*, 91; Alicia A. Garza, "Norias Ranch Raid," *Handbook of Texas Online*, http://www.tshaonline.org/handbook/online/articles/pqnbj, accessed October 14, 2016.
[463] Samponaro and Vanderwood, *War Scare on the Rio Grande*, 83-85, 88-89.
[464] Pierce, *A Brief History of the Lower Rio Grande Valley*, 96-97.
[465] "Hay abrumadoras pruebas de culpabilidad contra Chapa y J. Buenrostro," *La Prensa*, San Antonio, Texas, April 15, 1916, 5.

466 "First Executions of Border Raiders," *Arkansas Gazette*, Little Rock, Arkansas, May 20, 1916, 10.
467 "El Gobernador Raúl Gárate dice que el Estado de Tamaulipas es libre y soberano." *La Prensa*, San Antonio, Texas, February 18, 1916, 4.
468 "Hay abrumadoras pruebas de culpabilidad contra Chapa y J. Buenrostro."
469 "Ha sido observado un aeroplano misterioso en las cercanías de Brownsville, Tex," *La Prensa*, San Antonio, Texas, May 23, 1916, 4.
470 Pierce, *A Brief History of the Lower Rio Grande Valley*, 117.
471 "First Executions of Border Raiders;" Garza, "Norias Ranch Raid."
472 Attorney General Thomas Watt Gregory to President Woodrow Wilson, June 16, 1916, The National Archives, NARA M1085, Investigative Case Files of the Bureau of Investigation, 1908-1922, Mexican Files, 1909-21, Case Number 232-342, Roll Number 867, 201, https://www.fold3.com/image/5336767.
473 U.S. v Robert Runyon, Case No. 298, April 15, 1916, U.S. District Court for the Southern District of Texas, Brownsville, Texas, Division; Records of U.S. District Courts of the United States, Record Group 21; The National Archives at Fort Worth, Texas.
474 Copy of Guest Register, *La Tierra y Su Gente*, comment entry of Gloria E. Anzaldúa, Santa Cruz, CA, December 11, 1989, RFP.
475 Monica Muñoz Martinez, *The Injustice Never Leaves You: Anti-Mexican Violence in Texas* (Cambridge, Massachusetts: Harvard University Press, 2018), 235-237; Robert M. Utley, *Lone Star Lawmen: The Second Century* (New York: Oxford University Press, Inc., 2007), 33-34; Samponaro and Vanderwood, 60, 91.

Chapter 18
476 Pierce, *A Brief History of the Lower Rio Grande Valley*, 85-86; "Carranza and Blocksom Meet at Boundary," *The Brownsville Herald*, November 30, 1915, 1.
477 Pierce, *A Brief History of the Lower Rio Grande Valley*, 156.
478 Harris and Sadler, *The Plan de San Diego*," 262-263.
479 Interview with Amelia Leonor Medrano Longoria de Runyon, April 1987; Juan Montoya, "This Renaissance man unknown to many here," *The Brownsville Herald*, February 27, 1983, 1D.
480 Major James Longstreet to Robert Runyon, December 13, 1918, RRC, DBCAH Box 3B110; Runyon received permission from Commanding Officer Longstreet to sell eight photographs of buildings and the flag pole at Fort Ringgold. For more detail on Runyon's photography career during the buildup of troops along the border, see Samponaro and Vanderwood, *War Scare on the Rio Grande*, 99-125.
481 Runyon and Runyon, *Runyon Genealogy*, 32-33.
482 Terry, *Terry's Mexico*, 8.
483 Mike Gilbert, "Robert Runyons Celebrating Golden Wedding Date," *The Brownsville Herald*, June 30, 1963, 18.
484 Comisión Nacional Para Las Celebraciones del 175 Aniversario de la Independencia Nacional Y 75 Aniversario de la Revolución Mexicana, *Venustiano Carranza* (Mexico, Colonia Juárez, D. F., Mexico: Instituto Nacional de Estudios Históricos de la Revolución Mexicana, 1985), 32.
485 Robert Runyon to Amelia Leonor Medrano Longoria de Runyon, May 17, 1920, RFP.
486 "Lower Valley Had Grandstand Seat at Battle of Mexican Revolution."
487 T. R. Acres to Robert Runyon, July 31, 1920, RRC, DBCAH Box 2007-223/4.
488 Peterson, "From Commerce to History," 215.
489 "R. Runyon Studio is Open; New Work to Commercial Line," *Brownsville Herald*, March 13, 1920, 3.
490 "Invoice for £2, 11," Henry Greenwood & Co., Ltd., London, England, to Robert Runyon, Brownsville, Texas. October 18, 1921, RRC, DBCAH Box 2007-109/1.
491 Robert Runyon to Inspector in Charge, Immigration Service, Brownsville, Texas, May 1923, RRC, DBCAH Box 3B108.
492 Samponaro and Vanderwood, *War Scare on the Rio Grande*, 10; News Agency Telegrams. RRC, DBCAH Box 2007-223/4.
493 Robert Runyon, payment of $300 on note to General Francisco González Villarreal, RRC, DBCAH Box 2007-109/1.
494 Robert Runyon, "History, Data, and Information Relative to Robert Runyon, P. O. Box 11, Brownsville, Texas" and Runyon Perkins Notes, RFP..
495 Necah Stewart Furman, "Webb, Walter Prescott, *Handbook of Texas Online*, http://www.tshaonline.org/handbook/online/articles/fwe06, accessed October 20, 2016; Walter Prescott Webb to Robert Runyon, January 17, 1921, RRC, DBCAH Box 2007-223/4.
496 Peterson, "From Commerce to History," 216-217. In the 1920s Runyon printed close to half a million postcards, including souvenir packages, for sale.
497 J. M. Black to Robert Runyon, October 15, 1919, RRC, DBCAH Box 3B108.
498 Robert Runyon, Inventory of Postcards, March 30, 1929, RRC, DBCAH Box 2007-223/1.
499 T. R. Acres to Robert Runyon, July 31, 1920, RRC, DBCAH Box 2007-223/4.
500 Peterson, "From Commerce to History," 216.
501 Some historians believe Runyon used other photographers' work without authorization or acknowledgment at the same time he avidly protected his own work. Certainly, many of Runyon's copy negatives obviously were made for clients who wanted duplicate prints of a photograph. Yet these historians claim Runyon also pirated colleagues' historical photographs during the Mexican Revolution. See Samponaro and Vanderwood, *War Scare on the Rio Grande*, 14.
502 C. B. Gillespie to Robert Runyon, October 21, 1919, RRC, DBCAH Box 2007-223/4.
503 Robert Runyon to John H. Williams, March 18, 1928, RRC, DBCAH Box 2007-223/4.
504 "Runyon Case Set for Trial," *The Brownsville Herald*, December 11, 1928, 7; "Plea Charges Infringement of Copyright," December 16, 1928, clipping in Robert Runyon scrapbook, RRC, DBCAH Box 2007-223/5; "Runyon Suit Compromised," *The Brownsville Herald*, April 10, 1929, 10; R. B. Creager to Brownsville Mayor A. B. Cole., February 1, 1929, RFP.
505 Runyon and Runyon, *Runyon Genealogy*, 33; G. H. Pittman & Brother to Robert Runyon, September 9, 1926, June 30, 1927, RRC, DBCAH Box 3B107.

506 Peterson, "From Commerce to History," 216;" Order Blank, Robert Runyon to Curt Teich & Co., May 20, 1937, RRC, DBCAH Box 2007-223/3
507 Advertisement, "Matamoros: The Basket Place," *The Brownsville Herald*, November 13, 1927, 115.
508 Dewey, *Pesos and Dollars*, 86.
509 Robert Runyon to *The Brownsville Herald* staff, November 8, 1930, RRC, DBCAH Box 2007-109/1. "Basket Place Site Matamoros Landmark," *The Brownsville Herald*, December 15, 1930, 5.
510 Robert Runyon, "History, Data, and Information Relative to Robert Runyon, P. O. Box 11, Brownsville, Texas."
511 "Mexico Curios at Basket Shop," *The Brownsville Herald*, October 20, 1930, 3; Advertisement: "The Basket Place," *The Brownsville Herald*, October 27, 1930, 3; Robert Runyon to Julia C. Ford, August 26, 1937, RRC, DBCAH Box 2008-106/1; Robert C. Mayes to Amali Runyon, December 4, 1936, RFP.
512 "Our Founders." The Robert J. Kleberg, Jr. and Helen C. Kleberg Foundation. http://www.klebergfoundation.org/, accessed October 31, 2016.
513 Helen C. Kleberg to Robert Runyon, April 10 and April 26, 1933, RRC, DBCAH Box 2007-109/5.
514 Robert Runyon, "History, Data, and Information Relative to Robert Runyon."
515 "Local Bank Fails to Open," *The Brownsville Herald*, March 25, 1932, 1; Robert Runyon to U.S. Senator Tom Connally (D-TX), April 15, 1933, RRC, DBCAH Box 2007-109/1; "Mr. Creager, Let us Present," *Heraldo de Brownsville*, December 23, 1935, 5; Dewey, *Pesos and Dollars*, 185.
516 Interview. Amelia Leonor Medrano Longoria de Runyon, March 6, 1987, Brownsville, Texas.
517 J. Frank Dobie, "Writer Finds Coyote Lore, Men of Liberal Thinking in Brownsville," *Austin American-Statesman*, January 28, 1945, 2.

Chapter 19
518 E. J. Alexander, "Posidonia oceanica found in North America," *Torreya*, 37, No. 4, July-August 1937, 85.
519 Alfred Richardson and Ken King, *Neptunia Plena* (Fabaceae: Mimoisodeae) Rediscovered in Texas," *Journal of the Botanical Research Institute of Texas*, 2, No. 2, December 9, 2008, 1491-1493; Alfred Richardson and Ken King, *Plants of Deep South Texas* (College Station: Texas A&M University Press, 2011), 251.
520 George Kozmetsky, Piyu Yue, *The Economic Transformation of the United States, 1950-2000* (West Lafayette, Indiana: Purdue University Press, 2003), 80-82.
521 Robert Runyon. " Runyon Gives Hints on the Caring and Growing of Palms—One of the Valley's Trade Mark Trees," *The Brownsville Herald*, July 21, 1946, 5.
522 "Club Hears Valuable Talk on Shrubs by Mr. Runyon," *The Brownsville Herald*, August 18, 1946, 12.
523 Alexander, "Posidonia oceanica found in North America."
524 Richardson and King, *Neptunia Plena* (Fabaceae: Mimoisodeae) Rediscovered in Texas;" Richardson and King, *Plants of Deep South Texas*, 251.
525 Alfred Richardson, PhD, email to author, August 5, 2018.
526 Richardson and King, *Neptunia Plena* (Fabaceae: Mimoisodeae) Rediscovered in Texas."
527 Kozmetsky, Yue, *The Economic Transformation of the United States*, 80-82.

Chapter 20
528 Fannie Short to Robert Runyon, October 6, 1909, RRC, DBCAH Box 2008-106/1. The quote is actually Fannie Short's restating Runyon's comment on lower Rio Grande Valley flora in a letter he sent her that no longer exists. Fannie's full quote states: "Indeed I do wish Kentucky could be cheated out of my share of the cold weather as I would much rather spend the winter there than here, and as you say presume it is strange to see the tropical fruits growing there in that tropical climate during our winter months."
529 Robert Runyon. *Vernacular Names of Plants Indigenous to the Lower Rio Grande Valley of Texas* (Brownsville, Texas: Brownsville News Publishing Co., 1947), vi.
530 Runyon Perkins notes. RFP.
531 Runyon Perkins notes. RFP.
532 Luis Sánchez Osuna, *Explicando A Berlandier:Bicentenario de Luis Berlandier*, (Ciudad Victoria, Tamaulipas, Mexico: Instituto Tamaulipeco para la Cultura y las Artes (ITCA)/ El Consejo Nacional para la Cultura y las Artes (CONACULTA), 2004), 29-35, 111-128; Clinton P. Hartmann, "Berlandier, Jean Louis," *Handbook of Texas Online*, https://tshaonline.org/handbook/online/articles/fbe56, accessed April 21, 2017.
533 Rebert, Paula, "A Civilian Surveyor on the United States-Mexico Boundary: The Case of Arthur Schott," *Proceedings of the American Philosophical Society*, 155, No. 4, 2011, 447, JSTOR, www.jstor.org/stable/23208784.
534 George Yatskievych, PhD, curator, Billie L. Turner Plant Resources Center at The University of Texas at Austin, email to author, November 27, 2018. Data tabulated through the Texas database of the Turner Plant Resources Center shows that between 1870 and 1920—the latter year coinciding with Runyon's beginning plant study as a self-taught botanist—nineteen different individuals collected plant specimens from Cameron County, Texas, that today are part of The University of Texas herbaria.
535 "Ex-Brownsville Mayor Earns Nation-Wide Fame as Amateur Botanist Through His Specimens from Valley," *Valley Morning Star*, April 28, 1946, 6. In a genealogical research letter to his relative, Amos Runyon of Belfry, Kentucky, on May 2, 1946, Runyon included this article. Runyon told Amos: "It is butchered up as the newspaper stories usually are, but after all it will give you a fair idea of the amount of work I have done with my studies in botany." RFP.
536 Joe Ideker, "Robert Runyon, Pioneer Lower Rio Grande Valley Botanist," Teleconference with Delbert Runyon, *The Sabal*, 5, No. 8, December 1988, 3.
537 *Journey's Reward* manuscript edits by George Yatskievych, PhD, curator, Billie L. Turner Plant Resources Center at The University of Texas at Austin, November 27, 2018.
538 Runyon Perkins Notes, RFP.
539 Yatskievych direct message to author, November 27, 2018.
540 Runyon, "History, Data, and Information Relative to Robert Runyon."
541 B. L. Turner to Mrs. J. T. (Lillian Runyon) Mahoney, July 15, 1968, RRC, DBCAH Box 2007-223/3.
542 Robert T. Clausen to Robert Runyon, 1943, RRC, DBCAH Box 2007-223/1. Clausen, curator of the herbarium at Cornell University, was one of many scientists who asked Runyon to grow plants. In this correspondence,

Clausen asked Runyon to plant a leguminous vine with edible tubers and poisonous seeds in his Brownsville garden to test its cultural possibilities.
543 Runyon Perkins Notes, RFP.
544 J. R. Pemberton, "A Large Tern Colony in Texas," *The Condor*, Cooper Ornithological Society, XXIV, No. 2, March-April 1922, 37-48, http://www.jstor.org/stable/1362732; "Pemberton, John Roy 'Bill,'" Islapedia.com, http://islapedia.com/index.php?title=PEMBERTON,_John_Roy_%22Bill%22, accessed November 10, 2016.
545 "Expedition Finds Rare Plants on Mexico Side," *The Brownsville Herald*, April 14, 1926, 1-2; Robert Runyon to Fred G. Meyer, May 9, 1948, RRC, DBCAH Box 2007-223/3.
546 Robert Runyon to Scott Haselton, October 13, 1947, RRC, DBCAH Box 2007-109/1; The University of Texas herbaria, The University of Texas at Austin Billie L. Turner Plant Resources Center database. http://prc-symbiota.tacc.utexas.edu/collections/list.php, accessed November 3, 2016.
547 Robert Runyon to C. V. Morton, April 2, 1945, RRC, DBCAH Box 2007-223/3.
548 Elzada U. Clover, "Vegetational Survey of the Lower Rio Grande Valley of Texas," *Madroño*, California Botanical Society, 4, No. 2, April 1937, 42, http://www.jstor.org/stable/41422215.
549 J. Frank Dobie, "Writer Finds Coyote Lore, Men of Liberal Thinking in Brownsville."
550 B. C. Tharp and Fred A. Barkley, "The Genus Ruellia in Texas," *The American Midland Naturalist*, 42, No. 1, July 1949, The University of Notre Dame, 5.
551 B. C. Tharp to Jeanette MacConachie, March 30, 1950, RRC, DBCAH Box 2007-223/3.

Chapter 21
552 N. L. Britton, J. N. Rose, *The Cactaceae: Descriptions and Illustrations of Plants of the Cactus Family*, 13-4 (Washington, D.C.: The Carnegie Institution, 1922-1923).
553 Robert Runyon, *Vernacular Names Of Plants*, 8.
554 Chris Best direct message to author, September 25, 2018.
555 "Ex-Brownsville Mayor Earns Nation-Wide Fame as Amateur Botanist Through His Specimens from Valley;" J. N. Rose, "Runyonia Longiflora," *Addisonia*, 7, No. 1, March 1922, 39-40; Susan Verhoek, "Huaco and Amole: A Survey of the Uses of Manfreda and Prochnyanthes," *Economic Botany*, 32, No. 2, April-June 1978, 124-130., http://www.jstor.org/stable/4253919.
556 Yatskievych direct message to author, November 27, 2018.
557 William Scheick, "Echeverian Beauty Among the Rocks," *Texas Gardener*, July/August 2012, http://www.texasgardener.com/pastissues/julaug12/Echeverian.html, accessed April 24, 2017.
558 International Crassulaceae Network, Echeveria Runyonii Rose ex. Walther, 1935, http://www.crassulaceae.ch/de/artikel?akID=48&aaID=2&aiID=R&aID=1898, accessed November 9, 2016; Secretary of Agriculture Tom Vilsack, "Census of Horticultural Specialties (2014)," *2012 Census of Agriculture*, 3, Special Studies, Part 3. AC-12-SS-3, December 2015, 355; "Echeveria runyonii Rose, new species," *Cactus and Succulent Journal*, 7.1935, 69.
559 "Prominent Visitor," *Brownsville Daily Herald*, December 8, 1904; Julian W. Sauls, "The Texas Citrus Industry," Texas AgriLife Extension, January 2008, http://aggie-horticulture.tamu.edu/citrus/l2286.htm, accessed November 11, 2016. Stiles was working with citrus in California when he first learned about the Valley's potential for growing citrus at its exhibit during the 1904 world's fair in St. Louis.
560 Harry (sic) Stiles, *Esenbeckia runyonii*, TEX00302545, May 15, 1929, The University of Texas herbaria, The University of Texas at Austin Billie L. Turner Plant Resources Center database, http://prc-symbiota.tacc.utexas.edu/collections/list.php, accessed November 29, 2018.
561 Luttes v The State of Texas, Supreme Court of Texas, June 18, 1958.
562 Chris Best email to author, June 12, 2017.
563 Robert Runyon to Amali Runyon Perkins, January 15, 1958, RFP.
564 C. V. Morton, "A New Species of Esenbeckia from Texas," *Journal of the Washington Academy of Sciences*, 20 No. 7, April 4, 1930, 136.
565 Chris Best email to author.
566 Chris Best email to author.
567 "Endangered and Threatened Wildlife and Plants; 90-day Finding for a Petition To List the Plant 'Esenbeckia runyonii' (Limoncillo) as Endangered," 64, No. 124, *Federal Register*, 34755-34756, June 29, 1999; Chris Best email to author.
568 Robert Runyon to R. A. Young, December 17, 1943, RFP.
569 Robert Runyon, *"Esenbeckia runyonii,"* ND. RFP; Robert Runyon to Edwin A. Menninger et al, January 10, 1949, RRC, DBCAH Box 2007-109/1; Runyon to W. H. Friend, September 19, 1940, Box 2007-109/1; Runyon to Cyrus Lundell, November 1941, Box 2007-223/1; 2007-223/3; Runyon to R. A. Young, S. F. Blake to Runyon, March 1, 1949, John L. Creech to Runyon, December 30, 1948, USDA and Runyon to Robert A. Vines, October 9, 1951, RFP.
570 "Valley To Be Featured in Trees of Southwest," Old Dirt Dauber Garden Editor, *The Brownsville Herald*, September 6, 1976, 4A; R. A. Vines, *Trees, Shrubs and Woody Vines of the Southwest* (Austin, Texas: University of Texas Press, 1960).
571 Michael R. Heep email to author, January 28, 2013; "Proposed Rules," *Federal Register*, 64, No. 124, June 29, 1999, 34755-34776; Michael R. Heep and Robert I. Lonard, "Esenbeckia Berlandieri (Rutaceae) Rediscovered in Extreme Southern Texas," *The Southwestern Naturalist*, 31, No. 2, May 22,1986, 259-260, www.jstor.org/stable/3670574, accessed November 15, 2016.
572 U.S. Department of Homeland Security, U.S. Customs and Border Protection, U.S. Border Patrol, Environmental Stewardship Plan for the Construction, Operation, and Maintenance of Tactical Infrastructure, U.S. Border Patrol, Rio Grande Valley Sector, Texas, July 2008, 10-9.

Chapter 22
573 Michael E. Porter, *Competitive Strategy* (New York: The Free Press, 1980), 4.
574 Case No. 8000-129012; entry for Hauscher, German alien, World War Records: Old German Files 1909-1921, Investigative Reports of the Bureau of Investigation 1908-1922, NARA M1085. boi_german_257-850_0030, Fold3. www.fold3.com/image/1129467, accessed January 27, 2017.

575 Lorraine Owens to author.
576 Advertisement: "M.A. Newman Garage," *The Brownsville Herald*, September 4, 1929, 15.
577 "One-Point Margin Ousts Eagles from State Race," *The Brownsville Herald*, December 8, 1929, 8; "Scorps Hailed as Valley's Best Eleven of All Times," *The Brownsville Herald*, December 17, 1930, 5; "Athletes Coming And Going Here," *The Brownsville Herald*, January 30, 1931; "Five Valley Football Players Out for U. of T. Football," *The Brownsville Herald*, September 8, 1932, 5.
578 LOFP.
579 Robert L. Newman telephone interview with author, October 27, 2015.
580 Eustace, "Brownsville Aviation Pioneer Encountered Many Obstacles;" "In Our Valley," July 9, 1929; "Brownsville Man is Unsung Pioneer in Aviation," *The Houston Chronicle*, August 10, 1930, 8; Foehner, "Unsung Early Aviator Now Leads Quiet Life;" Foehner, "America's First Monoplane Was Constructed by Brownsville Man;" "Brownsville Machinist Made Motorless Biplane in 1908," *The Brownsville Herald*, December 31, 1950, 11-B.
581 "Nuptial Rites Solemnized Saturday," *The Brownsville Herald*, June 4, 1933, 21.
582 "William J. Earle Dies in Honduras," *Valley Morning Star*, June 28, 1953, 2.
583 Robert L. Newman telephone interview.
584 "In Our Valley," *The Brownsville Herald*, March 8, 1953, 4; March 20, 1953, 4.
585 Good, "Texas' First Airplane Flight." A rewrite by Good entitled "Conquering The Last Frontier—Aviation" ran in the same journal in March 1954.

Chapter 23
586 Runyon, "History, Data, and Information Relative to Robert Runyon."
587 Robert Runyon to Ladislaus Cutak, March 30, 1942, RRC, DBCAH Box 2007-223/4; "Ex-Brownsville Mayor Earns Nation-Wide Fame as Amateur Botanist Through His Specimens from Valley;" No Title, *The Brownsville Herald*, March 24, 1929, 37.
588 Quillin used Ellen D. Schulz as her author's name on *Texas Cacti*.
589 Runyon Perkins Notes, RFP.
590 Robert Runyon to Clyde T. Reed, March 31, 1930, RRC, DBCAH Box 2007-123/2; Texas Academy of Science, Publishing Agreement for Ellen Schulz Quillin and Robert Runyon, March 17, 1930, Box 2007-223/4; "'Texas Cacti' Printed in S. A.," *The San Antonio Light*, May 4, 1930, 12; Ellen Schulz Quillin to Robert Runyon, September 21, 1932, Box 2007-223/4; Runyon Perkins Notes, RFP.
591 Runyon Perkins Notes, RFP.
592 Robert Runyon, *Vernacular Names Of Plants*.
593 Landon Lockett, "Historical Evidence of the Native Presence of Sabal Mexicana (Palmae) North of the Lower Rio Grande Valley," *SIDA, Contributions to Botany*, 16, No. 4, December 1995, 711-719.
594 Seth Patterson, Lawrence V. Lof, editors, *El Valle: The Rio Grande Delta*, "Sabal Palm," Jimmy Paz (Brownsville, Texas: Gorgas Science Foundation, Inc., no date), 64-65.
595 Norman Rozeff and Lawrence Lof, "An Unusual Beginning to an Unusual Man: Part I," *Valley Morning Star*, February 14, 2014; Rozeff and Lof, "Frank Rabb: His life, political rise and fall: Part II," *Valley Morning Star*, January 4, 2014; Turner, Newman, Nauer, *Joseph and Rachel Rabb Newman*; Martin Bryan Glasscock, "Rancho Santa Maria," *Handbook of Texas Online*, http://www.tshaonline.org/handbook /online/articles/ qcr02, accessed April 25, 2017; Stambaugh and Stambaugh, *The Lower Rio Grande Valley of Texas*, 187.
596 Runyon Perkins Notes, RFP.
597 Robert Runyon, botany field notes at Rabb Palm Grove, December 15, 1939, RRC, DBCAH Box 2007-223/3; The University of Texas Herbaria; Robert Runyon to David Fairchild, June 14, 1945, RRC, DBCAH Box 2007-223/3.
598 Frank Rabb to Robert Runyon et al., June 5, 1926, RRC, DBCAH Box 2007-109/1.
599 John K. Small, "The Palmetto Palm—Sabal Texana." *Journal of the New York Botanical Garden*, XXVIII, No. 330, June 1927, 142-143.
600 "Famous Botanist Will Study Fauna of Valley," *The Brownsville Herald*, May 31, 1926, 1-2; Robert Runyon, 1940 Calendar, entry for Monday, April 22, 1940, RFP.
601 Small, "The Palmetto Palm—Sabal Texana;" Charles Sprague Sargent, *The Silva of North America* (Boston and New York: Houghton, Mifflin & Company, 1896), 43.
602 Robert Runyon, "Sabal Texana, Rio Grande Palmetto, Palma de Micharo," a paper read at the Kiwanis Club Luncheon, February 4, 1937, RFP.
603 Robert Runyon to David Fairchild, June 14, 1945, RRC, DBCAH Box 2007-223/3.
604 Robert Runyon to W. H. Friend, June 17, 1937, RRC, DBCAH Box 2007-109/1.
605 Runyon, "Sabal Texana, Rio Grande Palmetto, Palma de Micharo."
606 David Fairchild to Robert Runyon, June 9, 1945, RRC, DBCAH Box 2007-223/3; A. B. Hendry, Rotogravure Magazine, *Houston Chronicle*, August 15, 1958, 4.
607 Hendry, *Rotogravure Magazine*.
608 "Palm Grove Will Be Sanctuary," *The New York Times*, March 22, 1972; Rozeff and Lof, "The Downfall of Frank Rabb's Politicking: Part VII," *Valley Morning Star*, February 14, 2014.

Chapter 24
609 Dora L. Costa, "The Evolution of Retirement: An American Economic History, 1880-1990," National Bureau of Economic Research, University of Chicago Press, January 1998, 26-27, http://www.nber.org/chapters/ c6108, accessed February 16, 2017.
610 "Ex-Brownsville Mayor Earns Nation-Wide Fame as Amateur Botanist Through His Specimens from Valley."
611 "Mostly About San Benito," *San Benito Light*, March 8, 1939, RRC, DBCAH Box 2007-223/5.
612 Robert Runyon to Cameron County Judge Oscar Dancy and Cameron County Commissioners, October 4, 1966, RRC, DBCAH Box 2007-109/1.
613 Robert Runyon scrapbook, "Ideal Mounting Book Domestic Art," 11, RFP; "Democrats Express Their Indignation," *The Brownsville Herald*, April 5, 1912, 1.
614 Creager said Runyon's automobile was a 1912 model, but Runyon's grandchildren who rode in it state that it was a four-door 1915 Model T Touring Sedan; Robert C. Runyon email to Ginger Gilbert Liening, August

3, 2013, and R. D. Perkins to Robert C. Runyon and Ginger Gilbert Liening, August 3, 2013, RFP; "R. B. Creager Assails Yturria for Raising 'Race Prejudice' Here," *The Brownsville Herald*, December 5, 1935, RRC, DBCAH Box 2007-223/5.

[615] "Rentfro, Yturria Gird For Run-Off," *The Brownsville Herald*, December 11, 1935, RRC, DBCAH Box 2007-223/5. As "elite-class" businessmen, both Creager and Rentfro were two early investors behind Newman's Brownsville Aeroplane Company.

[616] Robert Runyon, "25 Long Years," July 15, 1936, RFP; "Six Candidates to Address Rally Here," *The Brownsville Herald*, July 15, 1936, 2.

[617] "Mayor Candidates State Election Platform," *The Brownsville Herald*, December 10, 1937, RRC, DBCAH Box 2007-223/5.

[618] "Defeated Mayoralty Candidate Appointed Brownsville Manager," *San Antonio Evening News*, December 27, 1937, RRC, DBCAH Box 2007-223/5.

[619] Robert Runyon to Julia Ford, December 17, 1937, RFP.

[620] Juan Montoya, "This Renaissance man unknown to many here." Anthony Gray, "Park may get a name change," *The Brownsville Herald*, January 31,1995, 3A.

[621] William L. Adams and Anthony K. Knopp, *Portrait of a Border City: Brownsville, Texas* (Austin, Texas: Eakin Press, 1997), 223.

[622] B. C. Tharp to Jeanette MacConachie.

[623] Robert Runyon to J. Edgar Hoover, February 13, 1939, RFP.

[624] Robert Runyon, *Glad Tidings*, Bulletins 1-4, Brownsville City Manager, February, March, May, June 1939; RFP; Wm. Brown, "What Is Runyonism?" *The Brownsville News*, September 15, 1938, RRC, DBCAH Box 2007-223/5.

[625] "City Attorney Maps Civil Service Plan," *The Brownsville Herald*, February 3, 1938, RRC, DBCAH Box 2007-223/5.

[626] "City Garden Clubs Approve Runyon's Plan for Parks," *The Brownsville Herald*, March 9, 1939, RRC, DBCAH Box 2007-223/5.

[627] Lincoln Park, with many trees and shrubs once planted by Runyon, disappeared after 1999 so that the land could provide highway access through the adjacent area for the Veterans International Bridge at Los Tomates. A new Lincoln Park was completed in 2001 a short distance away from the original. Ringgold Park is now Dean Porter Park.

[628] "NYA Project Offers Work To 50 Youth," *Valley Morning Star*, December 13, 1938; "City Garden Clubs Approve Runyon's Plan for Parks," RRC, DBCAH Box 2007-223/5.

[629] Robert Runyon to W. H. Feagin, March 11, 1939, RRC, DBCAH Box 2007-223/1.

[630] "Filmore Park Gets Variety Of Shrubs," *The Brownsville Herald*, May 14, 1939; "Filmore Park Being Improved By WPA," *The Brownsville Herald*, June 29, 1939; Robert Runyon to H. E. Snow, June 1, 1939, RRC, DBCAH Boxes 2007-223/5 and 2007-223/1.

[631] Runyon Declares Charter Gives Him Thirty More Days," *The Brownsville Herald*, May 23, 1940; "Mayor And City Attorney Clash," *The Brownsville Herald*, June 29, 1939, RRC, DBCAH. Box 2007-223/5.

[632] Robert Runyon, 1940 Calendar, entry for Monday, June 24, 1940, RFP.

[633] "$93,723," *The Brownsville Herald*, August 29, 1940; Robert Runyon, "Memorandum Data Prepared by Robert Runyon," RRC, DBCAH Box 2007-109/1.

[634] "$93,723," *The Brownsville Herald*.

[635] "Hot City Election," *The Brownsville Herald*, November 2, 1941, Robert Runyon scrapbook, RFP.

[636] Runyon Slate Victor Here By 400 Votes," *The Brownsville Herald*, November 5, 1941, RRC, DBCAH Box 2007-223/5.

Chapter 25

[637] Adams and Knopp, *Portrait of a Border City,* 223; "City Stops Fund For Chamber Here," *The Brownsville Herald*, January 1, 1942, and " City Declines Request For Nurse Change," *The Brownsville Herald*, January 9, 1942, Robert Runyon scrapbook, RRC, DBCAH Box 2007-223/5.

[638] Robert Runyon to Amelia Runyon, July 22, 1928, Perkins-Runyon Letter Files, RFP; "Our Policy," *The Brownsville Herald*, July 27, 1942; "Runyon Not To Run Again for Mayor and May Quit Politics," *The Brownsville Herald*, March 19, 1942; "Brownsville Mayor, Dr. Cole Cleared By Westervelt Rule," *The Brownsville Herald*, March 16, 1943, RRC, DBCAH Box 2007-223/5.

[639] "Brownsville's Street Car Rails Enough for 3 Tanks," *The Brownsville Herald*, August 2, 1942, RRC, DBCAH Box 2007-223/5.

[640] "Eucalyptus Is Ideal Tree for Brownsville says Runyon; It's Good for Beauty, Firewood, Fences and Even Lumber," *The Brownsville Herald*, May 6, 1942, 3.

[641] "History, Data, and Information Relative to Robert Runyon;" Robert Runyon to Captain Leo F. Crane, April 19, 1943, RRC, DBCAH Box 2007-223/4.

[642] "Memorandum data prepared by Robert Runyon."

[643] "'People's Ticket' Enters Brownsville Race," *The Brownsville Herald*, October 3, 1943, 1-2; "People's Ticket Elected Without Runoff Here," *The Brownsville Herald*, November 3, 1943, 1-2.

[644] "Runyon Now In Charge of Brownsville's Parks," *The Brownsville Herald*, February 17, 1944; "Political Repercussions Rumored in Park Strike," *The Brownsville Herald*, March 20, 1944; "Runyon Denies Any Strike Move," *The Brownsville Herald*, March 21, 1944, RRC, DBCAH Box 2007-223/5.

[645] Jack Rutledge, "In Our Valley," *The Brownsville Herald*, May 19, 1944, RRC, DBCAH 2007-223/5; "Fire Sirens To Announce D-Day in Brownsville," *The Brownsville Herald*, May 28, 1944.

[646] Lieutenant Robert A. Runyon to D. S. and Amali Runyon Perkins, August 13, 1944, RFP.

[647] Not until February 7, 1945, following seven months of combat duty, did Lieutenant Bob Runyon return to England on leave. On February 25, he underwent an operation to remove shrapnel from his shoulder. In April, he wrote that he took the European war's traditional "40 and 8 boxcars" in an effort to rejoin his unit. He finally reached it in Germany, where he was assigned to the ordnance branch for heavy automotive maintenance. He returned to Brownsville after the war and worked shortly for his father's Brownsville News Publishing Company. In 1947, he was named Brownsville postmaster and served that position until

his retirement in 1981. See "First Lieutenant Robert A. Runyon Citation from Headquarters, Fourth Armored Division, A.P.O. 254, US Army, 201 File," RFP; Robert Albert Runyon Genealogical Questionnaire, RFP; First Lieutenant Robert A. Runyon to D. S. and Amali Runyon Perkins, V-letters, June 17, 1944-July 4, 1945, RRC, DBCAH Box 2008-333/1.

[648] Ella Lawson to Robert Runyon, November 12, 1945, RFP.
[649] Robert Runyon to Amos Runyon, December 14, 1945, RFP.
[650] Runyon, "History, Data, and Information Relative to Robert Runyon."
[651] Curtis Vinson, "Anti-Administration Ticket for City Election Reported Forming," *The Brownsville Herald*, September 25, 1947, 1; "Administration Puts Complete Ticket in Race," *The Brownsville Herald*, October 5, 1947, 1; "Don't Split the Ticket," *The Brownsville Herald*, October 10, 1947, 4.
[652] Robert Runyon, Speech to Unions (Brownsville Local), October 28, 1949, RRC, DBCAH Box 2007-109/1.
[653] Kentucky Governor Earle C. Clements to Robert Runyon, May 31, 1949, and June 11, 1949, RRC, DBCAH Box 2008-333/1.
[654] "Lead Story," Robert Runyon biography, RFP; "Results Show Three Runoffs in County," *The Brownsville Herald*, July 28, 1952, 2; "Stokely Regains Mayor's Post," *The Brownsville Herald*, May 1, 1957, 1.
[655] "Good Government Ticket Has Responsibility Now," *The Brownsville Herald*, November 6, 1957, 6.
[656] "Bleier Wants To Sell Site To City," *The Brownsville Herald*, December 30, 1957, 5.
[657] Runyon, "History, Data, and Information Relative to Robert Runyon."
[658] "Robert Runyon, New Cameron County Democratic Chairman, Opposes Bolters."
[659] *Appellant's Brief, Robert Runyon, Appellant, Vs. A. M. Kent, Appellee*, appeal to Court of Civil Appeals, Fourth Supreme Judicial District of Texas, San Antonio (Brownsville: The Brownsville News Publishing Company, 1951), RFP.
[660] Robert Runyon, "Offers His Version;" "Dirty Words," *Valley Morning Star*, June 20, 1954, B-8.
[661] Oscar Dancy to Sam Rayburn, September 5, 1956, RRC, DBCAH Box 2008-333/1

Chapter 26
[662] "Charcot-Marie-Tooth Disease Fact Sheet." Office of Communications and Public Liaison, National Institute of Neurological Disorders and Stroke, National Institutes of Health, https://www.ninds.nih.gov/Disorders/Patient-Caregiver-Education/Fact-Sheets/Charcot-Marie-Tooth-Disease-Fact-Sheet, accessed February 1, 2017.
[663] Robert L. Newman.
[664] *Texas, Death Certificates, 1903–1982* for Prentice Alexander Newman, Ancestry.com, http://interactive.ancestry.com/Print/2272/40394_b062661-02424/2, accessed August 1, 2015.
[665] "Prentice A. Newman, Built 1-Wing Plane."
[666] Adams and Knopp, *Portrait of a Border City*, 223.
[667] Robert Runyon, "It's Impracticable," Letter to the Editor, *The Brownsville Herald*, June 29, 1960, 4.
[668] Robert Runyon, "Copy of A Report Made by Robert Runyon to the Citizens of Brownsville," June 20, 1940, 18, RFP.
[669] Robert Runyon to U.S. Rep. Joe M. Kilgore, March 15, 1961, RFP: *Handbook of Texas Online*, Thomas N. Campbell and Joseph R. Monticone, "Padre Island National Seashore," accessed August 12, 2018, http://www.tshaonline.org/handbook/online/articles/gkp01.
[670] Robert and Amelia Runyon Fiftieth Wedding Anniversary (1963) Guest List, RFP.
[671] Robert Runyon to Judge Oscar Dancy and the Brownsville City Commissioners.
[672] Montoya, "This Renaissance man unknown to many here."
[673] Donovan Stewart Correll and Marshall Conring Johnston, *Manual of the Vascular Plants of Texas* (Renner, Texas: Texas Research Foundation,1970), xi.
[674] B. L. Turner to Mrs. J. T. Mahoney.
[675] Robert Runyon to Book Mark; Robert Runyon to The Honorable Mayor and City Commission of the City of Brownsville; Paul K. Goode to Mrs. Robert Runyon, January 29, 1970, RRC, DBCAH Box 2007-223/4; Author email to Lori K. Atkins, Jernigan Library, Texas A&M University at Kingsville, October 19-20, 2016.
[676] Anthony Gray, "Park may get a name change," *The Brownsville Herald*, January 31,1995, 3A; Elizabeth A. Allen, "County commissioners table vote on new court," *The Brownsville Herald*, February 1, 1995, 17.
[677] Robert Runyon to Mrs. E. J. Walker, November 18, 1941, RRC, DBCAH Box 2007-223/3.
[678] "Lower Valley Had Grandstand Seat At Battle of Mexican Revolution."
[679] Clarence J. Roche, "Former Brownsville Mayor Ranks High as Scientist," *San Antonio Evening News*, April 11, 1947.

Epilogue
[680] Laura Morina Boria, "Robert Runyon: Texas Photography's Best Kept Secret?" *Reporting Texas: News and Features from UT-Austin's School of Journalism*, September 10, 2015, http://reportingtexas.com/robert-runyon-texas-photographys-best-kept-secret/, accessed January 22, 2016.
[681] Robert Runyon, "Copy of A Report Made by Robert Runyon to the Citizens of Brownsville," 8-9, 10-11, 17, RFP.
[682] "State Capital Is Destroyed;" Jeffry A. Timmons, *New Venture Creation: Entrepreneurship for the 21st Century* (Boston: Irwin McGraw Hill, 1999), Fifth Edition, 220-225.

Bibliography

Book
Adams, William L., and Anthony K. Knopp, *Portrait of a Border City: Brownsville, Texas,* Austin: Eakin Press, 1997.
Aiken, Bruce, *Ballots, Bullets and Barking Dogs: Brownsville Yesteryears,* Brownsville: D. Armstrong Co., Inc., 1996.
Allen, John Houghton, *Southwest,* Philadelphia and New York: J. B. Lippincott Company, 1952.
Anders, Evan, *Boss Rule in South Texas: The Progressive Era,* Austin: University of Texas Press, 1982.
Ashland Centennial Committee, *A History of Ashland, Kentucky 1786-1954,* Ashland: Graber Printing Company, 1954.
Babits, Lawrence E., and Joshua B. Howard, *Long, Obstinate, and Bloody: The Battle of Guilford Courthouse,* Chapel Hill: The University of North Carolina Press, 2009.
Baker, Thomas E., *Another Such Victory: The Story of the American defeat at Guilford Courthouse that helped win the War for Independence,* New York: Eastern Acorn Press, 1992.
Britton, N. L., and J. N. Rose, *The Cactaceae: Descriptions and Illustrations of Plants of the Cactus Family,* Washington, D.C.: The Carnegie Institution, 1922-1923.
Canseco Botello, José Raúl, *Historia de Matamoros,* Matamoros: Talleres Tipograficos de Litografica Jardin, S. A. de C. V., June 20, 1981.
Catlettsburg Centennial Committee, *History and Program Commemorating the Founding of the City of Catlettsburg, Kentucky,* Catlettsburg: 1949.
Chilton, Carl S., *From Steamboats & Stagecoaches to Jet Aircraft,* Brownsville: Brownsville Historical Association, 2011.
Collier & Son, editors, *The World's Great Events,* New York: P. F. Collier & Son Corporation, 1945, Vol. VIII.
Comisión Nacional Para las Celebraciones del 175 Aniversario de la Independencia Nacional Y 75 Aniversario de la Revolución Mexicana, *Venustiano Carranza,* Mexico D. F.: Instituto Nacional de Estudios Históricos de la Revolución Mexicana, 1985.
Correll, Donovan Stewart, and Marshall Conring Johnston, *Manual of the Vascular Plants of Texas,* Renner: Texas Research Foundation, 1970.
Dávila, Rosaura Alicia, and Oscar Rivera Saldaña, *Matamoros en la Guerra con los Estados Unidos,* Matamoros: Sociedad de Historia, 1996.
de la Garza, Ciro, *La Revolución mexicana en el Estado de Tamaulipas,* Mexico, D.F.: Librería de M. Porrúa, 1973-1975.
de la Torre, Toribio, et al., *Historia General de Tamaulipas,* Ciudad Victoria: Universidad Autónoma de Tamaulipas, 1986.
Dewey, Alicia M., *Pesos and Dollars: Entrepreneurs in the Texas-Mexico Borderlands 1880-1940,* College Station: Texas A&M University Press, 2014.
Ely, William, *The Big Sandy Valley: A History of the People and Country from the Earliest Settlement to the Present Time,* Facsimile Reprint Edition, Bowie, Maryland: Heritage Books, Inc., 1987.
Fyfe, H. Hamilton, *The Real Mexico: A Study on the Spot,* New York: McBride, Nast & Company, 1914.
Goodwyn, Frank, *The Magic of Limping John: A Story of the Mexican Border Country,* New York: Farrar & Rinehart, Inc., 1944.
Gouffé, Jules, *El Libro de Cocina,* Mexico, D.F: Dublan y Comp., 1893.
Guroff, Margaret, *The Mechanical Horse: How the Bicycle Reshaped American Life,* Austin: University of Texas Press, 2016.
Harris III, Charles R., and Louis R. Sadler, *The Plan de San Diego,* Lincoln: University of Nebraska Press, 2013.
Horgan, Paul, *Great River: The Rio Grande in North American History,* Vols. 1-2, Austin, Texas Monthly Press, Inc., 1984.
Janssens, Joe Lee, *Maneuver and Battle in the Mexican Revolution: A Revolution in Military Affairs, 1913,* Houston: Revolution Publishing, 2016.
_____, *Maneuver and Battle in the Mexican Revolution: A Revolution in Military Affairs, 1914,* Houston: Revolution Publishing, 2016.
_____, *Strategy and Tactics of the Mexican Revolution 1910-1915,* Houston: Revolution Publishing, 2019.
Jolly, Vijay K., *Commercializing New Technologies: Getting from Mind to Market,* Boston: Harvard Business School Press, 1997.
Kearney, Milo, editor, *Still More Studies in Brownsville History,* Brownsville: The University of Texas at Brownsville, 1991.
Kozmetsky, George, and Piyu Yue, *The Economic Transformation of the United States, 1950-2000,* West Lafayette, Indiana: Purdue University Press, 2003.

Lasater, Dale, *Falfurrias: Ed C. Lasater and the Development of South Texas*, College Station: Texas A&M University Press, 1998.
McCullough, David, *The Wright Brothers*, New York: Simon & Schuster, 2015.
Mauro, Garry, *Guide to Spanish and Mexican Land Grants in South Texas*, Austin: Texas General Land Office, 1988.
Marin, Mariano B., *Recuerdos de la Revolución Constitucionalista y La Rebelion Delahuertista en Tamaulipas*, Ciudad Victoria: Universidad Autonoma de Tamaulipas, 1977.
Mills, James W., editor, *Memories of Fort Brown and Other Select Interviews: an Oral History Project*, Brownsville: Border Press, 2012.
Mora Garcia, José Carlos, *La Revolución Mexicana en Tamaulipas: Raíces, Origen y Desarrollo de Movimiento Constitucionalista, 1913-1914*, Ciudad Victoria: Gobierno del Estado de Tamaulipas, July 15, 2009.
Muñoz Martinez, Monica, *The Injustice Never Leaves You: Anti-Mexican Violence in Texas*, Cambridge: Harvard University Press, 2018.
Nagle, James C., *Irrigation in Texas*, Washington, D.C.: Government Printing Office, 1910
Neal, Bill, *Sex, Murder and the Unwritten Law: Courting Judicial Mayhem, Texas Style*, Lubbock: Texas Tech University Press, 2009.
Nokes, Jill, *How to Grow Native Plants of Texas and the Southwest*, Austin: University of Texas Press, 2008.
Paredes Manzano, Eliseo, *Conmemoración del CXXV Aniversario de los Honrosos Titulos, de Heroica, Leal e Invicta*, Matamoros: Eliseo Paredes Manzano, October 30, 1976.
_____, *Homenaje a Las Fundadores de la Heroica, Leal e Invicta Matamoros en la Sesquicentenario de su Nuevo Nombre*, Matamoros: El H. Ayuntamiento de Matamoros, Tamaulipas, 1976.
_____, *La Casa Mata y Fortificaciones de la Heroica Matamoros, Tamaulipas*, Matamoros: Eliseo Paredes Manzano, 1974.
Patterson, Seth, and Lawrence V. Lof, editors, *El Valle: The Rio Grande Delta*, Brownsville: Gorgas Science Foundation, Inc., no date.
Perkins, Amali Runyon, *Just Another Family Cookbook*, San Antonio: Privately Printed, 2006.
Pierce, Frank Cushman, *A Brief History of the Lower Rio Grande Valley*, Menasha, Wisconsin: George Banta Publishing Company, 1917.
Porter, Michael, *Competitive Strategy*, New York: The Free Press, 1980.
Richardson, Alfred, *Plants of the Rio Grande Delta*, Austin: University of Texas Press, 1995.
Richardson, Alfred, and Ken King, *Plants of Deep South Texas*, College Station: Texas A&M University Press, 2011.
Rivera Saldaña, Oscar, *Diccionario Biografico de la Heroica Matamoros*, H. Matamoros: Librería Española, 2001.
Rocheleau, William F., editor-in-chief, *The Source Book*, Chicago: Perpetual Encyclopedia Corporation, 1926, Vol. I.
Roell, Craig H., *Matamoros and the Texas Revolution*, Denton: Texas State Historical Association, 2013.
Runyon, Robert and Amos Runyon, *Runyon Genealogy*, Brownsville: Privately Printed, 1955.
Runyon, Robert, *Supplement to Runyon Genealogy*, Brownsville: United Printers and Publishers, 1962.
_____, *Genealogy of the Descendants of Anthony Lawson of Northumberland, England*, Brownsville: The Brownsville News Publishing Company, 1952.
_____, *The Mirror Plater's Guide*, Catlettsburg: Privately Printed, 1906.
_____, *Vernacular Names of Plants Indigenous to the Lower Rio Grande Valley of Texas*, Brownsville: Brownsville News Publishing Company, 1947.
Samponaro, Frank N., and Paul J. Vanderwood, *War Scare on the Rio Grande: Robert Runyon's Photographs of the Border Conflict, 1913-1916*, Austin: Texas State Historical Association, 1992.
Sánchez Osuna, Luis, *Explicando A Berlandier: Bicentenario de Luis Berlandier*, Ciudad Victoria: ITCA/CONACULTA, 2003-2004.
Sargent, Charles Sprague, *The Silva of North America*, Boston and New York: Houghton, Mifflin & Company, 1896.
Schnitzler, Herman, compiler and editor, *The Republic of Mexico: Its Agriculture, Commerce & Industries*, New York: Nicholas L. Brown, 1924.
Schulz, Ellen D., and Robert Runyon, *Texas Cacti*, San Antonio: Texas Academy of Science, 1930.
Scott, Florence Johnson, *Historical Heritage of the Lower Rio Grande*, San Antonio: The Naylor Company, 1937.
Spence, Robert Y., *The Land of the Guyandot*, Chapmanville: Woodland Press, LLC, 2013.
Stambaugh, J. Lee, and Lillian J. Stambaugh, *The Lower Rio Grande Valley of Texas*, Austin: Jenkins Publishing Co./San Felipe Press, 1974.
Terry, Philip, *Terry's Mexico*, Boston and New York: Houghton Mifflin Company, 1911.
Timmons, Jeffry A., *New Venture Creation: Entrepreneurship for the 21st Century*, Boston: Irwin McGraw Hill, 1999.

Turner, Patty Newman, George Newman, and Betty Newman Nauer, *Joseph and Rachel Rabb Newman An Old Three Hundred Family of Texas and Their Descendants*, Wyandotte, Oklahoma: The Gregath Publishing Company, July 1998.
Utley, Robert M., *Lone Star Lawmen: The Second Century*, New York: Oxford University Press, Inc., 2007.
Valerio-Jiménez, Omar, *River of Hope: Forging Identity and Nation in the Rio Grande Borderlands*, Durham: Duke University Press, 2013.
Vines, R.A., *Trees, Shrubs and Woody Vines of the Southwest*, Austin: University of Texas Press, 1960.
Wells, H. G., *The Outline of History*, Garden City, New York: Garden City Books, Vol. II, 1956.
Wells III, John Britton, and James M. Prichard, *10th Kentucky Cavalry, C.S.A.*, Baltimore: Gateway Press, Inc., 1996.
Weniger, Del, *Cacti of Texas and Neighboring States*, Austin: University of Texas Press, 1984.
Wheelock, E. M., editor, *Reports of Cases Argued and Decided in the Supreme Court of the State of Texas During the Latter Part of the Second Annual Session of the Court, Commencing the First Monday of December, 1871*, Vol. XXXVI, St. Louis: The Gilbert Book Company, 1882.
Yturria, Frank Daniel, *The Patriarch*, Brownsville: The University of Texas at Brownsville and Texas Southmost College, 2006.
Zorrilla, Juan Fidel, Maribel Miró Flaquer, and Octavio Herrera Pérez, compilers, *Tamaulipas: textos de su historia 1810-1921*, Mexico: Gobierno del Estado de Tamaulipas, 1990.

Government Documents
"Annual Report of the Surgeon-General of the Public Health and Marine-Hospital Service of the United States for the Fiscal Year 1904," 58th Congress, Washington, D.C.: U.S. House of Representatives, 1904.
Bureau of Investigation, *Investigative Reports*, 1908-1922, accessed through Fold3.com.
_____, *Mexican Files*, 1909-1921, accessed through Fold3.com.
_____, *Old German Files*, 1909-1921, accessed through Fold3.com.
"Companies B, C, and D, Twenty-fifth United States Infantry: report of the proceedings of the Court of Inquiry relative to the shooting affray at Brownsville, Tex., August 13-14, 1906", Washington, D.C.: Government Printing Office, 1911, No. IV.
Federal Register, Vol. 64, No. 124.
Lavaca County District Court, The State of Texas v Arthur Newman.
Lavaca County District Court, The State of Texas v Prentiss Newman.
National Archives and Records Administration, *U.S. Passport Applications, 1795-1925* and *Nonstatistical Manifests and Statistical Index Cards of Aliens Arriving at Eagle Pass, Texas, June 1905-November 1929*; accessed through Ancestry.com.
_____, Fort Worth, Texas, Records of U.S. District Courts of the United States.
Supreme Court of Texas, Luttes v The State of Texas
U.S. Census Bureau, 1860, Eighth Census of the United States.
U.S. Census Bureau, 1870, Ninth Census of the United States.
U.S. Census Bureau, 1880, Tenth Census of the United States.
U.S. Census Bureau, 1900, Twelfth Census of the United States.
U.S. Census Bureau, 1910, Thirteenth Census of the United States.
U.S. Census Bureau, 1940, Sixteenth Census of the United States.
U.S. Department of Agriculture 2012 Census of Agriculture.
U.S. Department of Homeland Security, U.S. Customs and Border Protection, U.S. Border Patrol, "Environmental Stewardship Plan for the Construction, Operation, and Maintenance of Tactical Infrastructure," July 2008.
U. S. Patent and Trademark Office.

Journal Articles
Anonymous, "The Evidence Sufficient to Sustain a Conviction for Abortion," *Texas State Journal of Medicine*, Vol. III, No. 11, March 1908.
Arreola, Daniel D., "Plaza Towns of South Texas," *Geographical Review*, Vol. 82, No. 1, January 1992, http://www.jstor.org/stable/215405.
Brannstrom, Christian, and Matthew Neuman, "Inventing the 'Magic Valley' of South Texas, 1905-1941," *Geographical Review*, Vol. 99, No. 2, April 2009, http://www.jstor.org/stable/40377377.
Carrier, John P., "Medicine in Texas: The struggle with yellow fever, 1839-1903," *Texas Medicine*, November 1986.
Clover, Elzada U., "Vegetational Survey of the Lower Rio Grande Valley of Texas," *Madroño*, Vol. 4, No. 2, 1937, http://www.jstor.org/stable/41422215.
Costa, Dora L., "The Evolution of Retirement: An American Economic History, 1880-1990,", Chicago: University of Chicago Press, January 1998, http://www.nber.org/chapters/ c6108.

Esnault-Pelterie, Robert, "Expériences D'Aviation," *L'Aérophile*, June 1905
Good, Robert Earl, "Conquering The Last Frontier—Aviation," *The Junior Historian*, Vol. 16, No. 5, March 1956.
_____, "Texas' First Airplane Flight," *The Junior Historian*, Vol. 14, No. 6, May 1954.
González Gomez, César, "El Juego Liberal: Beisbol Mexicano En La Época Del Fin Del Segundo Imperio, 1866-1870," September 8, 2008, http://ciudadanosenred.com.mx/el-juego-liberal-beisbol-mexicano-en-la-epoca-del-fin-del-segundo-imperio-1866-1870/.
Haines, Lester, editor, "The Rio Grande Railroad Company 1870-1911," *Journal of Texas Shortline Railroads*, Vol. 1, No. 2, August-October 1996.
Heard, T. J., "Report on Medical Topography, Meteorology, and Epidemic Diseases of Texas," *The Galveston Medical Journal*, Vol. 3, No. 3, May 1868.
Heep, Michael R., and Robert I. Lonard, "Esenbeckia Berlandieri (Rutaceae) Rediscovered in Extreme Southern Texas, *The Southwestern Naturalist*, Vol. 31, No. 2, May 22, 1986.
Ireland, Robert M., "The Libertine Must Die: Sexual Dishonor and the Unwritten Law in the Nineteenth-Century United States," *Journal of Social History*, Vol. 23, No. 1, Autumn 1989, http://www.jstor.org/stable/3787563.
Lockett, Landon, "Historical Evidence of the Native Presence of Sabal Mexicana (Palmae) North of the Lower Rio Grande Valley," *SIDA, Contributions to Botany*, Vol. 16, No. 4, December 1995.
Meyer, Stephen, "Automobile in American Life and Society," University of Michigan, http://autolife.umd.umich.edu/Labor/L_Overview/L_Overview.htm.
Morton, C.V., "A New Species of Esenbeckia from Texas," *Journal of the Washington Academy of Sciences*, Vol. 20, No. 7, April 1930.
Myres, Sandra L., "Fort Worth, 1870-1900," *The Southwestern Historical Quarterly*, Vol. 72, No. 2, October 1968.
Pemberton, J. R., "A Large Tern Colony in Texas," *The Condor*, Vol. XXIV, No. 2, March-April 1922, http://www.jstor.org/stable/1362732.
Peterson, Linda, "From Commerce to History: Robert Runyon's Postcards of the Lower Rio Grande Valley and Brownsville, 1910-1926," *The Southwestern Historical Quarterly*, Vol. 102, No. 2, October 1998.
Rebert, Paula, "A Civilian Surveyor on the United States-Mexico Boundary: The Case of Arthur Schott," *Proceedings of the American Philosophical Society*, Vol. 155, No. 4, 2011, www.jstor.org/stable/23208784
Reuss, J. M., "An Outbreak of Yellow Fever in De Witt County," *Transactions of the State Medical Association of Texas*, 1904.
Rose, J.N., "Runyonia Longiflora," *Addisonia*, Vol. 7, No. 1, March 1922.
Small, John K., "The Palmetto Palm—Sabal Texana," *Journal of the New York Botanical Garden*, Vol. XXVIII, No. 330, June 1927.
Tharp, B.C., and Fred A. Barkley, "The Genus Ruellia in Texas," *The American Midland Naturalist*, Vol. 42, No. 1, July 1949.
Verhoek, Susan, "Huaco and Amole: A Survey of the Uses of Manfreda and Prochnyanthes," *Economic Botany*, Vol. 32, No. 2, April-June 1978, http://www.jstor.org/stable/4253919.

Unpublished manuscripts and brochures
(all from Runyon Family Papers)

"Industrial and Commercial Williamson, West Virginia's Youngest and Most Prosperous City," business promotional pamphlet, circa 1910.
Runyon, Robert, "Runyon Families Migrate to Eastern Kentucky and Southern West Virginia," unpublished paper, circa 1962.
_____, Copy of A Report Made by Robert Runyon to the Citizens of Brownsville, June 20, 1940.
_____, "Notes of the Data of the Runyon Family," no date.
_____, "Sabal Texana, Rio Grande Palmetto, Palma de Micharo," February 4, 1937.
_____, "The Old Board Walk," December 25, 1964.

Index

Boldface pages indicate illustration

Adams, William L., 183, 187
Adams-Farwell, 57, 70
Aerial Navigation Company, 70
Aeronautical Society of America, 51
Alamo Automobile Company, 43
Alert Base Ball Club, 98
American Association for the Advancement of Science, 176
American School of Art and Photography, 91
Armour & Company, 62
Armstrong, Captain John B., 62
Austin, A. L., 135
Austin, Charlie, 135
Austin, Stephen F., 10, 27
Automobiles: Cole "30" Touring Car, 5, **121**, 203; Model T Ford, 121, 141, 153, 157, 182; Pierce-Arrow, 74; Stoddard-Dayton, **48**, 49, 68
Ayres, Atlee B., 43

Bagby, W. T., 38
Bailey, Liberty Hyde, 157, 176, 179
Barragán, Miguel F., 108
Base Ball, 98
Basket Place, The, 145-147, 182
Battles of: Ciudad Victoria, 116-117, **118**, **123**; Matamoros, 105, 108-109, **110**, **111**, 119, 129; Monterrey, 126, **127**, 128-129
Bell, A. J., 38
Bellinghausen, William, 170
Bennet Ranch, 20-23
Bennet, Anne, 21
Bennet, Robert, 21
Berlandier, Louis, 154, 163
Best, Chris, 163, 165-166
Bissell Colleges-Illinois College of Photography, 91
Black, J. M., 144
Blanco, Lucio, 117, 119, 126, 133; Battle of Matamoros, 107-110; land redistribution, **114**, 115; ordered to Tamaulipas, 105; reassigned for insubordination, 115
Blériot, Louis, 51, 78, 80, 84
Blocksom, A. P., 133, **140**
Boone, Daniel, 15
Borglum, Gutzon, 177
Boyd, John, 27, 28, 34, 38, 40
British Journal of Photography, 142
Britton, Nathaniel Lord, 159, 179
Brodbeck, Jacob B., 70
Brown, Wm., 183
Brownsville Aeroplane Company, 73, 80, 81, 87; organization, 55; stockholders, 70, 71, 73, 74, 75, 78, 79, 80, 81, 83
Brownsville/Cameron County, Texas: A. Holms, photography studio, 94; airport, 168, 169; Bell Service Station, 168; Blue Bird Saloon, 94; Brownsville Affray, 65; Brownsville High School, 142, 168; Brownsville-Matamoros ferry, 4, 61, **94**-95, 100, 109; Brulay Plantation, 175; Burns Ranch, 175; Cameron County jail, 135, 136; Chamber of Commerce, 53, 68, 144-145, 187; ecotourism, 151, 166; Electric Theater, 78; first automobiles, 103; first motorized flight in Southwest, 80; first surveyed by Don Cayetano Medrano, 96; Galbert Curio Store, 94; Gateway Bridge, 95; Gladys Porter Zoo, 165, 197; Garza, Reynaldo G.-Vela, Filemon B. United States Courthouse, 84; Grover Singer Ranch, 175; Hargrove's Book Store, 144; Harry's Cigar Store, 144; home of South's first successful aeroplane, 75, **76**; homeseekers, 91, 146; International Bridge, 95, 139, **140**, 145, 182; Jackass Prairie, 77; Kiwanis Club, 177; land development companies, 144; Lincoln Park, 184, 197; list of parks, 184; Loma Alta, 77, 83; Maltby's print shop, 94; Merchants Bank failure, 147; Mesquite Station-Loma Alta flights, 77-80, 82-83; Midwinter Fair of 1912, 92; Old Board Walk, 4, 61, 94, 100; Palmito Ranch, 98; Park Board, 191; parks and resacas, 150, 151, 153, 182, 184, 185, 187, 189, 191; Piper Plantation, 175; Planning and Zoning Board, 191; Port of Brownsville, 182; Rancho El Salado, 175; Rancho San Tomás, 175; rice mill, **56**, 57, 67, 68, 71, 78, 80, 84; Ringgold Park, 184, 188; roads, 103-104; Runyon beautification plan, 181-185; Runyon's early promotion of, 85-86; San Carlos Hotel, 62; St. Charles street, 4, 66, 103, 133, 134, **142**, 143, 150, 155, 156, 168, 195; St. Joseph's College, 88; Texas Auto Sales Supply Company, 125; U.S. Customs Office, 94, 138, 144; U.S. Immigration Office, 94, 142; Veterans International Bridge, 197; Newman's west of city flights, 67, 71, 74, 81-82, 83
Bryan, William Jennings, 25, 132
Buenrostro, José, 135-136, **137**, 138, 144
Bull, J. K., 132
Burney, Lillian Runyon. See Mahoney, Lillian Runyon
Burns, John, 28, 33

Caballero, Luís, 117, 130, 133
Cactaceae, The, 159, 171, 172
Calderoni, Carlos, 100
Cameron Auto Company, 40
Cárdenas, Lázaro, 115
Carnegie Institution, 159, 172
Carranza, Jesús, 115, 125; Battle of Ciudad Victoria, 115-117; military convoy order, 117
Carranza, Venustiano, 105, 125, 130, 132, 133,

139; assassination, 141; Plan de San Diego, 139–**140**; Tamaulipas strategy changes, 115; Carrancistas: 5, 119, 132; Battle of Ciudad Victoria, 117; Battle of Monterrey, 128; hired as Newman-Runyon bodyguards, 120, **121,** 122, **203**
Carson, J. M., Jr., 41
Castro, J. Agustín, 107, 119
Caylor, Hutokah Dodson. See Newman, Hutokah Dodson Caylor
Caylor, Michael G., 10
Chapa, Melquiades, 135–136, **137,** 138, 144
Charcot-Marie-Tooth disease, 193
Chisholm Trail, 26
Christie, Edyth, 64, 86
Cincinnati, Ohio, 31, 59, 89
Clements, Earle C., 191
Clore, W. K. (Kenneth), 162
Connally, Tom, 147
Cornell University, 157, 176
Correll, Donovan S., 179, 195-196
Cox, Ibby, 132
Cox, Ira, 61
Cox, Norvin, 61
Cox, William B., 61; accused of counterfeiting, 132
Cracker Jack®, 91
Creager, R. B., 143, 145, 147, 182
Cueto, Andres, 79
Curt Teich: commercial postcard printer, 89
Curtiss, Glenn, 44, 51, 53, 56, 71, 75
Cutak, Ladislau, 171

Dahnke, Ethelyne, 13, 40, 43, 47, 48, 103, 170
Dahnke, J. L., 170
Dancy, Oscar, 192, 195
Davenport, Elizabeth Pettit, 187
Davenport, Harbert, 187
Davidson, Asbury Bascom, 38, 41
de Escandón, José, 93
de la Peña, Falcón B., 105–107
Decuir Latiolait, Luciano: Battle of Ciudad Victoria, 115, **118**; killed by sentries, 120; military convoy commander, 117–120, 122
Decuir, Cristina Dondé Valdés de, 117
Defensa Social: Ciudad Victoria, Mexico, 116; Matamoros, 108
DeWitt, Green, 27
Díaz, Félix, 114, 115; Felicistas, 134
Díaz, Porfirio, 114
Dixiecrats, 192
Dobie, J. Frank, 147, 158; famous Runyon description, 199

Earle, William J., 169-170
Echazaretta, Antonio, 108, 110, 138; executed, 109, **111**
Echazaretta, Hilario, 108, 109; executed, 110
Elite Postcard Company, 89
entrepreneurship, 5, 6, 200; actions at Ciudad Victoria, 120–124; first-mover advantage, 9, 52, 53, 83; intellectual property, 6, 12-13, 40, 45, 81, 89, 144–145, 172, 174; investor expectations, 71; new venture creation, 145–147; team selection value, 203
Earle, Lillian Newman, 81, 103, 169
Earle, William J., 169-170
Esenbeckia: *berlandieri*, 163; *pentaphylla*, 163; *runyonii*, 5, 161–166, 179, 197
Esnault-Pelterie, Robert, 46
Everson, Curtis, 74, 75, 119, 120

Fairchild, David, 177, 180
Falfurrias Machine Shops, 39–40, 48
Farman, Henri, 44, 51, 84
Feagin, W. H., 185
Ferguson, James, 136
Fernandez, E., 125
Fielding, Frederick J., 53
Flores, Manuela, 134
Ford, Julia C., 29, 87
Fort Brown, 65, 70, 73, 75, 77, 98, 129, 133, 134, 139, 140, 176
Fort Ringgold, 129, 139, 140
Fort Worth Auto and Livery Stable, 14
Fort Worth Stockyards: Exchange Building, 62
Forto, Emilio, 94
French, Anna, 62, 63
French, Evelyn, 62–66, 85, 86–88
French, Marcus, 62
French-Webb Live Stock Commission Company, 62
Freudenstein, Ben, 185
Frost, T. C., 43
Fulton, Robert, 56

Gárate, Raúl, 117, 120
Gavira, Gabriel, 125
George, B. F., 133
Gilbert, Virginia Runyon, birth of 140; **143,** 146, 175, 196, 198
Gilhousen, Charles, 75, **76,** 92
Ginn, R. L., 66
Gist, Christopher, 15
Givens, Ernest, 112
González Villarreal, Francisco (Pancho), 107–108, 109, 112, 114, 126, 130, 143; Battle of Ciudad Victoria, 115–117; death of, 188
González Villarreal, Leocadia Eduviges (Cayita) Medrano Longoria de, 107, 108
González, Pablo, Battle of Ciudad Victoria, 115–117; Battle of Monterrey, 126–130; vanguard at Padilla, 119
Good, Robert Earl, 170
Gorgas Science Foundation, 178
Gorgas, W. C., 176, 178
Gouffé, Jules, 113
Graham Nursery Company, 29
Green, E. H. R. (Ned), 70
Gregg, J.A., 61

Gregory, Thomas Watt, 136
Gulf Coast News and Hotel Company, 60, 64, 88, 89, 91
Gutiérrez, María Teresa, 96

Hagerman, Geertje (Charity). See Runyon, Geertje (Charity) Hagerman
Hague Convention, 128
Halff, G. A. C., 43, 45, **48**, 49, 50, 53
Hanning, J., 64
Harding, Warren, 142-143
Harris III, Charles H., 133
Harrod, James, 15
Hatfield, Anderson (Devil Anse), 17
Hatfield, Cap, 17
Hatfield-McCoy feud, 17
Head, George J., 55
Heep, Don, 165
Heep, Mike, 164-165
Henry, William D., 25
Herff, Adolph, 70
Herff, Ferdinand Von, 70
Herring, August, 71
Herring-Curtiss Company, 71, 73, 77
Hill, Lon C., 71
Hinkley & Batz, 102, 105
Hinojosa, María de, 96
Hoffman, Gertrude, 59
Holder Manufacturing Company, 89
Hood, L. T., 25
Hoover, J. Edgar, 188
Hotel Brazos, Houston, 59
Huerta, Victoriano, 105, 114, 117, 128
Hugh Ramsey Nature Park: Robert Runyon Garden, 197

Ideker, Joe, 164
International Correspondence School, 66

James B. Nellis & Company, 30
Janssens, Joe Lee, 116
Jara, Heriberto, 117
jopoy, 163

Kalamazoo Nursery Company, 30
Kelly Air Field, 170; Kelly Air Force Base, 170
Kenedy, Mifflin, 175
Kennon, M., 40
Kent, A. M., 192
King Ranch, 134, 146
King, Ken, 151
King, Richard, 146
Kitty Hawk, North Carolina, 1, 2, 14, 43, 44, 45, 71, 83, 84, 169; Kill Devil Hills, 83
Kleberg, Caesar, 134
Kleberg, Helen C., **146**
Kleberg, Robert Justus, Jr., 146
Knopp, Anthony K., 183, 187
knowledge: explicit, 12, 21, 23, 45, 51, 150, 151, 152, 156, 164, 170, 196-197; tacit, 11, 12, 16, 19, 25, 44, 45, 150, 151, 152, 161, 163, 164, 170, 195, 196-197; transfer, 6, 7, 11, 147, 151, 154, 156, 166, 173-174, 176, 196, 198, 202, 203

Lackey, Joseph, 28, 33
Lackey, S. C., 38
Lampton, W. J., 85-86
Lane Hotel, Yoakum, Texas, 26, 27, 35, 36, 39
Langley, Samuel Pierpont, 11, 44, 47
Lark, O. L., Mrs., 58
Las Norias, 134, **135**, 136, 144
Lasater, Ed, 39, 41
Lavaca County District Court, 2, 9, 40, 82
Lawson, Ann Bilton, 16, 17
Lawson, Anthony, 16-17, 24
Lawson, Ella, 58
Lawson, Elizabeth. See Runyon, Elizabeth Lawson
Lawson, Emily. See Smith, Emily
Lawson, George Washington, 17-18, 29
Lawson, Harry, 58
Lawson, John: Anthony Lawson's brother, 16; Anthony Lawson's son, 17
Lawson, Lafayette, 58
Lawson, Lucille G., 34
Lawson, Lucy. See Newman, Lucy Lawson
Lawson, Melvin, 17
Lawson, Thomas Jefferson, 34, 38, 42, 167-168
Leahy, Kate, 65
Leahy, Michael, 65
Leckie, Martha Newman, 34, 43
Leckie, W. H., 34, 36, 43
Libro de Cocina, El, 113
Lincoln, Abraham, 197; assassination, 98
Longoria Longoria, Felipa, 96
Longoria, José Matías, 96

MacMasters, K. W., 30
Madero, Francisco I., 105, 117
Mahoney, Lillian Runyon, 126, **143**, 146, 158, 175, 196, 198
Manual of the Vascular Plants of Texas, 196
Mason, Elmer S. See Mason, Shell
Mason, Frederick, 26, 36, 37, 40
Mason, James T., 37
Mason, Margaret, 26, 36
Mason, Rebecca Jane, 37
Mason, Shell, 9, 26-29, 38, 39, 40, 41, 76, 82, 202; funeral, 37; killing of, 33-36
Massey, Bruce, 45, 47
Matamoros, Tamaulipas, Mexico: 63, 78, 85, 104, 115, 116, 117, 126, 129, 130, 133, 139, 141, 142, 144, 154; as Constitutionalist headquarters, 115-122, 125; Basket Place, The, 145-147, 171, 176, 182;Battle of Matamoros, 105, 108-109, **110**, 119, 129; bullfights, 89, 92, 95, **97**, 144; Casa Mata, **90**, 109, **111**; Casino Matamorense, 108;

Catedral Nuestra Señora del Refugio, 112, 145; Hacienda Las Rusias, 108, 119; Los Borregos land redistribution, **114**–115; Medrano family in, 96-100, 107-108; Mexico Customs, 95; mule-driven rail cars, 95, **97**; Newman in, 168; Plaza de Gallos, **90**; Plaza Hidalgo, 4, 93, 95, **97**, 112, 144, 145, 146; Runyon in, 4, 61, 66, 94-96, 100, 108, 109-110, 112, 114-115, 138, 150, 153, 161; Santa Cruz ferry, 4, **94**-95; tradition of the paseo, 93; Union Base Ball Club de, 98; yerberías, 150, 153

Maynard, Jennie. See Runyon, Jennie Maynard

Maxim, Sir Hiram, 11, 44

McAfee: George, 15; James, 15; Robert, 15

McClung, Rupert, 31

Medrano Longoria, Amelia Leonor. See Runyon, Amelia Leonor Medrano Longoria de

Medrano Longoria, José Cecilio, 108, 145, 146; at Battle of Ciudad Victoria, 115–116

Medrano Longoria, Leocadia Eduviges (Cayita). See González Villarreal, Leocadia Eduviges Medrano Longoria de

Medrano Montalvo, José Telésforo, 96, 98, 99, 100, 116; attends Seton Hall College, 96; history's first Hispanic winning pitcher, 98

Medrano, Cayetano, 96

Medrano, José María, 96

Merchant & Planters Rice Milling Company. See Brownsville, Texas: rice mill

Metropolitan Museum of Art of New York, 75

Mexican Revolution, 105; Battle of Ciudad Victoria, 115–117, 157, 200-203; Battle of Matamoros, 107–110, 117, 119; Battle of Monterrey, 126–130; Las Virgenes, 116; Los Borregos land redistribution, **114**–115; Runyon's magic lantern presentation, 122; Santuario De Nuestra Señora De Guadalupe, 116

Mexican-United States Boundary Commission, 154, 160, 174

Mexico Boundary Commission, 154

Mims, John Diuguid, 23–24

Mims, Mary Louise. See Young, Mary Louise Mims

Mirror Plater's Guide, The, 30

Missouri Botanical Garden, 171

Monterrey Novelty Company, 141, 144

Montoya, Juan, 195

Morales, Miguel, 92

Morton, Conrad Vernon, 154, 163, 179

Morton, Stanley, 120

Múgica, Francisco, 115

Mulligan, James, 181

Murguía, Francisco, 116

Nafarrate, Emiliano, 139, **140**

National Audubon Society, 178

National Youth Administration, 184

Navarrete, Miguel, 107

Nelson, Margaret. See Newman, Margaret Nelson

Neptune grass. See *Posidonia oceanica*

New Orleans, Louisiana, 96, 112, 117; Audubon Park, 59; City Park, 59; Crescent Theatre, 59; Greenwall Theatre, 59; Hotel Richelieu, 59; Union Station, 59

New York Botanical Garden, 149, 154, 159-160, 164, 176; John Torrey Herbarium, 160

Newman, Ali, 10

Newman, Arthur, 9, **12**, **54**, 69, 81, 82, 167–168, 175, 194; acquittal, 41, 43; at Rio Grande Machine and Repair Shop, 42, 81; automobile repair, 14; bicycles, 13; birth of, 10; birth of Gladys, 81; birth of Lillian Lucille, 41; Brownsville garage, 168; death of, 169; drilling innovation, 40; entrepreneurial spirit, 11; in Alice, 27, 28, 33, 36; in Brooks County, 38-40, 42; in Brownsville, 41; in Laredo, 10–11; in Pettus, 168; in Runge, 12–13; in San Antonio, 167; killing of Shell Mason, 9, 33–36; love of Mexico, 11; marriage to Lucy Lawson, 34; promotes brother's aviation technology, 53–54; response to sister's death, 33; State of Texas v Arthur Newman, 40-41; unwritten law defense, 37–42

Newman, Elaine, 170, 194

Newman, Gladys, 81

Newman, Hutokah Dodson Caylor, 10, **12**, 13, 27–28, 33, 40, 43, 46; death of, 103

Newman, Joseph, 9-10

Newman, Joseph Austin, 10-11, 13, 27, 34, 43, 47, 48, 103; death of, 125

Newman, Lillian: See Earle, Lillian Newman

Newman, Lillian Lucille, 41

Newman, Lillian May (Lily), **12**, 27–29, 34, 36, 37, 38, 39, 41; autopsy, 33; birth of, 10; death of, 28; prize-winning essay, 11; funeral, 33; Goliad tornado care, 22; nursing school, 13; presented gold watch, 23; yellow fever care, 22–23

Newman, Lucy Lawson, 34, 39; birth of Gladys, 81; birth of Lillian Lucille, 41

Newman, Malcolm Arthur. See Newman, Arthur

Newman, Malcolm Arthur (Boy), Jr., 168, 170

Newman, Margaret Nelson, 10

Newman, Martha Ann Shedricks, 10

Newman, Martha. See Leckie, Martha Newman

Newman, P. A. See Newman, Prentice Alexander

Newman, Pearl P. Williams, 22, 43, 47, 81, 83, 103, 169; birth of Lillian, 81; birth of Prentice Alexander Newman, Jr., 14; birth of Thomas Cline, 126; in Dallas, 14, 40; in Fort Worth, 14; marriage to Prentice Alexander Newman, 13

Newman, Prentice Alexander, **2, 12**, 27, 28, **54**, 61, 81, 107, **169**, 175; acquittal for murder, 82; aero club secretary, 53; aeroplane photographs, 75; aeroplane refinements, 71; aeroplane specifications, 72; architect of America's first monoplane, 5, 80-82, 84 169, 194, 202; architect of America's fourth aeroplane, 51; arrival in Brownsville, 1, 9, 53-54; as automobile mechanic, 14; aviation dreams end, 83-84; aviation feats recalled, 169-170; aviation innovations, 46, 54-55, 78, 202-203; aviation legacy, 84; bicycles, 13, 45; birth of, 10; birth of Lillian, 81; birth of Prentice Alexander Newman, Jr., 14; birth of Thomas Cline, 126; business model, 9; Carrancista team formed, 120, **121**, 122; chauffeur, 103-104; court case continuances, 40, 46, 69, 82; death of, 194; dihedral wing design, 47, 78; entrepreneurship actions at Ciudad Victoria, 5, 120-124; entrepreneurial qualities and accomplishments, 1, 5, 6, 11, 53, 200, **201, 202**-203; entrepreneurship fades, 124, 167; exaggerated news coverage, 69; flight one, 1-2, 9, 43-50, **48**, 84; flight two, 68-69; flights three and four, 74, **76**; flight five (motorized), 78, 79, 80, 82, 84; Fort Brown Fourth of July 1909, 70, 77-78; in Dallas, 14, 40; in Fort Worth, 14; in Laredo, 10-12; in Runge, 12-13; in San Antonio, 43-53; intelligence work, 125-126, 131-134, 167-168; interest in aviation, 11; investor directives, 71; irrigation system innovation, 103; killing of Shell Mason, 2, 9, 33-36; letter from France, 69; love of Mexico, 11; marriage to Pearl Williams, 13; Mesquite Station- Loma Alta flights, 77-80, 82-83; military convoy chauffeur, 117-124; moves to Central America, 170; Newman's Perfection Radiator Compound, 126; *New York Times* recognition, 81, 194; and Plan de San Diego, 131-134; pledge to Brownsville residents, 73; post-aviation garage, 102; proven entrepreneur, 102; response to sister's death, 33-36; retired in San Antonio, 193-194; rotary drill innovation, 103, 168; starts Texas Auto Sales Supply Company, 125; steam engine patent, 12-13; steam engines, 11; unwritten law defense, 37-42; witnesses duel in Mexico, 105-107
Newman, Prentice Alexander, Jr., 14, 43, 47, 103, 170, 193
Newman, Rachel Rabb, 10
Newman, Robert L., 193-194
Newman, Thomas Cline, 126, 170
Newman, William, 10
Newspapers: *Brownsville Daily Herald*, 57, 72, 73, 79, 82, 83; *Brownsville Herald*, 68, 92, 122, 132, 170, 183, 185, 186, 190; *Brownsville News*, 155, 174, 183, 186; *Brownsville Sentinel*, 110, 122; *Catlettsburg Tribune*, 86; *Chicago Daily News*, 143; *Corpus Christi Caller*, 68; *Dallas Morning News*, 143; *Hallettsville New Era*, 38, 41; *Houston Chronicle*, 143, 144; *Houston Post*, 122; *New York Times*, 81, 143, 194; *New York World*, 56, 75; *San Antonio Express*, 122; *Sun* of New York, 69; *Washington Post*, 36
Nuevo Santander, 93

Obregón, Álvaro, 141
Old Three Hundred, 10
Olmito, Texas, 62, 134-135, 136, **137**, 161
Oman, J. W., 70
Owens, Lorraine, 11

Palo Alto Battlefield National Historical Park, 153-154
Pan American Airways, 168, 169-170
Paulhan, Louis, 84
Pearl Harbor, 186
Pemberton, J. R., 156
Periodicals: *Aeronautics*, 51, 52; *Automobile*, 51, 75; *British Journal of Photography*, 142; *Flight Illustrated*, 81; *Flight International*, 51, 69; *L'Aérophile*, 46; *Modern Electrics and Mechanics*, 126; *Monty's Monthly*, 174; *Popular Mechanics*, 125, 126
Perkins, Amali Runyon, 88, 140, **143**, 146, 156, 158, 172, 175, 196, 198
Pershing, John J., 130
Philadelphia Naval Shipyard, 170
Pierce, Frank Cushman, 105, 136-137
Pizaña, Aniceto, 135
Plan de Guadalupe, 105
Plan de San Diego, 131-138, 139
Plants of the Borderlands: *Acaulon runyonii*, 179; *Allium runyonii*, 179; betonyleaf thoroughwort, 155; *Bradburya virginiana*, 175; *Casparia runyonii*, 179; *Conoclinium betonicifolium*, 155; *Cooperia smallii*, 179; Corpus Christi fleabane, 155; *Coryphantha runyonii*, 159, **160**, 179; *Cuscuta runyonii*, 179; *Cyperus aristatus*, 179; dead-and-awake, 149; *Digitaria runyonii*, 179; ébano, 162, 183, 196; *Echeveria runyonii*, 161, 179; *Echinocereus runyonii*, 179; eel-grass, 148; *Erigeron procumbens*, 155; *Escobaria runyonii*, 159, 179; *Esenbeckia runyonii*, 5, 161-166, 179; *Euphorbia innocua*, 179; fresnos, 162; *Grindelia oolepis*, 179; *Helianthus debilis*,179; *Iresine palmeri*, 175; jopoy, 163; *Justicia runyonii*, 179,196; limoncillo, 161-166, 163; *Manfreda longiflora*, 161; naranjillo, 163; *Neomammillaria runyonii*, 179; *Neptunia plena*, 149, 151-152; olmos, 162; palma de micharos, 60, 176, 190, 191; Palmer's bloodleaf, 175; palo blanco, 162; *Plantago virginica*, 155; *Polianthes runyonii*, 161, 179; Prairie Mexican clover, 158;

Pseudobravoa, 161; *Richardia tricocca,* 158; *Rubus riograndis,* 179; *Ruellia runyonii,* 179; Runyon's Esenbeckia, 161-166, 197; Runyon's huaco, 159-161, 196; Runyon's water willow, 196; Runyon's Violet Wild Petunia, 197; *Runyonia,* 161, 179, 196; *Sabal texana,* 5, 60, 66, 174-178, 184, 197; *Scutellaria drummondi,* 179; *Selenia grandis,* 179; Topsy-Turvy, 161; *Utica chamaedryoides,* 179; *Verbena runyonii,* 179; Virginia plantain, 155; *Washingtonia robusta,* 60, 66, 177; water sensitive, 149; *Zostera marina,* 148
Point Isabel, Texas. See Port Isabel, Texas
Port Isabel, Texas, 77; lighthouse, 145; Tarpon Beach, 68
Porter, Dean, 189, 190
Porter, Mrs. R. A., 184
Posidonia oceanica, 148-49, 151

Quapaw Baths, 188
Quillin, Ellen Schulz, 172-173

Railroads: Chesapeake and Ohio (C&O) Railway, 59; División de Monterrey, 104; Frisco Railroad, 105; Illinois Central Railway, 59; International-Great Northern (I&GN) Railroad, 10, 64; Mexican National Railway, 10, 104, 105; Norfolk & Western Railway, 29, 58, 61; Rio Grande Railroad Company, 77, 91; Rio Grande Railway Company, 91; San Antonio and Aransas Pass Railway, 26, 35, 68; Santa Fe Railway, 59; Southern Pacific Railroad, 59, 189; St. Louis, Brownsville and Mexico Railway, 1, 3, 53, 60, 62, 63, 68, 134; Texas and Pacific Railway, 62; Texas-Midland Railroad Company, 70.
Rábago, Antonio, 116
Rabb Palm Grove. See Sabal Palm Sanctuary
Rabb, Frank, 138, 175-176, 177; Rabb Plantation, 175; Rancho San Tomás, 175
Rabb, Margaret McCormick, 177
Rabb, Mary Smalley, 9-10, 175
Rabb, Rachel. See Newman, Rachel Rabb
Rabb, William, 9-10, 175
Raemer, Betsy. See Runyon, Betsy Raemer
Ramos (telegrapher), 119
Rayburn, Sam, 192
Rees, J. W., 38
Rentfro, R. B., 182, 183, 184
Resaca de las Cuates, 161, 162
Resaca del Rancho Viejo, 62, 162, 165
Reuss, J. H., 21
Reuss, J. M., 21-23
Reyna, Eleuterio, 126
Richardson, Alfred, 151
Rio Grande Base Ball Club, 98
Rio Grande Machine and Repair Shop, 42, **56**
Rio Grande Palmetto. See Plants of the borderlands: *Sabal texana*
Robinson, S. S., 28-29
Rose, Joseph Nelson, 154, 157, 159
Rueckheim Bros. & Eckstein, 91
Runner, Betsy. See Runyon, Betsy Raemer
Runyon, Adron, 15
Runyon, Amali. See Perkins, Amali Runyon
Runyon, Amelia Leonor Medrano Longoria de, 107, **113**, 141, 147, 150, 153, 173, 175, 196, 198; assistance with herbarium, 155; birth of Amali, 140; birth of Delbert, 145; birth of Lillian, 126; birth of Robert Albert, 140; birth of Virginia, 140; buys St. Charles street house, 143; cooking skills, 113; courtship by Robert Runyon, 95; death of, 198; fiftieth wedding anniversary, 194; kinship to Francisco González Villarreal, 108; marriage to Robert Runyon, 112, **113**; opinion of politics, 195; photography assistance, 140
Runyon, Betsy Raemer, 15
Runyon, Delbert, 96, 121, 145, 158, 164, 196, 198
Runyon, Elizabeth Lawson, 16, 18, 24
Runyon, Floyd, 15, 18, 24
Runyon, Geertje (Charity) Hagerman, 15
Runyon, Isaac, 15
Runyon, Jennie Maynard, 15
Runyon, John, 15
Runyon, Lillian. See Mahoney, Lillian Runyon
Runyon, Mitchell, 15-16
Runyon, Nora Young, 30, 31; birth of, 24; death, 31; early married years, 23-25; funeral, 58; marriage to Robert Runyon, 25; sudden death, 4
Runyon, Margaret (Peggy) Taylor, 15
Runyon, Robert: **3, 18, 155, 195**; 812 E. St. Charles Street home and gardens, **142**, 143, 150, 155, 156; advocates preservation of Padre Island, 194; affinity for Mexico, 95; appointed Kentucky colonel, 191; arrival in Brownsville, 1, 3, 60; assimilation in Mexican culture, 98, 107; author of *Vernacular Names of Plants,* 173-174; birth of, 19; birth of Amali, 140; birth of Delbert, 145; birth of Lillian, 126; birth of Robert Albert, 140; birth of Virginia, 140; birth of William Thornton, 25; botanical library, 196; botanical observation skills, 148-152; botany autodidact, 153-158; botany over politics, 195-196; Brownsville city manager, 181-185; Brownsville mayor, 185-189; bullfight postcards, 89, 92, 95, **97**, 144; cacti, 60, 149, 154, 159, **160**, 172-173; Cameron County Democratic Party leader, 181, 192; Carrancista team formed, 120, **121**, 122, **201**, 203; table of Runyon flora discoveries, 179; city manager accomplishments, 183, 186; civic betterment, 181; Civil Defense coordinator,

187–189; closes photography studio, 145; co-author of *Texas Cacti*, 172–173; collaboration with Francisco González Villarreal, 108, 112, 114, 117, 126, 130, 143, 188; courtship of Amelia Leonor Medrano Longoria, 95–100; modern criticism of Runyon photography, 137–138; darkroom, 66; death of, 196; Depression bank failure, 147; early botanical interest, 19; early Kentucky settlers, 15, 23–24; early political interest, 19, 25; *Echeveria runyonii*, 161; entrepreneurship actions at Ciudad Victoria, 120–124; entrepreneurial qualities and accomplishments, 1, 5, 6, 25, 124, 200–203; *Esenbeckia runyonii*, 161–166; and Evelyn French, 62–66; fiftieth wedding anniversary, 194; first camera, 30; first photography assignment, 91; first visit to Matamoros, 61; flora business plan, 180–181; genealogical studies, 195; Gilhousen portrait, **3**, 75; Graham Nursery Company agent, 29; Greater Brownsville Party, 182; Gulf Coast News employee, 60, 64-65, 88, 89, 91; herbarium, 155–156, 174, 196; high school photographer, 142; importance of botanical knowledge, 196–198; in Boyd County, Kentucky, 19, 31; in Williamson, West Virginia, 29; inspiration for education, 16, 18; intellectual property, 89, 144–145, 172, 174, 182; International Law & Collection Company agent, 25; James B. Nellis & Company agent, 30; Kalamazoo Nursery Company agent, 30; Kentucky education, 19; Kentucky State Guard, 31, 63; knowledge transfer on flora, 173–174; Kodak contest, 88; Kodak Exposure Records, 30–31, 59, 60, 61, 66; *La Tierra y Su Gente*, 138; loyalty to Democratic Party, 192; marriage to Amelia Medrano Longoria, 112, **113**; marriage to Nora Young, 25; military convoy participation, 117–124; Model T Ford, 153, 157; native flora (see Plants of the Borderlands); Norfolk & Western Railway, 29; opposes Dixiecrats, 192; parks and resacas, 150, 151, 153, 182, 184, 185, 187, 189, 191; photography education, 91; photography services, 92, **143**; photojournalism coverage of: Battle of Ciudad Victoria, 5, 117-122, **123**, 124; Battle of Matamoros, 109, **110**, **111**, Battle of Monterrey, 126, **127**, 128–130, Las Norias, 134, **135**, Mexico's land redistribution, **114**–115, Warren Harding, 142; pioneer photojournalist, 4; and Plan de San Diego, 131–138;polymath, 1, 13, 18, 25, 110, 157, 198, 207; portrait studio, 145; postcards, 5, 30, 65, 86, **88**-89, **90**, 91, 92, **97**, 110, **123**, 126, 130, **135**, 139, 144, 145, 171, 198, 200; promotion of Brownsville, 85–86; proven entrepreneur, 102; Prudential Insurance Company agent, 25; published flora studies, 171–174; publisher of *Brownsville News*, 155, 183, 186; railroad news butch, 60; reinvents photography business, 139; relocation to Brownsville, 58–66; risk averse, 14, 201–202; runs for Texas Legislature seat, 191; Runyon Curio and Gift Store, 147; Runyon's huaco, 159–161; Runyonism defined, 183; *Sabal texana*, 60, 174–178; smuggling charges, 138; Southern Fire Insurance Company Inc. agent, 31; Spanish lessons, 66, 91, 107; The Basket Place, 145–147; *The Mirror Plater's Guide*, 30; travel in Mexico, 141, 146, 157; volunteers for park management, 189; West Virginia National Guard, 29; withdraws from political life, 194

Runyon, Robert Albert (Bob), 140, 196, 198; World War II, 188

Runyon, Virginia. See Gilbert, Virginia Runyon

Runyon, William Thornton (Willie), 25, 29, 30, 31, 58, 61, 62, 65, 86, 87, 95, 100, 112, 175, 196, 198

Runyon's Curio and Gift Store, 147

Russell, Royce, 184, 185, 186

Sabal Palm Sanctuary, 153, 178, 197

Sabal texana, Runyon's championing of, 174–178; also see Plants of the Borderlands, *Sabal texana* and palma de micharos

Sadler, Louis R., 133

SAHSA Airlines, 170

Salgado Jacobo, Santos, 165

Salome Hospital, 21, 22, 37

San Antonio Aero Club, 53, 55

San Antonio International Fair, 70

Santos-Dumont, Alberto, 80

Sargent, C. S., 176

Schott, Arthur Carl Victor, 160

Scott & White Hospital, 157

Scott, Viola, 31

Seton Hall College, 96, 100; base ball team, 98

Shedricks, Martha Ann. See Newman, Martha Ann Shedricks

Shinners, Lloyd Herbert, 161, 179

Shivers, Alan, 192

Short, Fannie, 61, 66, 85, 87, 153

Small, John Kunkel, 154, 176, 179

Smith, Emily, 17

Smith, George, 17

Smithsonian Institution, 154, 157, 159, 161, 163, 164, 176

South Padre National Seashore, 194

Spears, Ada, 62

Sperry, Elmer A., 46

St. John's College, 98

Starck, Lillian M., 175

Starck, María Vicenta Kenedy, 175

State of Texas v Arthur Newman, 40

State of Texas v Prentiss Newman, 82

Stevenson, Coke, 188

Stiles, Harvey, 161, 162
Stillman, Charles, 96
Stokely, H. L., 189, 191
Swift & Company, 62

Tamaulipas: first automobiles, 103; roads, 103–104; terrain, 104
Tandy family, 62–63, 88, 134
Taylor, Margaret (Peggy). See Runyon, Margaret (Peggy) Taylor
Terry's Mexico, 141
Texas A&I University. See Texas A&M University at Kingsville
Texas A&M University at Kingsville: Robert Jernigan Library, South Texas Archives, Robert Runyon Collection, 196
Texas Academy of Science, 172, 173
Texas Agricultural Experiment Station, 164
Texas bandit wars, **140**; Buenrostro-Chapa hangings, 135–136, **137**, 144; Olmito train derailing, 134–135, **137**; raid at Las Norias, 134, **135**, 144; P.A. Newman intelligence actions, 131–134
Texas Cacti, 172–173, 174
Texas Master Naturalist: Rio Grande Chapter, 197
Texas Rangers, 27, 131, 134, **135**, 136, 138, 144
Texas Research Foundation, 196
Texas State Historical Association: *Junior Historian*, 170
Tharp, Benjamin Carroll, 154, 157, 158, 177, 179, 183
Thrift, W. C., 28
Thurmond, Strom, 192
Toerck, Minnie, 21–23
Tom Jones Art Publishing Company: commercial post card printer, 89
Treaty of Guadalupe Hidalgo, 154
Trees, Shrubs and Woody Vines of the Southwest, 164
Trowbridge, J. T., 45
Tumlinson, Thos. R., 55, 67
Turner, Billie L., 156, 179

U. S. Immigration Service, 94, 142
U.S. Congress, 194
U.S. Customs, 94, 138, 144, 176
U.S. Department of Agriculture, 162, 164
U.S. District Court, 138, 145
U.S. Fish & Wildlife Service, 164
U.S. Library of Congress: copyrights, 89
U.S. State Department, 133
Underwood & Underwood, 143
Union Base Ball Club de Matamoros, 98
University of Southern California, 168
University of Texas at Austin, 138, 144, 146, 147, 154, 156, 183; Barker Texas History Center, 138, 198; Billie L. Turner Plant Resources Center, 149, 156, 196; Dolph Briscoe Center for American History, 198; Longhorns, 168
University of Texas at Brownsville. See University of Texas Rio Grande Valley
University of Texas Rio Grande Valley, 151

Vela, Petra, 175
Vernacular Names Of Plants Indigenous To The Lower Rio Grande Valley Of Texas, 173, 174
Viano, John, 94
Vicars, Margal L., 191, 196–197
Villa, Pancho, 130, 132-133, 139, 140; Villistas, 130, 132, 133, 134
Villarreal, Antonio, 116
Vines, Robert A., 164
Voisin, Charles, 44, 51

Wagener, Louis, 38
Walker, L. L., 84
War Production Board, 188
Webb, Walter Prescott, 144
Wherry, Edgar Theodore, 157, 176
Williams, C. U., Photograph Company, 89
Williams, J. F., 35, 36
Williams, Pearl P. See Newman, Pearl P. Williams
Williams, T. S., 13, 83
Wilson, Woodrow, 126, 136, 139, 140
Witte Museum, 172
Woer, C., 64
Wood, John, 197
Works Progress Administration, 184, 185, 202
Wright brothers, 1, 2, 9, 43–46, 47, 48, 51, 52, 53, 54, 56, 69, 70, 75, 78, 79, 81, 83, 84, 169, 194; bicycles, 13; first motorized flight, 14; wing warping, 45
Wright, Orville, 13, 44
Wright, Wilbur, 13, 14, 44, 57

Yarborough, Ralph, 192
Yellow fever, 20–23, 27, 33, 37, 176
Yoakum, Benjamin F., 26
Young, Edgar, 24
Young, Ella, 24
Young, Nora. See Runyon, Nora Young
Young, John M., 147
Young, Mary Louise Mims, 24, 58, 59
Young, William Thornton, 24, 32, 58, 59
Youngkin, S. I., 36
Yturria, Daniel, 98
Yturria, Fausto, 182
Yturria, Francisco, 98

Zimmerman & Company, 91

About the Author

Doug Perkins, a native of San Antonio, is a son of Douglas Samuel and Amali Runyon Perkins and a grandson of Robert and Amelia Medrano Runyon. He has spent a portion of every year of his life at or near his grandparents' former home in Brownsville, Cameron County, Texas. Perkins has a master of science in technology commercialization (2004) and a bachelor of journalism (1974), both from The University of Texas at Austin. In 2005, Perkins began working with entrepreneurs. He has helped start-ups raise millions of dollars in grant money and seed funding to commercialize their science and technology innovations. Over a thirty-year career as a professional journalist and free-lance writer, he wrote more than 800 feature-length business articles for regional-national agricultural publications. For a concurrent twenty years, he also marketed Texas agricultural products domestically and internationally. His work in entrepreneurship, journalism and marketing frequently took him to the lower Rio Grande Valley and, on multiple occasions, to the villages, towns and cities of Tamaulipas and Nuevo León that are part of the *Journey's Reward* story. Perkins and his wife, Susan, live in Austin.

www.ingramcontent.com/pod-product-compliance
Lightning Source LLC
Chambersburg PA
CBHW061216070526
44584CB00029B/3861